CULINARIA
HUNGARY

CULINARIA HUNGARY

Anikó Gergely
Text

Christoph Büschel · Ruprecht Stempell
Photography

Peter Feierabend
Art Director

Michael Ditter
Coordination and Layout

h.f.ullmann

Notes on abbreviations and quantities

1 oz	= 1 ounce = 28 grams
1 lb	= 1 pound = 16 ounces
1 cup	= 8 ounces *(see below)
1 cup	= 8 fluid ounces = 250 milliliters (liquids)
2 cups	= 1 pint (liquids)
8 pints	= 4 quarts = 1 gallon (liquids)
1 g	= 1 gram = $\frac{1}{1000}$ kilogram
1 kg	= 1 kilogram = 1000 grams = 2¼ lb
1 l	= 1 liter = 1000 milliliters (ml) = approx. 34 fluid ounces
125 milliliters (ml) = approx. 8 tablespoons	
1 tbsp	= 1 level tablespoon = 15–20 g *
	= 15 milliliters (liquids)
1 tsp	= 1 level teaspoon = 3–5 g *

The recipes:

The recipes serve four unless otherwise stated. Optional ingredients are shown as such. Preparation of individual ingredients is only described if it is different from normal.

Where measurements of dry ingredients are given in spoons, this always refers to the prepared ingredient as described in the wording following, e.g. 1 tbsp chopped onions BUT: 1 onion, peeled and chopped.

* The weight of dry ingredients varies significantly depending on the density factor; e.g. 1 cup flour weighs less than 1 cup butter. Quantities in recipes have been rounded up or down for convenience, where appropriate. Metric conversions may therefore not correspond exactly. It is important to use either American or metric measurements within a recipe.

© 2006 Tandem Verlag GmbH
h.f.ullmann is an imprint of Tandem Verlag GmbH

Concept:	Vince Books, Budapest
Studio photography:	Árpád Patyi, Budapest
Food styling (studio):	Péter Korpádi, Budapest
Food styling (on site):	Ursula Virnich, Cologne
Photographic assistant:	Sonja Büschel, Martin Kurtenbach, Cologne
Maps:	Astrid Fischer-Leitl, Munich
Cover design:	Claudio Martinez
Front cover photo:	© h.f.ullmann publishing/Ruprecht Stempell
Back cover photo:	© h.f.ullmann publishing/Günter Beer
Original title:	*Culinaria Ungarn* ISBN 3-8331-2184-X

© for this English edition: 2008, Tandem Verlag GmbH
h.f.ullmann, 2011
h.f.ullmann is an imprint of Tandem Verlag GmbH

Translation from German:	Mo Croasdale, Karen Green, Michele McKeekin and Elaine Richards in association with First Edition Translations Ltd
Editing:	Alison Leach in association with First Edition Translations Ltd
Typesetting:	The Write Idea in association with First Edition Translations Ltd
Project Management:	Andrew R. Davidson for First Edition Translations Ltd, Cambridge, UK
Project Coordination:	Nadja Bremse

Overall responsibility for production:
h.f.ullmann publishing, Potsdam, Germany

Printed in China
ISBN 978-3-8331-4996-2

10 9 8 7 6 5 4
X IX VIII VII VI V IV III II I

www.ullmann-publishing.com
newsletter@ullmann-publishing.com

CONTENTS

A country's cuisine says a lot about its history and culture. Hungary has been strongly influenced by eastern and western traditions. Cooking in kettles, which produces such typical Hungarian specialties as goulash and pörkölt (stews), is a legacy of the nomadic Asiatic Magyars, and its baking has been adopted from western European settlers. Over the centuries, Hungarians learned everything they could about the cuisines of both their peaceful neighbors, and their foreign conquerors. Recipes were adapted to suit their own tastes, which also gave the dishes a national flavor. Culinary expertise was also exchanged between social levels. Simplified versions of the delicacies served on the tables of the aristocracy, which frequently reflected the more discerning taste of foreign cuisines, found their way to the tables of the simple burghers. The reverse was also true, and many of the dishes which are today considered to be typically Hungarian hailed from the kitchens of the burghers. Unfortunately, it is still not possible to reproduce taste and smell, enclosing samples with a book, so instead let the photographs and words take you on a culinary voyage through Hungary. After all, where else would you learn more about a country and its people than from its food and drink?

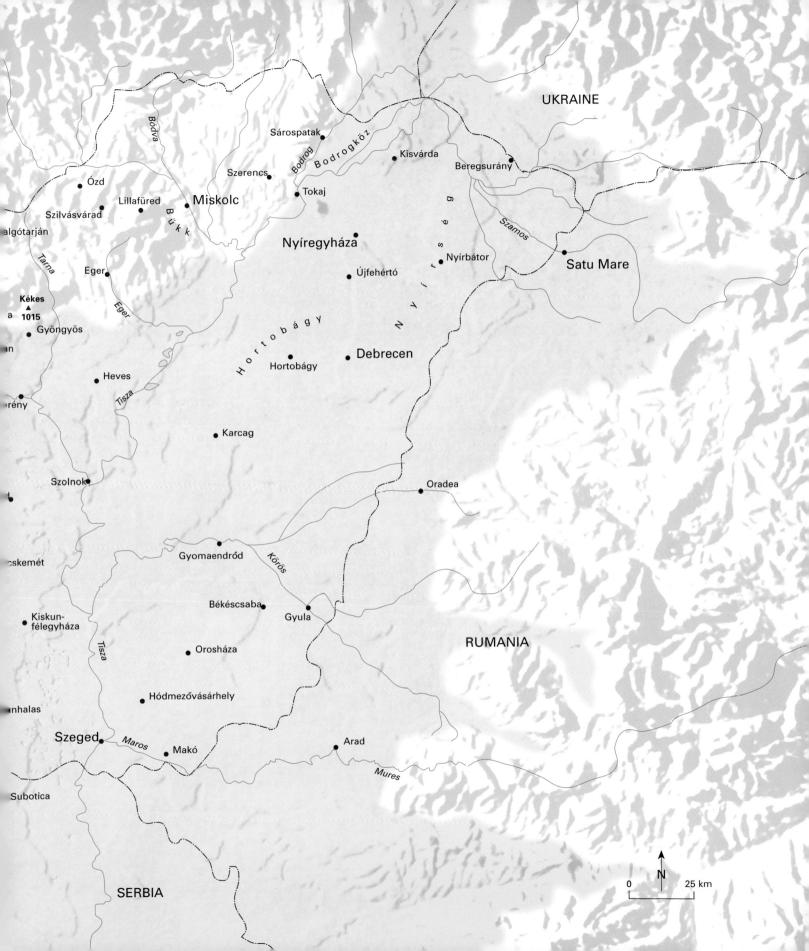

AZ ALFÖLD

THE GREAT PLAIN

The vast Great Plain of Hungary stretches to the east of the Danube, and, despite the remarkably unchanging landscape, consists of several regions with a variety of national groups and traditions.

The Great Plain is Hungary's larder – this is where most of the country's grain and vegetables are grown, and from here comes its famous fruit, which owes its unique aroma to the region's luscious, sandy soil and endless hours of sunshine.

Huge poultry farms and peaceful farmsteads are the homes of the geese that produce an excellent *foie gras* for gourmets. And herds of cattle and sheep still graze in the Puszta.

Today's cultural landscape did not develop until the 19th century, when the rivers that regularly used to flood the land were finally brought under control. The marshland disappeared and many years' hard labor by the farmers helped to prevent the land from becoming an infertile sand desert.

The Hungarians regard the Great Plain, with its frosty winters and tropically hot, dry summers, as the heart of Hungary. Perhaps this is because they owe the region so many of their delicacies: paprika, goulash soup, stuffed cabbage …

Peppers change color as they ripen: they start out green, then turn from light brown to dark brown, and finally, when they are fully ripe, to a rich, strong red.

The premier
PAPRIKA

"What spice do you associate with Hungary?" The answer to this question is unlikely to tax competitors in gastronomic quizzes anywhere in the world: paprika.

A lot of people believe that it is paprika which gives Hungarian dishes their typical heat – a heat that makes your eyes burn with the first mouthful, and forms a ball of fire in your stomach.

Others have heard that the feared Hungarian warriors of the early Middle Ages, who rode through Europe on the backs of wild horses, striking fear and terror in the hearts of the locals, were fired by paprika-laden dishes.

The latter is simply a legend; paprika was in fact completely unknown in Europe until the discovery of America. Ground paprika was first used in Hungarian cuisine during the Napoleonic Wars. The lower levels of society used it as a substitute for pepper, which had become scarce as the result of Napoleon's continental barrier, and they named it "Turkish" or "heathen" pepper. Prior to this, the pepper plants were used for decorative purposes in elegant gardens.

Pepper's cultural history is dogged by uncertainty and contradiction. Just about the only fact that seems fixed is that it was the doctor on Columbus' voyage of discovery who brought the first pepper seeds from Central America to Europe. However, some types of pepper are native to the Indian subcontinent, and some researchers believe that the Hungarian and Asian types are related. We do know that the first pepper plants arrived in Hungary during the 17th century, supposedly brought by the Turks, who occupied the country at the time. They grew the plants under strict guard in the central courtyards of their houses, and any Hungarians who considered growing pepper for their own use were threatened with decapitation. According to another theory, ethnic groups from the Balkans, fleeing north from the Turks, introduced pepper seeds to Hungary. This last theory is the most likely, since the

Young pepper plant

towns of Szeged and Kalocsa, which compete against each other for the title of "Paprika capital," are both in the southern part of the Great Plain, close to the Balkans.

Above: *Halászlé* (fish soup) is just one of many typical Hungarian dishes for which paprika is essential.

After this time, it becomes easier to chart the development of paprika. Records kept by pepper growers and old cookbooks both say the same thing: paprika has been used as a spice in Hungary only since the end of the 18th century.

Auguste Escoffier, the famous French chef, was responsible for introducing it to western European cuisine. In 1879 he had the red powder brought from Szeged on the river Tisza to Monte Carlo, where he brought fame and recognition to this "Hungarian spice" in the noble kitchens of the Grand Hotel.

How to use the red spice

In order for paprika to retain and develop its qualities in cooked dishes, quite a few points must be observed during preparation.

If using ground paprika in a roux (a mixture of flour and fat), or adding it to onions, first remove the pot from the heat. Do not return the pot to the heat until liquid has been added to the roux or the fat combined with any other ingredients that have a high water content, such as meat, potatoes, etc. This is essential, since paprika has a high sugar content and therefore burns easily. It then takes on an unsightly brown appearance and bitter flavor. Also, bear in mind that the flavor and color are released in hot fat, which is why sprinkling ground paprika over pale-looking dishes may improve their appearance, but does little for their flavor.

If you like to use paprika to add color to a prepared dish, always stir the red powder into a little hot oil, and then add

18

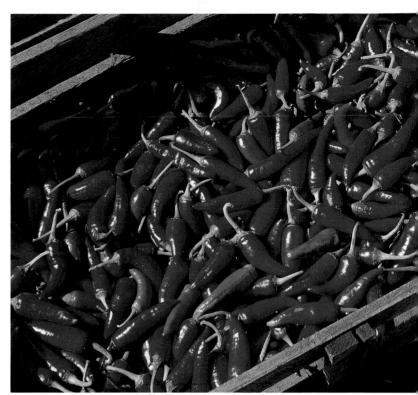

These bright red, hot pepper pods will be dried and then ground to a powder.

Peppers being picked by hand in a field near Kalocsa. This area, and Szeged to the south of the Great Plain, are the two main pepper-growing areas.

this to the dish. Paprika served separately at the table is not used as a seasoning in Hungary, but as an appetizing garnish – "a feast for the eyes."

Usually, sweet or slightly hot paprika are used, unless the cook knows for certain that the guests enjoy (and suffer no ill effects from) spicy dishes. Alternatively, fresh green or dried hot red pepper pods can be served with the meal. The ground powder can be used freely as a seasoning; most recipes call for teaspoons or tablespoons, rather than pinches. In powdered form, paprika also adds consistency as well as flavor.

Kept in a cool, dark place, paprika retains its flavor for six to eight months. After that, it begins to lose its color and aroma, but can still be used.

Drying peppers

The types of pepper that are particularly suited to drying are grown near Szeged on the river Tisza, and Kalocsa on the Danube. The plant needs plenty of nutrients and water, as well as care, to ensure a quality product. The growers' expertise and experience also help to ensure that the peppers are harvested at the right time: when they are ripe, but not too ripe. The peppers acquire their typical aroma and beautiful red color during the drying process. As they ripen, the peppers go through a range of attractive colors, from green to light brown, then growing ever darker until they are a deep black-brown – the Hungarians speak of them "rusting"; finally they take on the glorious, shiny red of the fully ripe fruit. In the villages around Szeged and Kalocsa, the peppers are still threaded onto long pieces of string and hung up to dry outside the houses and from garden fences. The length of the pepper chains, which varies from region to region, used to be a unit of measurement for the dealers: a Szegedinian chain measured 16 feet (some five meters).

Grinding peppers has a long tradition. At first, the dried pepper was simply crumbled into the cooked dish; later it was ground with a mortar and pestle. As demand increased, paprika became a successful commodity. Water and windmills began to grind more and more paprika, and less and less grain, and in time the manufacturing process became more refined. Today, peppers are ground in a closed system, between stones and steel cylinders. The warmth that is created by the friction releases the essential oils, and it is these which impart the flavor and color. Thanks to the high sugar content, the peppers also caramelize slightly, intensifying the flavor. In order to achieve the right flavor, a quantity of seeds is added to the pods before they are ground. The pepper millers use their experience to determine the exact quantities and ratios. After grinding, laboratory checks are carried out, and tasters make sure that quality remains consistent. If the ground paprika meets the requirements, it is filled into bags and stamped with a quality seal.

In the 19th century, the Pálfy brothers of Szeged received

1 The pepper growers spread the harvest out in the sun and leave it to dry.
2 The pods are then pierced with a thick needle and strung onto a thin piece of string …
3 … or placed in elongated nets.

4 The pepper chains and nets are hung outside the houses, and from walls and fences.
5 Drying the pods in the mild, warm fall sun helps to retain the flavor.
6 Early in the fall, every single house in and around Szeged and Kalocsa is decorated with bright red peppers.

awards for the quality of their ground paprika, and the world owes these brothers a debt of gratitude for the introduction of semisweet paprika. They removed the stalks and seeds from the pods before grinding them, as these contain capsaicin, which gives the paprika its heat. This not only resulted in a mild ground paprika, but also formed the basis for a number of different strengths.

The growers also contributed to paprika's fame throughout the world. They produced new types, such as the fairly mild "delikatess paprika," which contains no spiciness at all and can therefore be ground whole.

Capsaicin

Capsaicin, which is an irritant, is also used in medicine. It is particularly effective in the treatment of rheumatism: used in a cream, known as "Capsicum plaster," it promotes the blood supply to the skin.

1 Chopped dried peppers.
2 In commercial paprika production, the pods are dried in a closed system.

3 The heat that is created during the grinding process is essential for the development of the aroma.
4 The color of the end product and the degree of spiciness are determined by the quantity of seeds that is ground with the pods.

Ground paprika, served in dishes or sprinklers which are placed on the table, is used to garnish dishes.

Types of paprika

The following are the most widely available types of paprika in Hungary. "Sweet" means "not hot."

Special: Bright, shiny red, pleasantly spicy aroma, sweet or hardly hot, aromatic, the most finely ground.

Mild: Light red, pleasantly aromatic, not hot, not quite so finely ground.

Delicatess: Light red, pleasantly aromatic, slightly hot, medium coarse

Sweet: Dark, rich color, fairly mild, medium coarse.

Semisweet: Light, matte color, spicy, pleasantly hot, medium coarse.

Rose paprika: Lively red, spicy, medium coarse.

Hot: Light brown red to brick-red and yellow; very hot; slightly coarse.

Spices in Hungarian cuisine: then and now

One of the main features of Hungarian cuisine is that flavor is achieved by combining just a few, very carefully balanced, spices.

For some unknown reason, the former wealth of spices, which is documented in old records, has shrunk over the centuries. In recent times, however, it has been noted that the herbs, seeds, and roots that used to be in common use are now reappearing in the country as the result of foreign influences. These include tarragon, rosemary, basil, thyme, aniseed, juniper, saffron, and also ginger, which used to be just about the most important ingredient in Hungarian cuisine.

Gulyásleves
Goulash soup

1¼ lbs/600 g beef (neck or shoulder)
1 large onion
3 tbsp fat
½ tsp caraway
1 clove of garlic, crushed
Ground paprika (sweet)
Salt
1 medium carrot
1 medium parsley root
2 bell peppers (capsicum)
1 medium tomato
2 stalks of celery, including leaves
14 oz/400 g potatoes
Pasta pieces (see page 39)

Cut the meat into ¾ inch/2 cm cubes. Peel and finely chop the onion. Heat the oil in a large pot (12 cup/3 liter capacity), then cook the onions until translucent. Add the caraway and the crushed garlic, and cook briefly. Remove from the heat, then add the ground paprika and the meat, and season with salt. Cover with a lid and leave to cook gently, adding a little water if necessary. Add the diced root vegetables, the seeded and chopped bell peppers, the quartered tomato, and the celery leaves when the meat is half-cooked. Pour over 6½ cups/1.5 liters water, and simmer gently for 15–20 minutes.

Then add the peeled and chopped potatoes. Break some pasta into small pieces, and add to the soup once the meat and potatoes are cooked. Cook for another 5 minutes.

Serve hot. In Hungary, this soup is served with fresh white bread, dried hot paprika pods, and Kadarka (red wine). In restaurants, goulash soup is often served in small kettles as a reminder of its origins.

A plate of Hungarian history
GOULASH

Goulash is lauded as *the* Hungarian specialty all over the world, and it is no coincidence that an entire epoch of Hungarian history is referred to as "Goulash communism." The word *gulyás* originally meant only "herdsman," but over time the dish became *gulyáshús* (goulash meat) – that is to say, a meat dish which was prepared by herdsmen. Today, *gulyás* refers both to the herdsmen, and to the soup.

From the Middle Ages until well into the 19th century, the Puszta was the home of massive herds of cattle. They were driven, in their tens of thousands, to Europe's biggest cattle markets in Moravia, Vienna, Nuremberg and Venice. And the herdsmen made sure that there was always one "sickly" creature that had to be slaughtered along the way, the flesh of which provided them with a magnificent *gulyáshús*.

It was not until the end of the 19th century, during a period of burgeoning national awareness, that goulash moved from the herdsmen's kettles into the cooking pots of the wealthy. The Hungarians felt their cultural identity was threatened by the far-reaching reforms of the Holy Roman emperor and Hungarian King Joseph II, which were implemented after his mother's death in 1780. As the result, anything national came to have significance for them. It became imperative to protect the Hungarian tongue (German had become the national language), and to remember and pass down the traditional Hungarian dances, and their national costumes. The Hungarians wanted to assert their independence, the national characteristic of the Magyars, everywhere, even in their gastronomy, and so goulash became highly fashionable. The dish that had until then been eaten only by herdsmen using wooden spoons and from a shared kettle, was now served in the manor houses at elegant tables bedecked with porcelain and silver cutlery. And from there it moved on – or perhaps we should say back – to the simple folk outside the Great Plain, where it finally became common property.

A goulash soup can be prepared in a number of different ways, and each one has its own ardent supporters. However, all agree that the cook should be generous with both meat and potatoes. Under no circumstances should flour be used to bind the soup. If the soup, which should actually be quite thick, is a little too thin, one or two tablespoons of tomato paste may be added – although with care, so the soup does not become too tart. Ground paprika, which is always used in generous quantities, will also help to improve the consistency.

Kettle goulash (*Bográcsgulyás*): first braise the onions in some oil.

Then add the diced beef.

Cover the contents of the kettle with a thick layer of ground paprika.

Once the meat is half cooked, add the vegetables and water. Add the potatoes toward the end of the cooking time. Kettle goulash (above) has a creamier consistency than goulash soup.

National heritage
GRAY CATTLE

Gray Hungarian cattle, at home in Hungary's Puszta region, were saved from extinction.

The lot of the long-horned gray Hungarian cattle, which once were driven westward for sale by the Hortobágy-Puszta-based Heyducks, was far less happy than that of its present-day counterparts, which are thoroughly spoilt by comparison. Today, cattle are kept in comfortable stalls and given special feed. Gray Hungarian cattle are well able to cope with harsh conditions, however, and formerly grazed happily all year round on the meadows of the wide, marshy steppes, finding their own food, and surviving frost and heat. They were extraordinarily robust, and the cows calved without human intervention. The flesh was not only tasty, but of the best quality. On top of all that, the oxen were excellent draft animals. Gray Hungarian cattle fully met the economic requirement for "minimum investment, maximum yield."

It is no coincidence that the Hungarian word for "cattle" *(marha)* also means "treasure" or "wealth" in old Hungarian. For a long time, cattle were a form of payment. Legal statutes during the reign of Hungary's first king, Stephen the Holy (1000–38), called for fines measured in terms of young cattle. For example, murdering one's wife cost a knight or other wealthy person ten young cattle (a commoner could escape with a fine of only five).

Once "oxen power" was replaced by the "horse power" of machinery, milk yields became more important, and other breeds that were better at producing milk replaced the less productive gray cattle. In the 1950s, bureaucrats therefore decided to get rid of the gray Hungarian cattle. However, a number of committed experts made sure that the honorable old breed did not completely disappear. Gray Hungarian cattle are not only still being bred in Hungary, but their numbers are now steadily increasing.

Medieval packet soup

Although the old Hungarians had plenty of meat to eat, they also liked to preserve it. A 14th-century Italian chronicler tells us that the Magyars boiled heavily salted beef in vast kettles. When cooked, they removed it from the bones, and cut it into small pieces. The pieces of meat were dried in the sun or in an oven, then ground to a powder in a mortar and pestle, and the powder poured into small linen bags. When warriors went to battle, they sprinkled the powder onto boiling water – the original instant soup. The impressed chronicler goes on to say that this soup helped the soldiers to preserve their strength, and undoubtedly contributed to their victories. This old method of meat preservation continued in the Great Plain until fairly recently.

By contrast, there is another method of "meat processing" that is legendary. Medieval chroniclers report (not without horror) that riders would place slabs of meat beneath their saddles to tenderize it, and then eat it later. This legend is widespread even today, although research has shown that there is actually no truth in it. Horse-riding people did put pieces of raw meat on the backs of the horses – but only for healing purposes, as a sort of compress, on patches of skin rubbed raw by the saddle.

For many years, gray Hungarian cattle were bred primarily as part of the national heritage, to save them from extinction. Today, though, more and more people appreciate them, especially when the cattle are able to graze under ideal ecological conditions such as those in the protected Hortobágy-Puszta, where no chemicals, pesticides, or fertilizers are ever used. The Hortobágyan bullock, a highly desirable "bio-meat," is used in the manufacture of baby food.

The men's cooking pot
KETTLE

It's not a museum piece, nor is it an ethnographic rarity, but an item of everyday use in Hungary: the kettle. It holds the bubbling *paprikás* at the wine harvest, simmers the golden meat soup cooked at weddings, and Hungarians gather around it in friends' gardens or when camping.

Cooking in a kettle is men's work. Although the kitchen is traditionally held to be the women's domain, there have been many excellent male Hungarian cooks – especially among those who were otherwise occupied with hard physical work – even when the roles were shared more conventionally than they are today. Herdsmen who were often away from home for weeks on end, living in the Puszta, as well as farmers and laborers, who worked in the fields and vineyards from dawn to sunset, were perfectly capable of providing themselves with a hot meal.

These men had only a limited choice of ingredients. They prepared their meals almost "on the side" while carrying out their other duties. This meant that they had little time to refine their culinary talents, and so the dishes that were cooked in the vast kettles were very plain and simple. These are, however, ideal conditions for the ingredients to develop their true character: fish remains fish, pasta tastes of pasta, and the beef retains its aroma. This is highly typical of Hungarian cuisine: it allows the flavors of the individual ingredients to "speak for themselves," and does not appreciate any fancy touches that conceal their true nature.

Huge numbers of kettles in a wide range of sizes are offered for sale at Hungarian markets.

Kettlelike cooking pots were the norm among earlier peoples, and nomads and semi-nomads all over the world made similar items. However, the Magyars, who came from the Asian steppes 1100 years ago and moved into the Carpathian Basin, were already using clay pots that differed from similar vessels used by other peoples – much to the delight of archeologists, since these help to trace the wanderings of the Magyars.

The Hungarian kettle, which is used without a lid, is available in two different styles. One is compact with a wide base, and is the preferred choice for *pörkölt* dishes. The other version, which is taller and narrower, and tapers toward the top, allows the aroma of the fish soup to develop more fully.

One thing they both have in common is the handle, which, as with all buckets, is a semicircle attached at opposite

The kettle for fish soup tapers slightly toward the top.

sides of the kettle. It is not just used for holding the kettle, but also for hanging it over an open fire. The kettle can be suspended from a protruding tree branch or hung on a tripod.

Left: Goulash is still cooked over an open fire today, in a kettle with a wide base.

The goulash family
PÖRKÖLT, PAPRIKÁS, AND TOKÁNY

We don't always know exactly who the people are who have provided us with some great inventions. And we don't know who it was who first had the brilliant idea of combining fat, onions, and paprika to create that wonderful harmony of flavors so typical of *pörkölt* and *paprikás* dishes.

This masterpiece, still a defining factor in Hungarian cuisine today, can undoubtedly be traced back to cooking in a kettle. Fat and onions have been used since at least the Middle Ages. However, *gulyás*, *pörkölt*, and *paprikás* did not appear until the end of the 18th century, when people were just starting to season food with paprika.

The speedy development and enduring popularity of these dishes is easy to understand when you remember that pork fat was used almost exclusively in Hungary in former times, and that its flavor is what makes the fat/onion combination so delicious. That said, there is no cause for concern among the more health-conscious of us – most delicacies lose nothing if vegetable oil is used instead, which the latest nutritional research shows is better for us.

Apart from *pörkölt* and *paprikás*, there is another member of the family of dishes that are seasoned with the "trinity" of oil, onions, and paprika, and it probably originated from Transylvania: *tokány*.

Pörkölt is always made from poultry, pork, beef, mutton, or venison, with fresh beef

Clockwise from top left: polenta, dumplings, pasta pellets, *Borjúpaprikás* (veal *paprikás*), *Sertéspörkölt* (pork *pörkölt*), and *Borsos tokány* (pepper *tokány*).

being the preferred choice. *Paprikás* is made with lean meat, such as veal, chicken, or rabbit; *tokány* is usually made with beef, mutton, or venison.

The difference is in the detail. For *pörkölt*, the meat is usually diced, and for *tokány* it is cut into short, thin strips. *Pörkölt* usually has more sauce than *tokány*. Despite its name, *paprikás* usually contains less paprika than *pörkölt*, and it is made with sour cream for extra finesse. *Tokány* is almost always made without paprika; instead, it contains other seasonings, such as black pepper and marjoram, which are never found in *pörkölt* and *paprikás* dishes.

Regional *pörkölt*

The menus of smaller inns and restaurants often contain a separate column, entitled **zónaételek**. This column contains a number of dishes at lower prices. But just what is **zónaételek** – to say nothing of **zónapörkölt**? Simply, it's nothing more than a small portion. This column was introduced toward the end of the 19th century, when life moved at a slower pace, and clerks and businessmen had time to spend the morning in a local hostelry. They would sit in friendly social groups, drink a beer or two, and nibble a few delicacies. At that time, the railroad in Hungary was still under construction. Railroad stations, and especially railroad restaurants, became sociable meeting places – somewhere to see and be seen. It is said that when zone tariffs were first introduced and shorter distances cost less, a gentleman allowed himself a little joke and asked for a **zónapörkölt** or "zone pörkölt" …

Seed and chop the bell peppers.
Cut the tomato into 8 pieces.
Sauté the onion in the oil, and
remove from the heat. Add the
peppers and the meat. Return to
the heat and cook for a few
minutes, stirring continuously.
Season with salt, then add the
paprika and pieces of tomato.
Cover, and leave to cook in its
own juices.
Replace any of the juices that
evaporate with a little warm
water if necessary.
Garnish the cooked dish with the
sliced bell pepper.
Serve with dumplings or pasta
pellets, a fresh salad, or preserved
vegetables.

Borjúpaprikás
Veal paprikás

| 1¾ lb/800 g veal shoulder (boneless) |
| 1 medium onion |
| 3½ tbsp oil |
| ½ tsp rose paprika |
| Salt |
| 2 bell peppers (capsicum) |
| 1 medium tomato |
| 1¼ cups/300 ml sour cream |
| 2–3 tbsp flour |
| Sour cream to garnish |

Dice the meat (1¼ inch/3 cm or
bigger). Finely chop the onion,
and sauté in the oil until golden.
Remove from the heat, then
sprinkle the paprika and add 2–3
tbsp water. Let it bubble briefly.
Add the meat and salt to taste,
then cover with a lid. Cook
quickly, stirring frequently. Add a
little water if necessary.
Add the thinly sliced bell peppers
and the tomato to the half-
cooked meat. Combine the sour
cream with a little flour, stirring
until smooth. Add to the sauce,
and let it bubble briefly.
Garnish the prepared dish with a
few dollops of sour cream.

Borsos tokány
Peppered tokány

| 1¾ lb/800 g beef flank |
| 1 large onion, finely chopped |
| 2½ tbsp oil |
| Salt and pepper |
| 1 clove of garlic, crushed |
| ¾ cup/200 ml dry white wine |
| Tomato paste |

Cut the beef into strips of ¼ inch/
5 mm thickness, and 2 inches/
5 cm in length.
Sauté the onion in the oil until
golden. Add the meat, and brown
on all sides. Season with salt and
pepper.
Add the garlic and the wine, then
cover with a lid and simmer over
a low heat. Pour in a little water
if necessary.
Add the tomato paste when the
meat is half-cooked. Add a little
more water if required, and
continue cooking until the meat
is done. Let the liquid reduce as
much as possible.
This dish has a smooth, brown
sauce. It goes well with boiled or
mashed potatoes, rice, or polenta.

Sertéspörkölt
Pork pörkölt

| 1¾ lb/800 g pork (leg or shoulder) |
| 1 large onion |
| 2–3 bell peppers (capsicum) |
| 1 large tomato |
| 4 tbsp oil |
| ½ tsp ground paprika |
| Salt |
| 1 bell pepper (capsicum) for garnishing |

Cut the meat into ¾ inch/2 cm
cubes. Finely chop the onion.

CHICKEN PAPRIKA

In western Europe, chicken paprika (*Paprikás csirke*) became a prize-winning dish at the end of the 19th century, when Georges Auguste Escoffier (1846–1935), the famous French chef, put *Poulet au Paprika* and *Gulyás Hongroise* on the menu at the splendid Grand Hotel in Monte Carlo.

The popularity of *pörkölt* and *paprikás* made with chicken inspired chefs of the day to keep dreaming up new creations. One such development that is still popular today was created at the beginning of the 20th century in the elegant Hotel Arany Bika in Debrecen. It was named after the Hortobágy-Puszta, which comes under this town's administration: *hortobágyi palacsinta* – meat pancakes.

Hortobágyi palacsinta
(Hortobágyi meat pancakes with paprika sauce)

Pörkölt csirke
Chicken pörkölt

I chicken (about 2½ lbs/1.2 kg)
I large onion
2½ tbsp oil
I heaped tsp paprika (mild or sweet)
Salt
2 bell peppers (capsicum)
I large tomato

Divide the chicken into pieces (do not skin). Finely chop the onion. Heat the oil, and gently cook the onion, stirring occasionally. Remove from the heat, and sprinkle with the ground paprika. Add the chicken pieces and fry over a high heat for several minutes. Then reduce the heat, season the chicken with salt, and cover with a lid.

Remove the seeds from the bell peppers, and slice into rings, reserving a few for garnishing. Peel and seed the tomato, and chop. Add the pepper rings and the chopped tomato to the chicken and cover with the lid. Continue cooking until done, stirring from time to time. *Pörkölt* should ideally cook in its own juices. Add a little water only if you think it is going to burn. Toward the end of the cooking time, tilt the cooking pot from side to side instead of stirring the contents.

Arrange the chicken in a deep dish. Pour over the sauce and garnish with a few pepper slices. Serve with dumplings or pasta pellets, and a cucumber or green salad.

Paprikás csirke
Chicken paprika
(Photograph bottom right)

I chicken (about 2½ lbs/1.2 kg)
I large onion
2½ tbsp oil
I heaped tbsp ground paprika (mild or semisweet)
Salt
2 bell peppers (capsicum)
I large tomato
1⅔ cups/400 ml sour cream
I–2 tbsp flour

Prepare the chicken as for *Pörkölt csirke* (see above). Combine the cream with a little flour, and stir until smooth. Add the sour cream to the reduced juices at the end of the cooking time, and simmer gently for another 4–5 minutes. Serve with plain or quark dumplings, and a green salad.

Hortobágyi palacsinta
Meat pancakes with paprika sauce
(Photograph above)

8 unsweetened pancakes
14 oz/400 g chicken breasts (boned) or leg of veal
I small onion
2 tbsp oil
½ tsp ground paprika (sweet)
Salt
I bell pepper (capsicum)
I small tomato
1⅔ cups/400 ml sour cream
Parsley to garnish

Make 8 pancakes (see page 83), and prepare the meat as for *Pörkölt csirke* (see above). Dice the cooked meat, or push it through a meat grinder. Combine the meat juices with 1¼ cups/300 ml sour cream, and bring briefly to the boil. Add enough of this mixture to the ground meat to give it a spreadable consistency. Spread over the pancakes, and roll each one up individually. If you prefer, fold the edges over before rolling up the pancakes. The pancakes can also be shaped into little bags. Place in an ovenproof dish, and pour over the remaining cooking juices. Put the dish in a preheated medium oven, and heat thoroughly (10–15 minutes). Garnish with the remaining cream, sliced pepper, and parsley before serving.

Hortobágyi palacsinta are very filling, so serve only small portions.

Paprikás csirke (chicken paprika)

POPULAR CHICKEN DISHES

If you were to ask the Hungarians for their favorite dishes, breaded chicken (*Rántott csirke*) would undoubtedly be one of them. Although it looks fairly plain and simple, the preparation does require a little effort and skill. Breaded chicken was once a spring dish – and with good reason, since the main ingredient is a young, succulent chicken. Elek Magyar (1875–1947), the master of Hungarian cuisine, whose recipes and articles were published under the pseudonym of "Gourmet," emphasized the need for a freshly slaughtered, country chicken. In these times of mass production, the consumer is no longer at the mercy of the seasons, and not always too particular about the bird's origins. Chicken soup (*Tyúkhúsleves*) is served as a starter at traditional feasts. In many regions, the second course consists of cooked chicken served with some kind of sauce, perhaps made with tomatoes, gooseberries, dill, or garlic. A wedding feast without a golden, glistening chicken soup is simply unimaginable.

The cook is quite rightly proud of the beautiful golden color of the chicken soup, which used to be achieved by adding saffron. Today, however, saffron no longer really features in Hungarian cuisine.

Töltött csirke
(Stuffed chicken)

Rántott csirke
Breaded chicken
(Photograph center bottom)

I chicken (2¼–2¾ lbs/600–800 g)
2 eggs
Salt
¾ cup/100 g flour
¾ cup/100 g fine breadcrumbs
About 3½ cups/800 ml oil for deep-frying
Bunch of parsley

Wash the chicken. Pat dry with paper towels, and cut into eight pieces: 2 drumsticks and 2 wings (remove the tips), then halve the breast and back. Pierce the liver (to prevent splashing during cooking). Cut around the edge of the liver, and stuff into the wings. Lightly salt the chicken pieces. Beat the eggs in a deep dish with a little salt. Sprinkle the flour over one plate, and the breadcrumbs over another. Coat the chicken pieces with the flour, then dip in the beaten egg, and finally coat with the breadcrumbs. Make sure that the coating is equally thick all round.

Deep-fry the chicken pieces on both sides in plenty of very hot oil (cover with a lid at first). Watch the temperature: if it is too high, the breadcrumbs may burn, and the chicken will not cook; on the other hand, if the oil is not hot enough, the coating will come away from the chicken.

It is possible that the liver may splash during cooking, even though you have pierced it, so lower the liver-stuffed wings into the oil with care.

Place the cooked chicken pieces on paper towels to drain, and serve immediately.

Wash and shake dry the parsley. Sprinkle with a little flour, and dip briefly in the hot cooking oil (use a slotted spoon).

Traditionally, this dish is accompanied by potatoes cooked with parsley or steamed peas. It also goes well with a cucumber or green salad.

Petrezselymes újkrumpli
New potatoes with parsley

2¼ lbs/I kg new potatoes
Oil
Large bunch of parsley
Salt

Wash the potatoes. Leave the small ones whole, and halve the big ones. Heat the oil and stir in half the parsley, then add the potatoes. Season with salt, cover, and cook. Do not stir, but gently shake the pot from time to time. Sprinkle the remaining parsley over the potatoes, and continue to braise for another 1–2 minutes.

Tyúkhúsleves
(Chicken soup)

Rántott csirke
(Breaded chicken)

Sült csirke

Roast chicken

1 chicken (about 2¾ lbs/1.3 kg)	
Salt	
½ tsp marjoram (optional)	
Parsley, to taste	
¼–⅓ cup/60–80 g butter, melted	

Clean the chicken thoroughly. Rub salt over the inside and outside of the chicken, and sprinkle the marjoram or parsley into the cavity.
Truss the chicken with thread so that it keeps its shape while roasting. Place in a deep roasting pan, and pour over the hot butter. Place in a preheated medium oven, and roast for 45–60 minutes, basting occasionally. Add a little water if required. Reduce the cooking juices at the end of roasting.
Leave the chicken to rest before carving, then remove the wings and legs at the joints. Divide the chicken into the breast and back pieces. Finally, cut the back into 2–3 pieces, and slice the breast. A number of potato dishes, rice, steamed vegetables, and salads go well with this dish, and the juices are served as a sauce. *Sült csirke* is also delicious served cold.

Töltött csirke

Stuffed chicken
(Photograph top left)

2–3 slices day-old bread	
¾ –1¼ cups/200–300 ml milk	
1 chicken (1¾–2¼ lbs/800 g–1 kg)	
Salt	
½ tsp oil	
3–4 tbsp/50–60 g butter, melted	
1 tsp grated onion	
1 chicken liver (optional)	
Scant ½ tsp pepper	
Bunch of parsley	
2 eggs, beaten	

Soak the bread in the milk. Clean the chicken, and, using your fingers, gently loosen the skin around the neck opening, without damaging the skin. Season the chicken with salt on the inside and outside.
Heat the oil, then add the grated onion and fry gently without letting the onion turn yellow. Finely dice the chicken liver (if used), and add to the onion. Remove from the heat, and use a fork to combine with the bread. The bread does not need squeezing, since the heat will cause any surplus liquid to evaporate. Season with salt and pepper, and then add the finely chopped parsley and beaten egg. Combine well.
Push this stuffing gently between the chicken and the skin, and distribute evenly. Place the remainder inside the cavity. Close the openings, using a needle and thread, or skewers. Place in a roasting pan, then pour over the melted butter and place in a preheated (medium-hot) oven. Reduce the temperature after 3–4 minutes, and cook at a medium heat until crisp and golden. Baste frequently to prevent the flesh from becoming too dry. Leave to stand for a while, then remove the skewers or thread, and carve. Serve with potatoes or rice, braised vegetables, and salad. *Töltött csirke* is also delicious served cold.

Tyúkhúsleves

Chicken soup
(Photograph top right)

1 chicken (about 3¼ lbs/1.5 kg)	
Salt	
10 peppercorns	
2 large carrots	
2 large parsley roots	
1 small celery root	
1 small kohlrabi	
2 cloves of garlic	
1 small onion	

Cut the chicken into portions. Place in a high-sided pot, and pour over 4–5 pints (2–2.5 liters) cold water. Add salt and the peppercorns. Bring the water to the boil once, and then simmer over a low heat. There is no need to remove the scum.
Meanwhile, wash the carrots and the parsley roots, and cut into strips. Peel the celery and the kohlrabi, and leave whole. Peel the garlic, and leave whole. Remove only the brown outer skin from the onion, to give the soup a pleasant color.
Add the vegetables to the pot after 30 minutes. The soup is ready after 1–1½ hours total cooking time.
Leave the soup to stand for a few minutes, then pass through a strainer. Do not pour the soup into the strainer, but use a ladle, as this will keep the soup clear. Like any other soup, this chicken soup is also delicious if you add some pasta, rice, or semolina dumplings.
At a wedding, this soup is traditionally served with pasta crescents made by the bride's friends.

1 Clockwise from top: flour, eggs, salt, pasta pellet strainer
2 Combine the eggs with water and salt.
3 Add some of the egg/water mixture to the flour in the wooden trough.

4 Knead well. Add more egg/water to the dough, and continue to knead.
5 Repeat this process until the dough has the desired consistency.
6 Using all your strength, press the dough through the strainer.

The pasta pellets are spread over a clean tablecloth to dry.

PASTA PELLETS

"And where do pasta pellets grow?" – a question the Hungarians like to ask their children, in fun. After all, the shape, which is similar to that of grains of barley or rice, does seem to indicate botanical origins.

The Hungarian name for pasta pellets is *tarhonya*, and is Turkish-Ottoman in origin. The Hungarians are supposed to have adopted the art of pasta pellet-making while under the despotic rule of the Ottomans in the 16th and 17th centuries. However, others would have it that they brought the recipe with them from their original home in Asia. In fact, Balkan and Turkish countries, and even Persia, all have similar pasta products, the names of which are all derived from *tarhonya*. However, pasta pellets are more popular in Hungary than anywhere else. Today, pasta pellets, which actually came from the cuisine of the Puszta, are a classic accompaniment that is found on every Hungarian family's menu. Twice a year on the Great Plain, in the spring and in the fall, the women set about kneading vast quantities of eggs and flour with a little salt water to make a very firm dough. The dough is then pushed through a special strainer with large holes, and spread out in the garden to dry, first in the bright sun, and later in the shade. Finally, the pasta pellets are put into finely woven linen bags and hung in a dry place. Stored this way, they will keep for several months.

Field workers, herdsmen, and then also farmers and railroad workers, all used to take the pasta pellets to work and prepare their midday meal from them. They were cooked in kettles and the flavor improved by the addition of onions, ground paprika, and smoked bacon (and later potatoes). Although this dish, which is still extremely popular today, is actually called a soup, it is really more of a stew – it should be so thick that the spoon stays upright in it.

In the 19th century, increasing numbers of impoverished farmer's wives offered pasta pellets for sale in markets or to other families in their villages as a way of improving the family's finances. The pearl-like grains gained substantially in popularity during World War I, and in 1928 the production from the Szeged area filled more than a hundred freight cars.

Today, only a few housewives still know how to make pasta pellets. However, of all the types available commercially, the most popular (and the most expensive) are the ones that look handmade – unevenly shaped, and with a rough surface. Their close relatives, *reszelt tészta* (grated pasta), are more likely to be made by hand today.

Tarhonyaköret
Pasta pellets as an accompaniment

½ small onion
2½ tbsp oil
1¼ cups/250 g pasta pellets
Pinch of ground paprika
Salt

Finely dice or grate the onion. Heat the oil and sauté the pasta pellets in the hot fat until golden, stirring continuously. Add the onion, and cook together for a few minutes. Remove from the heat, and sprinkle with the ground paprika and salt. Add twice the amount (about 2 cups/500 ml) of boiling water. Cover and cook in a preheated (medium) oven for about 15 minutes.
Serve the pasta pellets with *pörkölt*, *paprikás*, and *tokány*. If served as a side dish, the pasta pellets should be light and fluffy, like rice.

Szegedi tarhonyás hús
Szegedinian meat with pasta pellets

1¼ lbs/600 g pork (lean shoulder or knuckle)
1 large onion
5 tbsp oil
1 tsp ground paprika (sweet)
Salt
2 bell peppers (capsicum)
1 large tomato
1¼ cups/250 g pasta pellets

Cut the pork into ¾ inch/2 cm chunks. Finely chop the onion. Heat half the oil and fry the onions until golden. Remove from the heat, and sprinkle over the paprika. Add ½ cup/100 ml water, and let the liquid evaporate over a low heat.
Then add the meat and salt, and cover with a lid. Leave to simmer gently, adding a little more water if necessary.
Cut the prepared peppers and the tomato in half lengthwise, and add to the half-cooked meat.

Fry the pasta pellets in the remaining oil until golden, stirring continuously. Then add to the meat when it is almost ready. Add enough warm water to cover.
Season with salt if required. Cover and place in a preheated oven for about 15 minutes. Serve with a fresh seasonal salad or preserved vegetables. Pickled gherkins, pickled peppers, or mixed pickles go extremely well with this dish.

Tarhonyaleves
Pasta pellet soup

1 tomato
1 bell pepper (capsicum)
10 oz/300 g potatoes
2 tbsp oil
3½ oz/100 g pasta pellets
½ small onion
½ tsp ground paprika
1 heaped tsp chopped parsley to garnish

Dice the tomato, pepper, and the peeled potatoes. Heat the oil, then sauté the pasta pellets until golden, and put aside.
Sauté the finely chopped onion. Remove from the heat, sprinkle over the paprika, and add 5 cups/1.25 liters hot water. Add the tomato and the pepper, and cook for a few minutes. Then add the potatoes and the pasta pellets, and cook over a low heat.

Reszelt tészta
Grated pasta

2¼ lbs/1 kg flour
4–5 eggs

Knead the flour and the eggs to a very firm dough, without adding any water. Grate, and spread over a wooden board or a tablecloth to dry. Store in a screwtop jar, and cook as for pasta pellets.

Lebbencs: a poetic Hungarian name for a down-to-earth ingredient

Apart from pasta pellets, the Great Plain of Hungary also boasts another type of pasta: *lebbencs* (small wafer-thin pasta). It too keeps well, and does not mind being transported. Connoisseurs of traditional recipes use it to conjure up the most wonderful dishes. Farmer's wives on the Great Plain used to make vast quantities of the dough for this pasta in the spring. They would roll it out into thin sheets, and then hang these over rods, or poles, in an airy place in the storeroom to dry, with a clean tablecloth spread out below to catch the pieces that dropped off. Drafts of air would cause the pasta sheets to flap (*lebben* in Hungarian) like washing on a line, hence the poetic name – *lebbencs*.

Lebbencsleves
Lebbencs soup

1 tomato
1 bell pepper (capsicum)
7 oz/200 g potatoes
2 tsp oil
3½ oz/100 g *lebbencs*
2oz/50 g smoked bacon
½ small onion
½ tsp ground paprika
3 stalks of celery leaves
1 hot chili pod (optional)

Chop the tomato, the bell pepper, and the peeled potatoes. Heat the oil, sauté the pasta until golden, and set to one side.
Dice the bacon, and sauté in the pan until the fat starts to run. Add the finely chopped onion, and sauté until golden. Remove from the heat, then sprinkle over the paprika and add 5 cups/1.25 liters hot water. Return to the heat, add the tomato and the pepper, and cook for a few minutes. Then add the potatoes, the pasta, and the celery leaves (tied together), and cook over a low heat. Remove the celery leaves before serving.
Those who like spicy soups may like to add a piece of dried hot chili to their soup.

PASTA

Pasta is almost as important in Hungarian cuisine as it is in Italian. The midday meal usually consists of soup, followed by a hot, hearty, or sweet pasta dish. Pasta may well be served both as a main course and as dessert. Many Hungarian families have a pasta day once a week. This is usually Friday, which, according to Christian tradition, is a day of fasting. So deeply entrenched is this custom that even during the anti-religious periods of the communist regime, many business and school canteens served pasta as a main course on Fridays – more out of habit, it has to be said, than as a sign of tolerance.

It has become quite unusual for Hungarian housewives to make their own pasta, since a wide range of different types are available commercially. Although most of these are mass-produced, some are still made by small businesses. The latter still use traditional production methods and have the wording *házi* (homemade) on their packaging. The packaging also provides information on the egg content: two to eight eggs are used for every 2¼ lbs (1 kg) of flour. The more eggs that are used, the better the quality of the pasta.

The great variety of types of pasta in the country is due to a Hungarian peculiarity: a strict rule which states that every dish must have its own specially shaped type of pasta.

Gyúrt tészta
Homemade pasta
(Photograph)

3⅓ cups/400 g flour
3 eggs
Pinch of salt
Butter

Sift the flour into a bowl, and make a well in the center. Break the eggs into the center of the well, and sprinkle over the salt. Gradually add ¾–1¼ cups/200–300 ml of water. First, combine everything with your fingers, and then firmly knead the dough on a floured work surface until it no longer sticks to either your fingers or the work surface. Halve the dough, and shape each half into a loaf. Brush some melted butter over each piece of dough, then cover and leave to rest for 10–15 minutes. Roll the dough out evenly; if necessary, sprinkle some flour over the work surface, the dough, and the rolling pin. The dough should be as thin as parchment for square pasta (*csusza* and *lebbencs*). For ribbon pasta, it should be as thick as the blade of a knife.

Place the pasta sheets on a clean dish towel and leave to dry a little, so they do not stick together when you roll them up. Then roll the individual pasta sheets onto the rolling pin, and cut through them lengthwise. Cut these pieces into the required shape. Ribbon pasta should be no more than ¼ inch/5 mm wide, and square pasta should be cut into ⅔–¾ inch/1.5–2 cm squares. You can also simply tear the pasta with your fingers into slightly larger, irregularly sized pieces. Boil the pasta in plenty of lightly salted water, stirring it occasionally. Do take care not to overcook the pasta; like its Italian cousins, it should still have a certain "bite" to it. Finally, briefly coat it in some hot fat, and add any other ingredients your recipe requires. Serve immediately.

1 Roll the dough out thinly.
2 Carefully roll the sheet of dough around a rolling pin.
3 Use a kitchen knife to cut lengthwise through the dough.

4 Carefully remove the dough from the rolling pin.
5 Cut the sheets of pasta into the required size.
6 Ribbon pasta is the most popular type.

Mákos metélt
Poppyseed pasta

⅔ cup/100 g ground poppyseeds
Scant 1 cup/100 g confectioners' sugar
Pinch of grated lemon rind
Ribbon pasta (made from 2⅔ cups/350 g flour and 4 eggs)
Melted butter

Combine the poppyseeds with the sugar and lemon rind. Stir the cooked pasta in some melted butter and add half the poppyseed mixture. Sprinkle the other half over the pasta serving.

Diós metélt
Nut pasta

¾ cup/100 g grated walnuts
Scant 1 cup/100 g confectioners' sugar
Ribbon pasta (made with 2⅔ cups/350 g flour and 4 eggs)
Melted butter

Combine the walnuts and the sugar. Stir the cooked pasta in some melted butter and sprinkle over half the nut mixture. Sprinkle the other half over when serving.

Grízes metélt
Semolina pasta

¾ cup/120 g semolina
⅓ cup/80g butter
Salt
Ribbon pasta (made from 2⅔ cups/350 g flour and 4 eggs)

Stir-fry the semolina in the hot butter until golden, then add 1½ times the same amount of lightly salted hot water. Bring to a boil. Cover, and place in a preheated (medium) oven to absorb the liquid. Then combine with the cooked pasta, and reheat.
Serve either as a savory dish with pickled vegetables, or with a little thinned, hot jelly.

Káposztás kocka
Cabbage pasta squares

2¼ lbs/1 kg white cabbage
Salt
1 tsp sugar
3½ tbsp/50 g butter
½ tsp pepper
Large square pasta (made from 2⅔ cups/350 g flour and 4 eggs)

Grate the cabbage, then salt it and leave to stand for 15–20 minutes. Let the sugar caramelize in the melted butter, then add the well-drained cabbage and stir-fry until brown: Season with the pepper, and combine with the cooked, well-drained pasta (add a little oil to the cooking water for the pasta).
Serve hot. If you have a sweet tooth, add a little sugar when serving.

Sonkás kocka
Ham pasta squares

Large square pasta shapes (made from 3⅓ cups/400 g flour and 4 eggs)
12 oz/350 g cooked ham
3½ tbsp/50 g butter
3 eggs
¾ cup/200 ml sour cream
Salt and pepper
1 cup/50 g breadcrumbs

Cook and drain the pasta. Finely chop the ham (you may want to do this in a meat grinder). Butter an ovenproof dish. Combine the remaining butter with the egg yolks, stirring until smooth. Add the ham and the sour cream, and season with salt and pepper. Beat the egg whites until stiff.
Carefully add the pasta, then the beaten egg whites to the ham mixture. Coat the buttered dish with the breadcrumbs. Spread the ham mixture evenly over the dish. Bake in a preheated medium oven until golden. Serve hot.

Soup garnishes

Pasta: Small pasta shapes that are added to soup to cook (see below).

Dumplings: The dough for these is slightly different from that for the dumplings which are served as an accompaniment (e.g. *Daragaluska* and *Májgaluska*; see pages 40–41). They are added to soups to cook.

Thin pancakes: Cut into wide ribbons, and added to consommés and meat soups.

Toasted breadcrumbs: Day-old bread is cubed, and fried in a little oil or butter until crispy. Used in oven-baked, cumin-flavored, and cream soups.

Semolina: One or two teaspoons of semolina are sprinkled into vegetable soups to cook. This makes the soup creamier, and adds flavor. Good low-fat choice.

Cérnametélt, kockatészta, eperlevél
Ribbon and square pasta

1 egg
About 1 cup/120 g flour
Pinch of salt

Combine the egg and flour with a pinch of salt, and knead to a firm dough (as in the recipe for *Gyúrt tészta*; see page 38). The exact quantity of flour required depends on the size of the egg. The flour should absorb all of the liquid without the addition of water.
Roll the dough out very thinly without sprinkling flour over the rolling pin, and cut into the desired shapes: parchment-thin ribbons (*cérnametélt* = ribbon pasta), or squares (*kocka* = squares). The sides of the squares should measure at least ¼ inch/ 5 mm. If you cut them with a pastry wheel, the edges will look like the edges of a leaf, which is why this shape is also called *eperlevél* (strawberry leaf). In

Hungary, a small stick and ribbed board are sometimes used to shape the plain square pasta into little horns or snails (see page 234). Place the pasta in the soup when it is ready, and leave for a few moments to cook. Ribbon and square pasta are added mainly to meat soups, but they can also be added to any other variety.

Csipetke
"Plucked" pasta

Make a dough using the above recipe, and leave to rest. Then roll out to a thickness of ¼ inch/ 5 mm, and "pluck" into pea-size pieces. As a general guide, allow ¾ oz/20 g per person.
Ideal for goulash and bean soups.

Eperlevél (strawberry leaves)

Kiskocka (small square pasta shapes)

DUMPLINGS

Small semolina dumplings, known as *galuska* and *nokedli*, are not only the most popular accompaniment to all *pörkölt* dishes, but – made from a different kind of dough – the most frequent addition to vegetable soups.

As an accompaniment (Photograph):

2 eggs
Pinch of salt
About 3⅓ cups/400 g flour
3½ tbsp oil

Beat the eggs with the salt and ¾ cup/200 ml water. Add enough flour to make a smooth, viscous dough. Beat well with a wooden spoon. Push the dough through a dumpling strainer into a pot containing a generous quantity of salted boiling water. Remove the cooked dumplings with a slotted spoon when they rise to the surface of the water. Rinse with lukewarm water, and drain well. Finally, stir in hot oil.

As soup garnish:

1 egg
Pinch of salt
Small pinch each of pepper and finely chopped parsley (optional)
¾ cup/100 g flour

Combine the egg with the salt and the parsley and pepper, where used. Add enough flour to make a viscous dough. Using a teaspoon, scoop out tiny "dumplings," and cook in the gently simmering soup for a few minutes.

1 The ingredients, clockwise from top right: water, salt, eggs, dumpling strainer, flour.
2 Beat the eggs in a bowl. Add the water and a pinch of salt, and mix well.

3 Add the flour and combine thoroughly.
4 Place the dumpling strainer over the saucepan and push the dough through the openings in the strainer into the boiling water.

Using a slotted spoon, remove the cooked dumplings from the water and drain well.

Tojásos nokedli
Egg dumplings
(accompaniment)

For the dough:

2 eggs
Pinch of salt
3⅓ cups/400 g flour

For the egg mixture:

4 eggs
Scant ½ cup/100 ml milk or sour cream
Salt
2½ tbsp/40 g butter

Prepare the dough as given in the recipe for "Dumplings as an accompaniment" (page 40). Beat together the eggs, milk (or sour cream), and the salt. Melt the butter in a large skillet, and pour in the egg and milk mixture. Add the freshly cooked dumplings when this mixture is just beginning to set. Combine carefully, and leave to set for a few minutes.
Egg dumplings are usually served, after a soup appetizer, as an independent course, and accompanied by a salad.

Májgaluska
Liver dumplings (for soups)

2 chicken livers (or scant 4½ oz/120 g veal or pork liver)
1–2 slices day-old bread
1 egg
Salt
Pinch of pepper
Pinch of marjoram
½ tsp grated onion
1 tsp oil
Half a bunch of parsley, chopped

Finely chop the liver, or pass it through a meat grinder. Soak the bread in water. Squeeze it well, then combine with the egg and liver. Season with salt, pepper, and marjoram.
Sauté the onion in the oil. Add the parsley, and fry quickly. Add to the liver mixture, and combine everything well.

Using a teaspoon, scoop out tiny "dumplings," and drop into the simmering meat stock or soup to cook. At first, drop just a few dumplings into the stock. If they disintegrate, add a little flour to the liver mixture.

Daragaluska
Semolina dumplings (for soups)

4 tsp butter
2 eggs
Pinch of salt
1¼ cup/200 g semolina

Beat the butter and egg until fluffy. Season with the salt, and combine with the semolina. Place in the refrigerator for 30 minutes. Using a teaspoon, scoop out tiny dumplings and drop into the strained, simmering meat stock. Cook gently over a medium heat. These dumplings are a popular addition to meat soups. You will know your semolina dumplings are a success if they "puff up", and are light and fluffy. It is best to cut one in half to check whether it is cooked. Since semolina dumplings absorb a lot of liquid, they are usually prepared in a separate pot of stock. Do this by dissolving a bouillon cube (or as many as required) in plenty of boiling water.
Add the dumplings to the soup just before serving.

Debrecziner sausages with bread

A famous pair
DEBRECZINER

Debrecen, the third largest city in Hungary and the cultural and economic center of the Great Plain, is the namesake of a popular type of sausage that is famous well beyond the country's borders.

This delicacy is a lightly smoked sausage that is made from beef and pork, its red color due to the mild paprika used in its manufacture. Debrecziner, which are always sold in pairs, can be simmered or fried. They are used in many Hungarian dishes, where they are appreciated for the spicy, slightly smoky flavor they

The Great Church of the Reformed is the town's main landmark.

add. Unlike most dried sausages which become hard when cooked, Debrecziner remain soft and juicy even after extensive

cooking. This is due to the garlic stock, which is added to the meat during the manufacturing process.

Debreceni krumpli egytál
Debreczin potatoes

3½ oz/100 g smoked bacon or lardons
2 small onions
½ tsp ground paprika
2 pairs Debrecziner sausages (about 14 oz/400 g)
1¾ lbs/800 g potatoes
About ¾ cup/200 ml oil
Salt
Small bunch of parsley

Cut the bacon into thin slices, and place in a skillet until the fat begins to run. Finely chop the onions, and sauté in the fat until they turn golden. Remove from

the heat. Sprinkle over the ground paprika and add a little water. Add the sausages (with the skins), then cover and simmer for 7–8 minutes. Remove the sausages, and cut into thick slices. Return to the pan, and cook until the juices thicken.
Peel the potatoes, and cut into slices of the same thickness as the sausage. Fry the potato slices in plenty of hot oil over a high heat until they are brown and crispy, then drain well on paper. Season with salt, sprinkle over the chopped parsley, and add to the sausages. Serve immediately.

Proud and free
HEYDUCKS

The Heyducks (*hajdú*) were originally drovers (*hajtó*) of vast herds of cattle. Their work was hard, and required extensive experience and expertise, as well as strength and endurance. They also had to protect their herds against thieves and armed robbers. Skilled in battle, they were often employed as coachmen and bodyguards.

During the Turkish wars, however, they lost their work as drovers, and as a result many Heyducks turned to highway robbery or became mercenaries. In 1605 István Bocskai, prince of Transylvania, moved several thousand of them to his lands around Debrecen, and awarded them certain privileges. The Heyducks did not have to pay taxes, but instead had to accompany the prince into battle.

The Heyducks settled, and soon developed their own independent culture in their villages and towns. They became famed for their saber dances, of which many travelers spoke with great enthusiasm, and their hearty, solid fare has also found many admirers.

Hajdúkáposzta
Cabbage served in the Heyduck tradition

2 medium onions
4 tbsp oil
2 tsp ground paprika
1 clove of garlic
2 small cured pork knuckles
4 large potatoes
1¾ lbs/800 g sauerkraut
4 slices smoked bacon with rind (each 2 oz/50 g)
Ground paprika to garnish

Sauté the finely chopped onions in the oil. Remove from the heat. Sprinkle over the ground paprika and add the crushed garlic. Return to the heat and fry for several minutes, stirring continuously.

Add the prepared knuckles. Pour over a little water, then cover with a lid and cook.

Peel the potatoes. Add the potatoes and the sauerkraut to the half-cooked knuckles, and finish cooking.

Thicken the juices at the end of the cooking time to make a smooth, creamy sauce. Meanwhile, slit the rind on the slices of bacon at ½–¾ inch/1.25–2 cm intervals, to a depth of ½–1 inch/1–2 cm (to make a "cockscomb"), and fry until crispy. Finally, dip the "cockscomb" in the ground paprika.

Remove the meat from the bones, and arrange the sauerkraut on top of the meat. Place the "cockscomb" on top, and arrange with the halved cooked potatoes.

This 17th-century engraving shows some Heyducks performing one of their famous saber dances. Kapronca castle is in the background.

Mulberry tree

If you have never picked the berries of this tree, which grows all over Hungary, you are unlikely to be familiar with them. Similar in appearance to blackberries, they are generally unremarkable – except when consumed as the highly popular "Schnapps." Although the fruit does have its admirers, the sweet, delicate berries are not available commercially apart from, occasionally, at weekly markets.

The deep-blue berries are preferred for making compotes, jellies, and juices, since they are far more aromatic than their creamy yellow cousins.

The mulberry tree, which arrived in Europe some 2000 years ago via the Silk Route from China, thrives in the wild and provides fruit in abundance, without human intervention. It was briefly cultivated in Hungary in the 18th century, when it was hoped that economic problems could be resolved by cultivating silkworms, so the mulberry tree was grown to provide food for the caterpillars.

Inhabited islands
ISOLATED FARMS

The isolated farm (*tanya*) is the traditional style of housing on the Great Plain of Hungary. The main house, consisting of residential and agricultural buildings, is surrounded by extensive fields and meadows, not unlike an island in an ocean. The family spends most, if not all of the year here, tending the garden, fields, and stock.

In bygone days, it was disparaging to say that someone "came from an isolated farm," since it implied that the person was poor, backward, or even slow-witted. Now, however, the meaning of the phrase has changed and it awakens feelings of nostalgia. If poultry and eggs offered for sale on markets are *tanyasi* (from an isolated farm), this is desirable, since it brings to mind idyllic scenes of hens scrabbling freely in open fields, rather than of poultry factories and battery farms. And increasing numbers of stressed city-dwellers spend vacations with friendly farmers in the countryside, to seek peace and rest.

1 A typical isolated farm with mulberry trees and a draw well, a relic from a bygone age.
2 Living on a farm is hard work for the farmers.

3 The mangalica pig is happiest in the open air.
4 Food for the winter from one's own garden.

VEGETABLES

Vegetable dishes are a central feature of the plain, homely fare of Hungary. They consist of one or any number of vegetables, usually sautéed in fat, and cooked in a small amount of liquid, usually marrow stock. Depending on the particular recipe, the dish is seasoned, and thickened with flour, a *roux*, or soured cream. Although the preparation looks easy, and not particularly refined, a certain degree of instinctive flair is required for the dish to be a success. The right amount of seasoning and thickening are the secrets of success (the dish must not be too thick), so that the particular flavor of each vegetable is allowed to develop.

A vegetable dish is always served as an accompaniment to something else. A roast or breaded meat goes with green peas, kohlrabi, or carrots; spinach, sorrel, green beans, and pumpkin are excellent with fried eggs, and *pörkölt* is particularly delicious with the latter two.

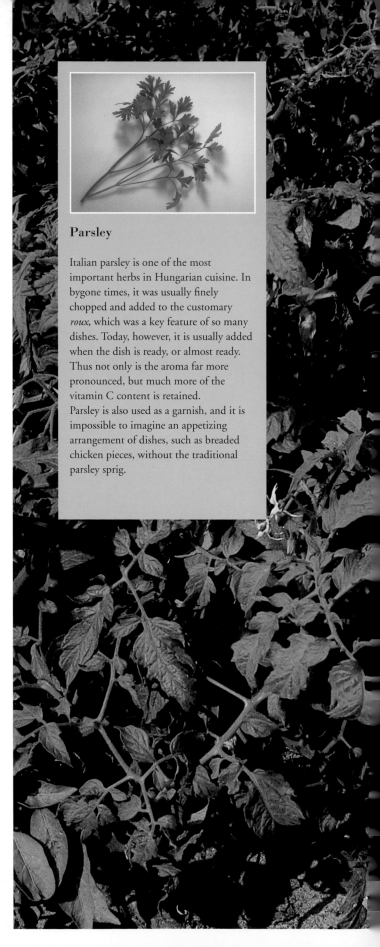

Parsley

Italian parsley is one of the most important herbs in Hungarian cuisine. In bygone times, it was usually finely chopped and added to the customary *roux*, which was a key feature of so many dishes. Today, however, it is usually added when the dish is ready, or almost ready. Thus not only is the aroma far more pronounced, but much more of the vitamin C content is retained.

Parsley is also used as a garnish, and it is impossible to imagine an appetizing arrangement of dishes, such as breaded chicken pieces, without the traditional parsley sprig.

Carrot-shaped, creamy white parsley roots are used in soups.

Fresh country vegetables in a Hungarian market

Sárgarépafőzelék
Creamed carrots
(Photograph below)

2¼ lbs/1 kg carrots
Bunch of parsley
2½ tbsp/40 g butter
2 tbsp sugar
Salt
½–¾ cup/100–200 ml marrow stock
5 tbsp flour
¾ cup/200 ml milk

Peel and thinly slice the carrots. Finely chop the parsley. Sauté the carrots in hot butter, and season with sugar, parsley, and salt. Add a little stock or water, and cook. Let the liquid reduce, and sprinkle over the flour. Add the milk, and heat through.

Sóskafőzelék
Creamed sorrel

2¼ lbs/1 kg sorrel
Salt
2½ tbsp/40 g butter
5 tbsp flour
Marrow stock
½–¾ cup/100–200 ml light cream
About 3 tbsp sugar

Remove the stalks and thick veins from the sorrel, and the stalks from the delicate leaves. Sprinkle a little salt over the leaves, and stir-fry in hot butter until the leaves are almost creamy. Sprinkle with the flour, and continue to stir over the heat. Add the stock and the cream, and stir. Season with a little sugar, but remember this dish should still be a little "sour." Serve with boiled potatoes.

Karalábéfőzelék
Creamed kohlrabi

2¼ lbs/1 kg young kohlrabi
Bunch of parsley
2½ tbsp/40 g butter
Salt
Marrow stock
5 tbsp flour
½–¾ cup/100–200 ml milk

Peel and thinly slice the kohlrabi. Finely chop the parsley. Melt the butter and stir-fry the kohlrabi. Sprinkle with the parsley, and season with salt. Cover with a lid and continue to cook the kohlrabi over a low heat, ideally in their own juices, but adding a little marrow stock (or water) if necessary. Finally, increase the heat to evaporate the liquid until only the melted butter remains. Sprinkle with the flour, and stir for several minutes until the flour has turned golden. Then pour over a little cold water and the milk, and heat through for a few minutes.

Sárgarépafőzelék (creamed carrots)

Zöldbabfőzelék
Green beans
(Photograph bottom right)

1¾ lbs/800 g tender green beans
Salt
1 small onion
Bunch of parsley
3½ tbsp/50 g butter
6 tbsp flour
1 clove of garlic
½ tsp ground paprika
⅔ cup/150 ml sour cream
½ tsp sugar
Vinegar

Wash the beans, and cut into 1 inch/2.5 cm lengths. Place in a pot, cover with salted water, and cook.
Finely chop the onion and parsley. Melt the butter, add the flour, and combine well. Remove from the heat and add the onion, crushed garlic, parsley, and ground paprika. Add about ¾ cup/200 ml cold water, then whisk until smooth, and combine with the cooked green beans. Stir in the sour cream.
Season the dish with sugar and vinegar (it should taste slightly sour), and simmer for another 3–4 minutes.

Tökfőzelék
Creamed pumpkin
(Photograph top right)

2½ lbs/1.2 kg pumpkin
Salt
1 small onion
Bunch of dill
3½ tbsp/50 g butter
7 tbsp flour
1 tsp ground paprika
1 bell pepper (capsicum)
2–3 tsp vinegar
¾ cup/200 ml light or sour cream

Peel the pumpkin, and remove the seeds. Roughly grate the pumpkin flesh, then sprinkle with some salt and leave to stand for 10–30 minutes. Pour off the liquid. Finely chop the onion and the dill.

Heat the butter in a large pot, then stir in the flour and cook until just brown. Add the onion and sauté. Remove from the heat, and season with the dill and paprika. Add some water, then the pumpkin and the seeded pepper.
Return to the heat and cook. After 10–15 minutes, when the vegetables are half-cooked, season with the vinegar. Cook until ready, making sure the pumpkin retains some "bite."
Finally, stir in the cream and heat through. Remove the onion before serving.
The vinegar stops the pumpkin from disintegrating. Add a little more vinegar if using sour cream. Served cold on hot days, this dish is extremely refreshing.

Spenót
Creamed spinach
(Photograph center right)

2¼ lbs/1 kg leaf spinach
Salt
1 day-old bread roll
About 2½ cups/600 ml milk
3 tbsp/40 g butter
½ cup/60 g flour
1–2 cloves of garlic
Pinch of pepper

Remove the stalks and thick veins from the spinach, or just the stalks from tender leaves. Bring a generous 3 quarts/3 liters lightly salted water to a boil, then cook the spinach, uncovered, for 3–4 minutes. Drain in a strainer and leave to cool, then squeeze gently. Soften the roll in milk, and pass through a grinder with the spinach.
Melt the butter, then sprinkle over the flour and cook until just brown. Add the crushed garlic and a little milk, and stir until smooth. Add the spinach and stir well. Pour over the remaining milk, and stir until the desired consistency is achieved (not too runny).

Season with a little salt and pepper.
This dish is usually served with boiled potatoes, but it is also delicious with fried eggs, meatloaf, or fritters.

Zöldborsófőzelék
Garden peas

1¾ lbs/800 g garden peas
3 tbsp/40 g butter
Salt
5 tbsp flour
2 tbsp sugar (optional)
Bunch of parsley

Stir the peas in the hot butter and season with salt. Cover with a lid, and let the peas cook in their own juices. Sprinkle over the flour, and, stirring continuously, cook until the flour turns golden. Add a little cold water, and simmer for several minutes. Season with a little sugar if required.
Finely chop the parsley and add to the dish before serving.

Bundáskenyér
Bread fritters

Bread
Egg
Salt
Milk as required
Oil

Cut the bread into slices. Beat the eggs and season with the salt; thin with a little milk if required. Dip the bread in the beaten egg and fry in the hot oil until crispy on both sides.
Serve hot.

Tökfőzelék (creamed pumpkin)

Spenót (creamed spinach)

Zöldbabfőzelék (green beans)

VEGETABLE SOUPS

Soups play an important part in Hungarian cuisine. The midday meal is traditionally the main meal of the day, and it is impossible to think of it without a soup being served. People are not generally prepared to forego a first course of soup, which stimulates the gastric juices and thus the appetite. There are also soups that are served as a main course, and soups that are eaten to soothe a troubled stomach "the morning after."

The *leitmotif* in the symphony of soups is vegetable soup, for which only the freshest ingredients are used. The Hungarians like to make their vegetable soups with marrow stock rather than water. Not only does this make them more nutritious, but it also improves the flavor; these do, however, also require more elaborate preparation.

Zöldbableves
Green bean soup

| Generous 1 lb/500 g green beans |
| 1 small onion |
| 1 tomato |
| 1 bell pepper (capsicum) |
| Salt |
| 2 tbsp/30 g butter |
| 4 tbsp flour |
| ½ tbsp mild paprika |
| Bunch of parsley, finely chopped |
| Vinegar to taste |
| ⅔ cup/150 ml sour cream |

Wash and trim the beans. Cut the beans diagonally into 1 inch/2.5 cm lengths. Bring 6 cups/1.5 liters water to a boil, and gradually add the beans without letting the water stop boiling. Leave the onion, tomato, and bell pepper whole, and add to the beans (they are removed before serving). Season when the beans are half cooked.

Melt the butter, add the flour, and stir. Remove from the heat, then stir in the paprika and use to bind the soup. Finish cooking the beans, and season the soup with finely chopped parsley and a little vinegar.

Add the sour cream to the soup when ready to serve, or else serve separately for diners to help themselves.

Below: Farmers' wives offering their wares for sale at the market. Only the very freshest ingredients are used to make soup.

Zöldborsóleves (garden pea soup)

Karfiolleves (cauliflower soup)

Zöldségleves (vegetable soup)

Zöldségleves
Vegetable soup
(Photograph center)

½ small onion	
2 tbsp/30 g butter	
2 medium carrots	
2 medium parsley roots	
Salt	
4 tbsp flour	
½ tsp ground paprika (mild)	
1 tomato	
1 bell pepper (capsicum)	
Pinch of pepper	
Bunch of parsley, finely chopped	
Dumplings, liver dumplings, or pasta shapes	

Finely chop the onion, and sauté in the butter. Add the sliced carrots and parsley roots, and season. Cover, and sauté until the vegetables are a pleasant shade of reddish-yellow, stirring frequently. Sprinkle over the flour, and stir until it turns the same color. Remove from the heat, then season with the paprika and add 5½ cups/1.3 liters water. Add the tomato and the bell pepper (which are removed from the soup before serving), and continue cooking. When ready, season with pepper and finely chopped parsley.
Little dumplings (see page 40), liver dumplings (see page 41), and square pasta shapes (see page 39) are delicious in this soup. They are added to the soup toward the end of the cooking time.

Karfiolleves
Cauliflower soup
(Photograph top right)

Generous 1 lb/500 g cauliflower florets	
Salt	
2 tbsp/30 g butter	
6 tbsp flour	
½ tsp ground paprika (sweet)	
Bunch of parsley, finely chopped	
¾ cup/200 ml sour cream	

Parboil the cauliflower florets in 6 cups/1.5 liters lightly salted water. Melt the butter, add the flour, and cook until light golden. Remove from the heat, then stir in the paprika and use to bind the soup. When the cauliflower is cooked, add the finely chopped parsley and half the cream, and let the soup come to the boil again briefly. Garnish the soup with the remaining cream before serving.

Karalábéleves
Kohlrabi soup

1¼ lbs/600 g tender kohlrabi	
2 tbsp/30 g butter	
5 tbsp flour	
Salt	
Generous pinch of pepper	
Bunch of parsley, finely chopped	
Scant ½ cup/100 ml sour cream	

Peel the kohlrabi and chop into small dice. Melt the butter in a pot, and braise the kohlrabi for 2–3 minutes, stirring continuously. Sprinkle over the flour and stir until golden in color. Add 5½ cups/1.3 liters water and bring to a boil. Season with salt and pepper, and cook the kohlrabi over a low heat until done.
Finally, stir in the finely chopped parsley and the sour cream.

Zöldborsóleves
Garden pea soup
(Photograph top left)

2¼ lbs/1 kg fine peas in pods	
2 tbsp/30 g butter	
5 tbsp flour	
About ½ tsp ground paprika (sweet)	
Bunch of parsley	
Dumplings or liver dumplings	

Shell the peas, keeping a few of the better pods to one side (they will be used later in the soup), and rinse them. Melt the butter in a pot and sauté the peas briefly, stirring continuously. Sprinkle over the flour, and when it is golden in color, remove the pot from the heat and season to taste with the paprika. Add 5½ cups/ 1.3 liters water and the pods, and cook until done.
Stir in the finely chopped parsley, and add some dumplings (see page 40) or liver dumplings (see page 41) to cook before serving.

PICKLED GHERKINS

It is impossible to imagine a Hungarian summer without these large, pot-bellied jars, which are placed in the sun to let the pickled gherkins mature. Whether stored under the eaves of the farmhouses, in a corner of a terrace, or on the kitchen window ledge of a city apartment, these gherkins, which are preserved by the process of lactic acid fermentation *(kovászos uborka)*, are simply everywhere.

Some 4½ pounds (two kilograms) of cucumbers are needed for a 6½-pint (3-liter) jar. The right gherkins (or cucumbers) are four to five inches (10–12 centimeters) in length, two fingers thick, and crispy fresh. They are sold on markets and in numerous delis with one other vital ingredient: half-dried dill (several stalks are required, with flowers if possible). And that's the end of the shopping list, since the remaining ingredients are usually to hand in every household: a thick slice of bread (dark is better), two cloves of garlic, and salt.

First, place the cucumbers in a large bowl with lukewarm water to remove any sand on the skins. Clean thoroughly under running water, using a brush if necessary. Discard the two ends and slash the skins. It is worth testing every single cucumber, since a single bitter one can ruin the whole jar.

Pickled gherkins are preserved without an acidifier such as vinegar or lemon.

Add a heaped tablespoon of salt to a good two pints (one liter) of water, and bring to a boil. Leave to cool for about five minutes. Meanwhile, place half the dill and a peeled, sliced clove of garlic in the bottom of the jar, then layer the cucumbers on top. When the jar is half full, add a second layer of herbs and garlic; the bread is placed on top. Then pour the salt water over the cucumbers to cover them, and moisten the bread. Put a lid, a small plate, or a piece of cheese-cloth over the jar, and place in the sun. The cucumbers will have ceased fermenting after three or four days. The water turns cloudy during the fermentation, becoming opaque and milky.

People who prefer their pickled gherkins with a little more spice add half an onion, a piece of peeled horseradish, some sour cherry leaves, and marjoram and/or basil, as well as the dill and garlic.

It is worthwhile testing the gherkins before ending the fermentation process. Pickled gherkins should always be pleasantly sour and not too soft, giving a little resistance when bitten into.

Now discard the bread, remove the gherkins, and rinse them. Pack them into smaller, well-sealing jars and cover with the fermentation water, passing it through a very fine sieve. Stored in the refrigerator in airtight jars, they will keep for up to three weeks.

Pickled gherkins are served ice cold, and without the liquid. In Hungary, on hot summer days, they are often served on crushed ice. Chilled gherkin liquid, diluted with soda water if preferred, is welcome at this time of year as a healthy and refreshing drink.

Left: Hungarian consumers prize these organically grown "warty" cucumbers.

Summer salads – the essential accompaniment

Salads are not served as an independent course in traditional Hungarian cuisine, but as an essential accompaniment to many hearty dishes, especially meat dishes. Salads emphasize the flavor of the main dish, aid the digestion, and add a touch of color to even the plainest table. A small plate of salad is therefore an important part of plain home cooking.

Fejes saláta: Quartered lettuce with a dressing, sometimes includes hard-boiled eggs and slices of lemon.

Káposztasaláta: Finely grated white or red cabbage is salted for one hour, then pressed, and seasoned with chopped onion dressing and caraway.

Paprikasaláta: Bell pepper (capsicum) rings. Leave to absorb the dressing for one hour before serving. The rings are sometimes blanched in salted water first.

Paradicsomsaláta: Sliced tomatoes with a dressing, if desired seasoned with pepper, chopped fresh parsley, and oil, sometimes topped with onion rings.

Uborkasaláta: Cucumber salad, preferably from thick cucumbers with a "warty" skin. The cucumber slices are salted for 30 minutes, then pressed. The dressing is poured over the cucumber slices, and garnished with pepper, paprika, or finely chopped parsley. A dollop of sour cream is placed on top of the paprika. Sometimes the cucumber is flavored with garlic or combined with finely chopped onion.

Salátaöntet
Salad dressing

¾ cup/200 ml water
3½ tbsp vinegar (6%)
2 tbsp confectioners' sugar
Salt

Combine the ingredients thoroughly. Vary the proportions of the individual ingredients to suit your own taste; the main thing is the dressing should taste slightly sour.

"There's still an onion in the provisions sack …"
ONIONS AND GARLIC

The most important ingredient in Hungarian cuisine is not paprika, but, in fact, the onion. Peeled and finely chopped, sautéed in hot fat, and often, but not always, seasoned with paprika, the onion imparts the decisive flavor to many different variations in the range of *gulyás* and *pörkölt* dishes – the "basic tone," perhaps.

Of course, the onion is also used elsewhere: for example, finely chopped and added to a *roux*, or left whole and added to soups and vegetable dishes during cooking. The light-colored skin is also sometimes added to meat stocks and soups to add a golden color.

The Hungarians also enjoy eating onions raw. In fact, until fairly recently, the basic farmer's breakfast consisted of bacon, bread, and raw onion. All that is required for this simple menu, which also served as the midday meal for laborers in the vineyards and fields, is a clasp knife (which every Hungarian carried; most men still carry a pocketknife with them wherever they go today). The bacon and the bread provided the raw energy, and the onion provided the vitamins and minerals, and aided digestion. And anyone who was too poor to buy the bacon could fill up on bread and onion, as is confirmed in countless Hungarian fairy tales and folk songs. And if there was no bread, then the song went, "There's still an onion in the provisions sack, if a little bitter on its own …"

Onions from Makó

It is hard to understand why the ubiquitous onion so very rarely appears as a dish in its own right. And even when it does, it is not in traditional Hungarian dishes, but rather in the creations of professional chefs. One such onion dish that is found on the menus of Hungarian restaurants is exceptionally delicious: stuffed onions à la Makó (see page 56).

Below: A farmer from Makó enjoying a traditional onion meal. He uses his knife to cut off bite-size pieces of onion, which he eats immediately.

Bread, bacon, and onion are held in one hand, the knife in the other.

A simple piece of machinery was used in the past to sort the onions according to size.

In former times, the onions were placed on a special grid over the oven to dry.

Onions and garlic from Makó

Every Hungarian knows that the country's best onions are grown in the Makó region. The local onions are full of trace elements and have quite a high sugar content, so they have a delightful aroma. They are also very hard, which makes them ideal for storage and transportation, and, last but by no means least, they are eye-catching in appearance, with bright white flesh and a warm, bronze skin.

Onion-growing began here more than 200 years ago. Due to the fact that the region was always flooded, and as the result of competition from the traditional wine-growing regions, it was becoming increasingly difficult for the residents in and around Makó to feed themselves. So, despite the ban imposed by the landowners, they decided to try their luck with vegetable-growing. Onions and garlic quickly proved to be extremely popular and gradually took over from other vegetables. Thus it came about that the humble onion family, originally planted as an intercrop, gradually spread throughout the land.

A unique method of cultivation developed in the Makó region where the onion is not just planted in a special way with the appropriate implements, but which has also marked the lives of native families. What makes this method of cultivation so special is the heat treatment the onion receives. In Makó, the tiny bulbs that spring forth from the seeds sown early in the year are taken from the soil in the fall, then dried in a warm place to be replanted in the following spring. This process prevents the onion from shooting in the second year, instead producing huge bulbs of the best quality. The same method of replanting the onions, rather than growing them from seeds, is also used in other countries, but the process of treating the onions with heat when drying them was first invented in Makó. It is said that a particular farmer stored the onions on a bench by the oven in the parlor throughout the winter to protect them from frost, and harvested huge onions the following year. Word soon traveled, and this new practice quickly spread throughout the region.

Onion-growers in Makó also practice various other tricks of the trade. The harvested goods are first gathered in a large pile, and then left on the fields in the sun and fresh air for a few days. The individual bulbs are then rubbed off, during which the cracked outer skin, which is almost turned gray by the adhering soil, is removed. This gives the Makó onions their glossy sheen, which distinguishes them from their counterparts even at a distance.

Töltött hagyma makói módra
Stuffed onions à la Makó

1 bread roll
A few parsley stalks
8 medium onions
3½ tbsp oil
9 oz/250 g lean ground pork
1 egg
Salt
3 tbsp/40 g butter
4 tbsp flour
¾ cup/200 ml milk
White pepper
Scant ½ cup/100 ml light cream
1 egg yolk
¾ cup/80 g grated cheese

Soak the roll, then squeeze it. Finely chop the parsley. Remove the outer brown skin from the onions, and cut off the bases so they can stand. Cut a "lid" from the top (about ¼ of the onion). Carefully scoop out the center of the onions. Finely chop the onion flesh, and sauté in hot oil until golden. Combine with the pork, bread, egg, parsley, and a little salt, then spoon into the hollowed-out onions. Place the onions in a greased ovenproof dish, pour in a little water, and bake in a preheated medium oven until soft.

Meanwhile, melt the butter and stir in the flour. Add the hot milk and whisk until smooth. Season with salt and white pepper, then reduce until it has the consistency of a sauce.

Remove from the heat and stir in the cream and egg yolk.

Place the roast onions in a flat ovenproof dish, then pour over the sauce and top with the cheese. Return to the oven until the cheese has melted and is nicely brown.

Onion field near Makó

56

When dried, the garlic bulbs are braided together in strings.

The bulbs are trimmed off neatly, and the shape of the string adjusted.

Above: Market stall with garlic strings.
Left: Garlic hanging up to dry.

The international career of this vegetable, which in the beginning was known only in Hungary, began in 1858 in the Naschmarkt in Vienna, after the expansion of the railroad network. Vegetable merchants from Germany and other western European countries became aware of the excellent properties of the Makó onion, and two wagonloads were sold in the first year. As before, the growth and sale of the onions still determine life and prosperity in this little town on the Great Plain today.

Garlic also plays an important part in the vegetable culture of Makó, and it is impossible to imagine Hungarian cuisine without it. It is just as good for us as the onion, and adds finesse and flavor to even the humblest dish – the Hungarian "Hussar's roast" is evidence of this. Slices of day-old bread are fried until crispy in lard and garlic – simply delicious!

Garlic

Different types of peppers

1 **Tölteni való paprika** (paprika for stuffing)
  Sweet or medium hot peppers, eaten raw or
  used in cooking.

2 **Bogyiszlói** (banana chili)
  Aromatic, very hot peppers, eaten raw or used
  in cooking.

3 **Almapaprika** (apple paprika)
  Whether sweet, mild, or very hot, this type is
  often pickled in vinegar.

4 **Kosszarvú** (ram's horn)
  Sweet, aromatic peppers that are popular raw,
  but also used in cooking.

5 **Cseresznyepaprika** (cherry paprika)
  Very hot, good fresh or dried for adding aroma
  to dishes, and also for eating as they are.

6 **Hegyes erös** (cayenne peppers)
  Use as *cseresznyepaprika*

7 **Paradicsompaprika** (sweet bell pepper)
  Pleasantly sweet aroma, high in vitamin C,
  used raw.

Paprika isn't always paprika
PAPRIKA

When Hungarians speak of "paprika," they could be referring either to the whole pods of different members of the capsicum family or to the spice obtained from them. Fresh bell peppers, for example, feature just as largely in many Hungarian dishes as the spice does, and they are equally popular raw. And it's not surprising that they should be so popular; they are available in such a range of colors, shapes, and flavors, that it is impossible to tire of them. Stroll across any market and admire the brightly colored, endless variety on display, from the acid-green, hot "pods," which the stallholders describe as "atom-hot," to the innocuous-looking but almost lethal yellow "banana chili," to the countless yellow, green, and bright red sweet peppers.

Hungary produces exceptionally tasty peppers, and because they have thin skins, they are easy to digest as well. Just try them once, and you will understand why the Hungarians are so enthusiastic about them.

The aroma must be due to the ideal conditions in which they are grown on the Great Plain. The climate and soil conditions are practically predestined for vegetable-growing in general, and paprika-growing in particular: fertile loessial soil, long hot summers with little rain, and some 2000 to 2200 hours of sunshine every year.

Opposite: Hungary's abundance of hot and mild paprikas and peppers.

Töltött paprika
Stuffed peppers

8 medium bell peppers (capsicum)	
1 medium onion	
4 tsp oil	
⅓ cup/60 g rice	
Salt	
5½ cups/600 g ground pork	
Generous pinch of pepper	
For the sauce:	
4¼ cups/1 liter tomato juice	
Some celery leaves	
3 tbsp flour	
2 tbsp/30 g butter	
1–2 tsp sugar to taste	

Hollow out the peppers. Finely chop a quarter of the onion, and sauté in the hot oil. Add the rice with a little salt, and just cover with water. When almost cooked, set aside to cool.

Add the ground pork to the rice, and season to taste with salt and pepper. Fill the peppers with the meat mixture (to about ½ inch/1.25 cm below the edge, as they expand during cooking). Bring the tomato juice to a boil, and pour around the stuffed peppers. Add the remaining onion and the celery leaves. Cover, and finish cooking over a medium heat (for about 50 minutes). Remove the peppers from the tomato liquid and discard the celery leaves and onion. Add the flour to the hot butter, stirring continuously until it turns golden. Use to thicken the tomato juice, and season with sugar.

Finally, carefully return the stuffed peppers to the sauce and leave to stand for 10 minutes. Serve with boiled potatoes.

The "paprika" prize

These were the words used by the world's press to describe the 1937 Nobel Prize for Science, which was awarded to Albert Szent-Györgyi (1893–1986), the only Hungarian scientist to receive acknowledgment for his successes in Hungary. The highlight of his career came about in 1932, and began with a fresh bell pepper, which his wife served with the evening meal.

"I didn't really want it, and as I looked at it, I realized I had never experimented on a pepper," he later recalled. Instead of eating it, he took it to his laboratory for investigation. After the initial results proved to be much better than anyone had expected, all other work was stopped. Within three weeks, over three pounds (1.5 kilograms) of pure vitamin C had been obtained. This was a sensational success, since only a few grams of the vitamin had ever before been isolated.

The Nobel prizewinner sent the vitamin to the WHO to be used in the treatment of scurvy, and he sent it to his colleagues throughout the world as a base for additional research. This was also the dawning of a new industrial boom: vitamin production. Later, the scientist also managed to isolate flavonoids, whose health benefits had only recently been recognized.

Szent-Györgyi also invented a paprika paste, which became commercially available first under the name of "Vitaprik," and later of "Pritamin," and both names are still synonymous with paprika paste in Hungary to this day.

Boxes, filled to overflowing with locally grown tomatoes, arrive in August and September.

The tomatoes are poured into a long water channel, where they slowly bob along …

… on their way to the washing drum.

Tomatoes in the washing drum.

Tomatoes on a conveyor belt, where rotten and unripe tomatoes are sorted and removed.

The tomatoes are made into tomato paste in a closed system.

The end product is subject to quality checks in the in-house laboratory.

Paradise apples
TOMATOES

The Hungarians used to call this popular vegetable "paradise apple," which had probably come to them via the Balkans from its American home. In time, the "apple" was dropped, and only *paradicsom* remained, which today means "tomato" as well as "paradise."

Large, juicy tomatoes with a thin skin are the most suitable for cooking. The smaller, firm, decorative ones are usually preferred for serving fresh. And despite the rapture with which greenhouse-grown tomatoes are greeted in winter, they cannot compete with freshly picked, sun-ripened field tomatoes.

The Kecskemét canning factory has been processing regional products for more than a century.

Until fairly recently, the ritual of turning tomatoes into tomato juice (for a winter drink or for cooking) was even more important in many Hungarian households than making apricot jam. The ceremony was the same every year. Choosing the right time to buy the tomatoes; the family occasion of buying them; washing them; cooking them; passing them through a sieve; and putting them into jars and bottles, which were wrapped in paper and stored between cushions and blankets until the juice had cooled. A lack of time means that ever more consumers are turning to high quality, commercially produced tomato products today.

Fresh tomato sauce

Chop 2½ lb/1.2 kilograms of fresh tomatoes, and pass the uncooked flesh through a sieve. Stirring continuously over a high heat, cook until the sauce has reduced to the consistency of a sauce, and then season with salt and sugar. This delicious sauce retains the full aroma of the raw tomatoes.

Canned products are becoming increasingly popular with the Hungarian consumer.

LECSÓ

Lecsó is a typical Hungarian dish that consists of tomatoes, peppers, and onions. How *lecsó* turns out can differ, depending on the type of pepper used. Some swear by the bitingly hot *bogyiszlói* (banana chili), others prefer the sweet, mild varieties. However, there is always room for compromise by adding a few hot ones to the milder ones. However, care should be taken when adding very hot peppers, since just a single one can ruin a dish for an unaccustomed palate.

In winter, fresh tomatoes and peppers for many Hungarian dishes, such as *pörkölt*, are traditionally replaced by preserved or deep-frozen *lecsó*. To preserve it, the hot cooked mixture is spooned into sterilized jars, and a tablespoon of fat poured over the top. The jars are immediately sealed, and dry-sterilized by wrapping them in paper. If using *lecsó* as a seasoning for other dishes, it should immediately be poured into small jars, whereas larger preserving jars are more suitable for winter provisions for complete meals.

To freeze it, the *lecsó* is prepared using the basic recipe and portions placed in tightly sealed containers, which can then be put in the freezer.

Clockwise from left: *Paprikás krumpli* (paprika potatoes), *Gránátos kocka* (March of the Grenadiers), *Lecsó*

Lecsó
Basic recipe
(Bottom of photograph)

2¼ lbs/1 kg bell peppers (capsicum)
Generous 1lb/500 g tomatoes
1 large onion
4 tbsp oil
1 heaped tbsp ground paprika
Salt

Remove the stalks and the seeds from the peppers, and cut into finger-width strips or rings. Remove the stalks from the tomatoes, and squash or slice them. Finely chop the onion and fry in the hot oil, stirring continuously, until translucent. Remove from the heat and stir in the paprika.
Add the peppers and salt, and cover with a lid. Simmer gently for about 10 minutes, then add the tomatoes and cook until soft.

Lecsó with sausage
Add 7 oz (200 g) sliced or mild smoked sausage (Debrecziner) to the *lecsó* just before it is ready, and cook for a few minutes. The sausage can also be left whole; use one pair for each person.

Lecsó with rice
Fry ½ cup (80 g) rice in a little oil. Prepare the *lecsó* according to the basic recipe. Then add the rice and leave to swell in the vegetable juices, adding a little water if necessary. Extra salt is usually required if you add more water.

Lecsó with pasta pellets
Sauté ⅓ cup/80 g pasta pellets in a little hot oil, then proceed as in previous recipe.

Lecsó with bacon drippings
Prepare the *lecsó* in accordance with the basic recipe, using bacon drippings instead of the fat. Dice about 5 oz/150 g smoked bacon and heat until the fat runs, then remove the cracklings.

Lecsó with egg
Beat the eggs (1–2 per person) until smooth, and add a little salt. Pour over the cooked *lecsó*, and heat the mixture, stirring continuously, until the egg begins to set.
Both the basic recipe for *lecsó* and the versions using bacon drippings and sausage are suitable for this recipe.

PAPRIKA POTATOES, MARCH OF THE GRENADIERS

The simple, inexpensive *Paprikás krumpli* (paprika potatoes), the ingredients for which are always to be found in any Hungarian household, is a culinary delight that consists of lard or drippings, onions, and ground paprika.

The story of how the potato and pasta dish *Gránátos kocka*, which is more widely known as *grenadírmars* (March of the Grenadiers), got its name is highly amusing. It appears that at the time of the Napoleonic Wars, the Austrian army was running low on provisions, and the cook found himself with only dried pasta and a few potatoes left, from which he had to prepare a meal. The Hungarians who were serving in the Imperial Army "refined" their portions with ground paprika, which lent color and flavor to the dish. This dish, created from need, has been passed from generation to generation, and is still popular today.

little water, and cook through over a high heat. Do not stir the potatoes once they have started to cook, but carefully tilt the pot from side to side. Only add as much water as is required; the sauce should not be too thin.
In winter, the tomatoes and peppers can be replaced by several tablespoons of *lecsó*.

Variations
Prepare the dish with a little more sauce, and add some broiling sausages just before the end of the cooking time.
Stir a few tablespoons of sour cream into the hot dish just before serving.
Prepare a dumpling dough (see page 40) for soup and cook in plenty of sauce. Add a little sour cream if required.

Gránátos kocka
March of the Grenadiers
(Photograph top right)

1¼ lbs/600 g potatoes
1 medium onion
3½ tbsp oil
½ tsp mild, sweet paprika
Salt
14 oz/400 g large, square pasta shapes (see page 38)

Peel the potatoes and cut into small dice. Finely chop the onion and sauté in the oil. Remove from the heat, then sprinkle over the paprika and salt. Add the potatoes, pour over a little water, and cook, stirring frequently.
Press the cooked potatoes with a fork, but not too much; they should still be lumpy.
Cook the pasta and add to the potatoes. Season with salt, if required. Heat the mixture again and serve hot.
Serve with sour gherkins.

Paprikás krumpli
Paprika potatoes
(Photograph top left)

3½ lbs/1.5 kg potatoes
2 bell peppers (capsicum)
2 tomatoes
5 oz/150 g smoked bacon (or ⅓ cup/80 ml oil)
1 large onion
2 cloves of garlic (optional)
Generous pinch of ground caraway (optional)
1 heaped tsp mild, sweet paprika
Salt

Peel the potatoes and cut into quarters lengthwise. Slice the trimmed peppers and chop the tomatoes.
Dice the smoked bacon and heat until the fat runs (or heat the oil, if used). Finely chop the onion and add to the diced bacon or oil. Add the crushed garlic and caraway, if used. Remove from the heat and sprinkle over the paprika, then add the potatoes, peppers, and tomatoes. Season with salt and combine well. Add a

Once the cooking juices have been thickened with a *roux*, the stuffed cabbage leaves are carefully returned to the pot on a slotted spoon to continue cooking.

STUFFED CABBAGE

"Meat and cabbage are the coat of arms of Hungary." Only a few people today still know this old saying, which was in frequent use in the 17th and 18th centuries. Nowhere else in the world was any other dish served as frequently as this one in Hungary – sometimes every day. Whether rich or poor, aristocrat or burgher, cabbage and meat was always right at the top of the menu, and today it is regarded as one of the country's national dishes.

The Hungarians learned how to make sauerkraut from their neighbors to the north, the Slovaks. The meat filling was copied from the Balkans, and in particular from the Turks. They combined sauerkraut with fresh and smoked pork, and with sour cream, thus adapting it to their own taste. Preparation varies according to region and family. Sometimes, the sauerkraut is replaced by blanched cabbage leaves. In some areas, the stuffed cabbage is not thickened with a *roux*. In Transylvania, bunches of dill and savory are added to the pot and removed before serving. Hungary's first opera diva, Róza Széppataki-Déry (1793–1872), waxed lyrical about stuffed cabbage à la Transylvania, which was served at a banquet given in her honor in Klausenburg in 1815. In fact, she was so delighted by the dish that she published the recipe in her memoirs.

Opera singer Róza Széppataki-Déry, a great star in her day, was immortalized in porcelain.

"Only stuffed cabbage tastes better re-heated," goes an old Hungarian saying that usually refers to a couple that has separated, but is now reunited. The extent to which it actually applies for lovers is open to debate, but stuffed cabbage, like so many other sauerkraut dishes, continues to improve every time it is re-heated. And in Hungary, the discomfort which it is known to cause is counteracted with a cumin soup, which is served as an appetizer.

Köménymagos leves
Cumin soup

1–2 tbsp/10–20 g butter
4 tbsp flour
1 tsp caraway seeds
Salt

Melt the butter and fry the flour in it. As soon as the flour starts to change color, add the caraway and stir. When the caraway seeds start to "jump," or the *roux* starts to turn darker, add 5½ cups/1.3 liters of water. Season with salt and bring to a boil. Pass through a sieve, and serve with a dish or basket of croutons.

Töltött káposzta
Stuffed cabbage
(Photograph)

10 oz/300 g smoked pork ribs
2¼ lbs/1 kg sauerkraut
8 sauerkraut leaves
1 medium onion
⅓ cup/50 g cooked rice
4½ cups/500 g ground pork
Salt and pepper
¼ cup/60 g butter
3 tbsp flour
2 tbsp mild, sweet paprika
¾–1¼ cups/200–300 ml sour cream

Make a meat stock with the ribs (see page 301).
Rinse the sauerkraut under running water. Finely chop the onion. Combine the rice, ground pork, half the onion, and the salt and pepper with a little butter. Flatten the cabbage leaves or remove the thick stalks from the center. Place a small amount of the meat mixture on each leaf, and roll it up firmly, folding the edges under. Sauté the remaining onion until translucent, and spread half the sauerkraut over it. Layer the stuffed cabbage leaves on top, and cover with the remaining sauerkraut. Pour over enough meat stock to just cover the contents, and simmer over a low heat for 1 hour.
Make a *roux* from the remaining butter, the flour, and the paprika, and use to thicken the sauerkraut. Remove the stuffed cabbage leaves before doing this, and return them to the sauerkraut when it has been thickened. Cook for another 10 minutes.
Serve hot, accompanied by a small dish of sour cream.

1 The ingredients for stuffed cabbage leaves.
2 Place the ground pork mixture on the cabbage leaves.
3 Take care not to put too much mixture on the leaves, as otherwise they are difficult to roll.

4 Roll the leaf up firmly.
5 Fold over the ends of the leaves.
6 Add the paprika *roux* to the sauerkraut.

Only the best quality pork is used.

The salami is smoked before it goes into the maturing chamber.

After three months, the salamis have acquired a protective bloom.

In summer and in winter
SALAMI

Téliszalámi, known all over the world as Hungarian salami, is one of the "aristocrats" of all sausages. Its typically delicate aroma, good shelf life, and worldwide popularity have gone to ensure its pre-eminent position among the hierarchy of Hungarian meat products.

The first salamis to be produced in Hungary came from Szeged on the river Tisza in the south of the Great Plain. One Márk Pick decided to try his luck at making a certain type of Italian sausage that was at the time unknown in Hungary. He started small and, after highly promising success in 1883, soon went into "mass production." After a while, the Pick salami ceased to bear any resemblance to the Italian version that originally inspired it, since Hungarian butchers worked to give it a typically Hungarian flavor.

So what is the special touch that makes this salami unique? Well, as always, only natural ingredients are used. The best pork and pork fat are not chopped in machines, but expertly by hand, using specially designed knives. The excellent aroma of the salami is not solely due to the combination of spices (which is, of course, a closely guarded secret) but also to the protective bloom that coats the sausage during its three-month maturing period after it has been smoked. This white, uneven coating protects the salami from becoming rancid, and so helps to ensure a long shelf life.

Márk Pick later moved his business to its present location on the banks of the river Tisza, since he understood the role played in the maturing process by the cool air that rose from the river. As recently as the 1950s, salami was produced only during the colder months of the year, namely from October to March (hence its name of *téliszalámi* – winter salami), since that was the only time the basic method of heat regulation (which required extensive knowledge and expertise) could be applied. This called for the windows on the drying level being opened or closed. The bloom was twice removed with a brush, and the sausages moved to ensure that they all matured evenly and simultaneously.

A butcher in the Pick salami factory. The fact that the names of the two leading salami manufacturers – and competitors – correspond with terms for suits of playing cards – Herz ("heart") and Pick ("spade" is "Pik" in German) is not a marketing strategy thought up by card-playing advertising agencies, but sheer coincidence.

Once mature, *téliszalámi* is traditionally given a banderole in the Hungarian national colors of red, white, and green. The ends are secured with string and given a lead seal.

The unopened salami should not be refrigerated, but stored in a cool place, out of the sun. Kept this way, it will retain its delightful flavor for at least three months.

Over the years winter salami has acquired a number of different relations, including newer developments such as *paprikás szalámi* (paprika salami), which was given a Hungarian flavor, and *csemegeszalámi* (fine salami), which also contains beef and thus tastes slightly different. The continued success of Pick salami appealed to several other would-be producers, but the only salami to rival it was itself produced at the Herz-Salami works, established in 1888 on the banks of the Danube at Pest.

The land of milk and honey – and sausages
GYULAER AND CSABAER

Sausages are among the most delicious products that are made from fattened pigs. A Hungarian fairy tale tells how a good fairy granted a poor boy three wishes. His first, which involved no hesitation on his part, was for a plate of sausages. And small children are told how the land of milk and honey has fences made of sausages – still a symbol of wealth in Hungary today.

In the hierarchy of sausages, the smoked varieties are right at the top. Care and expertise are required for the preparation, and stored in the right conditions they will keep almost indefinitely. At the most, they become a little drier and harder over time. Hungary boasts a wide range of different types of sausage, each containing different herbs and spices.

Smoked sausages are always sold in pairs.

Sausage "à la maison" simply contains a few basic spices, such as salt, paprika, pepper, and garlic. Cumin sausage contains cumin, pepper, and lemon rind. Another extremely popular variety is marked by the penetrating aroma of garlic, and in yet another, it is the smell of pepper. Smoked lemon sausage is seasoned with pepper and ground cumin, as well as lemon juice and grated lemon rind.

The best-known Hungarian unsmoked sausages come from Békécseba and Gyula in the south of the Great Plain, and are known simply as Csabaer and Gyulaer. Cattle-breeding has flourished in this region since the early Middle Ages, and vast cattle markets were staged under the protection of Gyula castle and attended by dealers from as far away as Munich, Dresden, Nuremberg, and Vienna. Whole butcher dynasties grew up in this traditional meat center, who were constantly dreaming up new products to tempt their customers. Hungary's first abattoir was also opened here, in 1868. At the beginning of the 20th century, when improved traffic conditions meant better sales opportunities, countless small meat-processing businesses sprang up like mushrooms, including the meat factory of András Stéberl. This master butcher was so proud of his meat products that he boldly decided to exhibit them at the 1935 World Exhibition in Brussels. His bravery paid off, since his products received the highest recognition: the gold medal. The company was nationalized in 1948, and Stéberl sausage became known as *Gyulai kolbász* – Gyulaer hard-smoked sausage.

This sausage is still as popular as ever, although it now contains beef as well as pork, which, for the tradition-conscious Hungarian, should be the only type of meat allowed in a sausage. The secret of its success is moderation in the seasoning; although Gyulaer is piquant, it will not upset a sensitive stomach. A careful balance of selected spices, such as the best quality Hungarian paprika, pepper, cumin, and garlic, and above all else, very finely chopped Hungarian bacon, combine to produce the unmistakable aroma. The smoking process adds the final touch to a perfect flavor.

First-class animals from the region.

Long sausages …

… are shortened, and cut off in pairs.

The sausages are hung on racks and wheeled into the smoking chamber.

Gyulaer hard-smoked sausage would still receive a gold medal from connoisseurs all over the world today, just like it did at the 1935 World Exhibition.

Give us this day our daily bread
BREAD

Bread is ubiquitous in Hungary, and no table is complete without it, since Hungarian meat, sausage, and sauerkraut delicacies demand it. It is sometimes also served with fruit, vegetable, and pasta dishes. A true Hungarian will happily travel even to remote parts of the town or city, or to neighboring villages, for the delicious wares produced by a particular baker.

Wheat dominates the grain cultivated in the Great Plain, the "corn chamber" of the country, as it does in other regions, and so white bread is the main type of bread in Hungary. It is not as sweet as its counterparts in western and southern Europe. The modern, health-conscious Hungarian prefers the darker types, however, which used to be the reserve of the poor, and so were eaten by the better-off only in times of need.

The "Cookbook of the Hungarian Nation," written by István Czifray, and published in 1816, contains a description of what bread should be like that still applies today: "We deem the bread to be good if it is nicely rounded in shape. Its crust is neither too hard nor too soft; it is yellow or brown on the outside, but never burned black, and nor does it break away from the bread. Good bread should not crumble, and if pressed against with a finger, should regain its shape immediately. It is fine-pored, tasty, and should not spoil after a few days."

Before both master bakers and the factories that followed conquered the market, every household baked its own bread. Many Hungarians regard a particular old custom as a symbol of the continuity of life: in bygone days, a bride was given a

Left: Long ago, wheat was ground in windmills on the Great Plain.

Bread-baking is still mainly a manual process today.

The unbaked loaves are scored before baking to prevent the crusts from splitting.

Lots of different types of bread are baked in today's bakeries.

piece of sourdough by her mother on her wedding day, which she would then use to bake her first loaf for herself and her new husband. The young wife would then continue to keep a piece of dough week after week, and would in turn pass a piece on to her own daughter. Bread was usually baked once a week, on Saturday, so there would be fresh bread for the holy day. Tradition has it that "a decent woman bakes on Saturday, and launders on Monday."

Bread-baking was hard work. Not just the kneading, which took a good two hours and required considerable strength, but the whole process was arduous. Once the sourdough had risen, it was kneaded – at around midnight. The unbaked loaves were then placed in bread baskets to rise, before being baked in the early morning – before sunrise. Bread was therefore treated with a certain amount of reverence.

Right: The smell of freshly baked bread lures us into the bakery.

Giant loaves

In his accounts of his travels, Evliya Celebi, the Turkish world traveler, describes the largest loaf ever baked on Hungarian soil. In 1663, Transylvanian Prince Mihály Apafi invited the entire Ottoman army to be his guests after a battle, from the Grand Vizier down to the humblest infantryman. "He put on such a magnificent feast, the like of which had never been seen before," Celebi tell us. "The meadows were covered with Hungarian carpets, onto which forty giant loaves were placed. These forty loaves were so big that each one had to be drawn on an oxcart. Each loaf was twenty paces long, and five paces wide, and as high as a full-grown man. And I tell the truth – or may Allah strike me down! I asked how they kneaded and baked the bread, and this is what they told me. Vast quantities of flour were kneaded in baking troughs numbering several hundred times hundred. Then ditches were dug, as big as a castle moat. Here they laid fires, and the dough was placed in the glowing embers, with ash on top. They then lit more fires above and beside, which were put out seven hours later. Now countless men came with rods, and fetched the baked loaves out. They cut off the charred crusts, and carried the bread to the place of the banquet …" Although Celebi was by no means exaggerating in this account, it was a long time before anyone believed it, when renowned researchers proved that people of the Near East were baking bread in this way long before those elsewhere even began to measure time.

Popular rolls

Kifli
(croissant)

Mákos kifli
(poppy seed croissant)

Vajas kifli
(butter croissant)

Tepertős pogácsa
("pompons" with cracklings)

Tekert mákos kifli
(poppy seed knot)

Sós magos stangli
(salt roll with seeds)

Zsemle
(bread roll)

Above: The gifts that decorate the table on the "Day of the New Bread"
symbolize the country's wealth.

Usually the man of the house had the honorable task of cutting into the bread, and in Catholic areas of Hungary he would mark it with the sign of the cross before doing so. Any slices of bread that were dropped would be kissed in apology when they were picked up.

The success – or otherwise – of the bread does not just depend on the baker's ability, but above all on the quality of the ingredients. Up until a hundred years ago, the flour produced in the mills still contained the bran, most of which was sieved out at home, and this resulted in a wonderful flour for bread-baking. Later, rolling mills were started up, in whose development and distribution Hungary played a considerable role. Soon, only a very fine, white flour was available, which

The "Day of the New Bread," which is also the day of Christian King Stephen, is celebrated with much enthusiasm. Open-air concerts are held in good weather.

initially was mixed with a little bran to increase the shelf life of the bread and to retain the accustomed flavor.

Some towns and regions became famous throughout the land for the ability of their bakers. In the 19th century, bread from Orosháza, a town in the south of the Great Plain, was highly desired, and it is first mentioned by Robert Towson in his "Travels in Hungary," which appeared in London in 1797: "… nowhere else did I eat bread that was lighter, whiter, and tastier than this …" The small, round loaves from Debrecen were also prized.

There are still festivals to mark the grain harvest all over Hungary today, of which the biggest is the "Day of the New Bread," which is celebrated on August 20. This is also the "Day of Constitution," when Hungarians remember Saint Stephen, their king and founder, who brought Christianity to the country at the end of the 10th century. Every year on this day, the president of the country is ceremoniously given the first loaf baked from new flour and decorated with a band in the national colors. This bread, which is of a prescribed size, and baked with a golden crust, represents the traditional flavor of bread in Hungary.

LÁNGOS

Lángos is the Hungarian name of a flat cake that today is deep-fried from a potato-based dough. It was originally made from a piece of bread dough that was kept back when baking the family's bread, and cooked at the front of the oven close to the flame (*láng*) to provide breakfast for the whole family on baking day. Spread with cream cheese, it was a great treat. But times have changed, and now few Hungarians bake their own bread. *Lángos* made from bread dough is now usually served only at events of a historical nature.

At home, potato-based *lángos* are served at the evening meal, usually with tea, and sometimes with mulled wine. However, it is most often eaten away from home, since it is Hungary's cheapest and most popular snack. *Lángos* stalls are found wherever there are lots of people – weekly markets and fairs, on railroad stations, on beaches, and at tourist attractions. Prospective diners are well advised to check the facilities carefully, as it is unfortunately not unknown for unsuspecting customers to be sold old, stale cakes that taste of oil or lard and are at best lukewarm, at worst cold.

Popular variations
Basic recipe: see next page.

Lángos with dill
Flatten the piece of dough on the palm of your hand and cover with finely chopped fresh dill. Fold the cake in half, then tweak it into shape, and deep-fry.

Lángos with ewe's milk cheese
Make a slightly thicker cake, and crumble a walnut-size piece of ewe's milk cheese in the center. Fold the cake in half and deep-fry.

Lángos with dill and ewe's milk cheese
Season the ewe's milk cheese with finely chopped fresh dill. Continue as shown in the previous recipe.

Lángos with ham I
Pass cooked or raw ham through a grinder, and combine with sour cream to make a smooth, creamy mixture. Place 1–2 teaspoons on the center of the cake, and continue as in the ewe's milk cheese recipe.

Lángos with ham II
Make the dough with water obtained from boiling a ham instead of the milk (see smoked meat broth, page 301), and add a small amount of finely chopped ham.

Lángos with cabbage
Prepare the cabbage as in the recipe for cabbage pasta squares (page 39), and season well with pepper. Place the filling on the cake and fold in half, then deep-fry.

Lángos are twice as nice with sour cream. They can also be sprinkled with garlic juice.

1 Using your hands, shape a round, flat cake from a piece of dough.
2 Deep-fry the cake in hot oil.

3 Turn the cake over when the underneath is brown and crispy.
4 Drain off excess oil, or place the cake on paper towels.

Zsírban sült lángos
Lángos basic recipe

5 oz/150 g mealy potatoes
1¾ cakes/30 g fresh compressed yeast
3 tbsp confectioners' sugar
1⅔ cups/400 ml milk
3⅓ cups/400 g flour
3½ tbsp oil
Salt
Oil for deep-frying

Cook the potatoes in their skins. Dissolve the yeast and the sugar in a scant ½ cup/100 ml of lukewarm milk, and stand in a warm place for 10 minutes. Peel the potatoes and mash while still warm. Sift the flour into a bowl. Make a well in the center, and pour in the milk and yeast mixture. Add the potatoes and the oil, and knead to a smooth dough with the remaining lukewarm milk, adding a little salt. Sprinkle over a little flour, and cover with a dish towel. Leave in a warm place for about 1 hour until the dough has doubled in size.

Pour some oil into a skillet of about 2½ inches/6 cm height. Tear off a piece of the risen dough, and shape it into a round, flat cake about ¾ inch/2 cm thick. Fry in the hot oil (do not cover the skillet) until golden, then turn over carefully and fry the cake on the other side.

Season with salt, and eat while still hot. Delicious spread with sour cream or garlic juice.

Left: *Lángos* is a popular snack, and tastes best while still hot.

A rediscovered tradition
ROAST OX

"Master Antal once roast an ox. Inside the ox, he placed a fat, mature sheep. Inside the sheep, he placed a tender calf. Inside the calf, he placed a juicy capon. When the ox was roast, he removed the capon – and knew that if the capon was ready to eat, the ox was too." Master Antal was chef to a Transylvanian aristocrat, and this account comes from a number of his colleagues who were discussing a wedding feast. It has to be admitted that several of them doubted whether an ox could actually be roasted in this manner. The quotation is taken from what is probably Hungary's oldest cookbook, entitled *Szakács tudomány* (The Science of Cooking). The name of the author is unknown, only that he was at court in the middle of the 16th century, in the heyday of the Transylvanian princedom, and that he treasured the specialties produced by the indigenous chefs. However, from his recipes it is clear that he was also familiar with the most sophisticated dishes created in other parts of Europe.

A number of men work together to skewer the ox.

Smaller skewers are used to secure the heavy animal.

The back is larded with slices of bacon.

Wood is stacked in a great pile, and set alight.

Once the fire has burned down to the glowing embers, it is time to roast the ox. The very long skewer serves two purposes: the men can use it to turn the ox by hand, and it helps to keep them at a safe distance from the heat of the embers.

The head chef personally cuts off a piece of meat from the neck to check whether the meat is cooked.

Later accounts inform us that it was customary to roast oxen at folk festivals and celebrations with large numbers of guests. In time, though, the custom dwindled away, and people gradually forgot the finer culinary points.

However, in the 1970s a Hungarian chef rekindled the old tradition, first experimenting with piglets and lambs. In time, he became bolder, and finally decided to try his luck with an ox – with great success. He then passed his knowledge on to a number of his colleagues, and now roast ox is once again a popular tourist attraction and specialty at fairs, street parties, and club gatherings – provided there are enough guests: it is not worth roasting an ox unless there are at least a hundred hungry mouths to feed.

Well-known Hungarian chefs prefer the Hungarian gray cattle for roasting. The live animal should weigh 770–1100 pounds (350–500 kilograms), and be neither too lean nor too fat. Preparations commence five or six days before the event. Once the animal has been slaughtered and gutted, it is rubbed inside and out with a mixture of oil, mustard, salt, and pepper before being marinated in a mixture consisting of many different vegetables and spices. The marinade is also injected into the thicker parts of the animal using a huge "syringe."

On the big day, the animal is skewered and its legs bound together. The tail is wrapped in aluminum foil, and the body larded with bacon and pieces of garlic. An acacia wood fire is laid in an appropriately sized ditch, and then set alight. Once the fire has burned down to the glowing embers, the animal is placed on a skewer that is as thick as an arm, and rotated over the embers for 10–14 hours. During this time, it is basted frequently with the marinade, and finally with light beer. When the meat is crispy, it is sliced while still on the skewer, then served.

RACKA SHEEP

For centuries, the Hungarian landscape has been dominated by vast flocks of sheep. The "racka" sheep used to be the most common variety, but it is now found only in the Hortobágy-Puszta National Park. It is instantly recognizable by its slightly alarming corkscrew horns. The racka sheep gives plenty of milk, and its meat is very tasty. Its coarse fleece makes it impervious to snow and cold, but this also the reason why it has gradually been replaced by soft-fleeced varieties, particularly the merino sheep.

Working shepherds rely on their sheepdogs.

Top: Dried sheep dung is still used for fuel today.
Right: Racka sheep

What used to be a matter of course in Hungary is now a rarity: not many people drink ewe's milk any longer. Nor are lamb or mutton everyday fare; at most they are served on special occasions, such as vintage festivals or at Easter. A number of innkeepers spotted this gap in the market, and decided to open a nationwide chain of restaurants (*birkacsárda*) that serve lamb and mutton specialties.

Hortobágyi ürügulyás
Mutton goulash

2¼ lbs/1 kg mutton on the bone (breast)
2 medium tomatoes
2 medium bell peppers (capsicum)
Generous 1 lb/500 g potatoes
4 tbsp oil
2 large onions, chopped
2 cloves of garlic, crushed
½ tsp caraway
1 heaped tbsp ground paprika
Salt
¾ cup/200 ml dry red wine

Cut the meat into bite-size pieces. Quarter the tomatoes, slice the seeded bell peppers, and dice the potatoes. Heat the oil and fry the meat, stirring continuously. Add the onions and the garlic, and season with caraway, paprika, and salt, then cook for a few more minutes. Add enough water to cover the contents of the pot. Cover with a lid, and simmer over a low heat for about 1½ hours. Add the vegetables just before the end of the cooking time, and pour over 4–6 cups/1–1.5 liters water. Cook until the vegetables are done. At the end of the cooking time, pour over the wine, and boil up briefly.

Spárgás bárányborda
Lamb cutlets with asparagus
(Photograph below)

10 oz/300 g asparagus tips
Salt
5 oz/150 g mushrooms
Bunch of parsley
8 lamb cutlets (each weighing 2–3 oz/60–80 g)
5 tbsp flour
2–3 tbsp oil
2–3 tbsp/40 g butter
Pinch of pepper

Blanch the asparagus tips in salted water and drain. Trim and dice the mushrooms. Finely chop the parsley. Gently pound the cutlets, then season with salt and coat with the flour. Heat the oil and sauté the cutlets on both sides, then place them in another skillet. Melt the butter in the remaining meat juices, and braise the mushrooms. Season with salt and pepper. Add the parsley and the asparagus. Add the vegetables to the cutlets, and cook for about another 10 minutes.

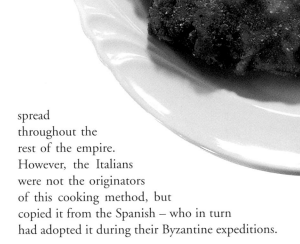

Sunday lunch
BREADED DISHES

On high days and holidays, most Hungarians' preferred choice for the midday meal is a breaded meat dish. What is simply referred to as *rántott hús* (breaded meat), is actually closely related to the well-known *Wiener Schnitzel*. The only difference is that the Hungarian version is made with pork rather than veal. Coating food with breadcrumbs is so popular a method in Hungary that it is also used with fish, cheese, and vegetables, as well as different kinds of meat.

This cooking method actually dates back to the Danubian monarchy, to which Hungary once belonged. While marching through Italy, Field Marshal Count Josef Radetzky (1766–1858) wrote to Emperor Franz Joseph not just of military events, but also to tell him that the Milanese coated escalopes in breadcrumbs before frying them. This recipe was immediately tested at the Viennese court, and soon it had spread throughout the rest of the empire. However, the Italians were not the originators of this cooking method, but copied it from the Spanish – who in turn had adopted it during their Byzantine expeditions.

1 The ingredients: cutlets, salt, flour, egg, and breadcrumbs.
2 The cutlet is coated in flour, then dipped in the salted beaten egg.
3 Finally, the cutlet is coated in breadcrumbs.

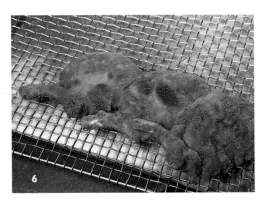

4 The meat must be well coated on both sides.
5 The breaded meat is fried in plenty of hot oil, and turned once.
6 When the cutlets are cooked through and golden, they are placed on a rack to drain.

Rántott sertésborda
Breaded pork cutlets
(Photographs left and below)

8 pork cutlets (each weighing about 3½ oz/100 g)
Salt
¾ cup/100 g flour
3½ cup/200 g fresh breadcrumbs
2 eggs, beaten
1¼ cups/300 ml oil for deep-frying

Gently pound the cutlets, and season with salt. Sift the flour and breadcrumbs onto two separate plates. Beat the eggs and a little salt in a deep dish. Pat the cutlets dry with paper towels, and turn in the flour. Dip in the beaten egg, then coat on both sides with the breadcrumbs. Place in the hot oil immediately. Cover with a lid when the cutlets start to turn golden. When the underneath is golden, turn the meat over and fry the other side (do not cover). Place on paper towels or a rack to drain, and serve immediately.

Rántott karfiol
Breaded cauliflower

2½ lbs/1.2 kg cauliflower
Salt
About 1 cup/120 g flour
3 eggs, beaten
1¼ cups/300 ml oil for deep-frying

Divide the cauliflower into florets. Blanch in salted water, and drain. Then carefully turn in the flour, dip in the salted beaten egg, and finally coat with the breadcrumbs.
Place in a slotted spoon and dip into the hot oil, frying until golden on all sides. Place on paper towels to drain, and serve hot.
Serve the breaded cauliflower with rice and a tomato sauce, or with tartar sauce. Whole mushrooms, slices of tender pumpkin, celery, and eggplant can also be cooked in this way.

Rántott sertésborda
Breaded pork cutlets

PANCAKES

The origin of these thin pancakes (*palacsinta*), which are extremely popular in Hungary, is not entirely clear. Most probably they developed from the Roman *plazenta*, a small, round cake that was eaten instead of bread. Pancakes are served in a wide range of varieties, both sweet and savory. They are served as an appetizer, a main course, and a dessert. As well as the familiar round, they are also made as pasta or even cakes, and are even breaded and deep-fried in hot oil.

What makes this "quick-change artist" so popular with rich and poor alike is the easy availability and affordability of the ingredients.

Pancakes are eaten hot. The more genteel diner will use a fork to shred it into pieces, but others will make life easier by using a knife as well.

Sift the flour into a bowl. Add the egg, salt, and milk.

Whisk the ingredients well.

The batter should be thin and smooth.

Ladle scoops of the batter into an oiled skillet.

Ideal for cooking pancakes: a long-handled skillet with 1½ inch (3 cm) high sides, made of iron, with a flat base and rounded edges. New skillets need to be seasoned before using. To do so, make a few dark-brown, slightly burned pancakes (not intended for consumption). Finally, lightly wipe over the skillet with a sponge soaked in water and detergent, then rinse in clear water, and dry well. Pancakes take a little longer to cook in nonstick pans, and are not quite as tasty.

Top: Pancakes taste best when cooked in a simple, long-handled, iron skillet.

Bottom right: The favorite choice of filling: jelly or jam, preferably apricot.

Pancake batter I
(Makes 10 pancakes)

1⅔ cups/200 g flour
Pinch of salt
2 eggs
1 cup/250 ml milk
2 tsp sugar (optional)
Scant ½ cup/100 ml soda water
Oil for frying

Combine the flour, salt, eggs, and milk, to make a smooth batter. Add the sugar if the pancakes are to have a sweet filling.
Pour enough soda water into the batter to give it a thick, creamy consistency. Brush a skillet with some of the oil, and ladle a small amount of batter into it. Tilt the skillet to distribute the pancake batter, and fry on both sides over a high heat.
Use a spatula or similar implement to turn the pancake. Brush some more oil into the skillet for each new pancake so that they will not burn.

Pancake batter II
(Makes 12–15 pancakes)

Generous 2 cups/250 g flour
Pinch of salt
3 eggs
¾ cup/200 ml milk
3½ tbsp oil
2 tsp sugar (optional)
About ¾ cup/150 ml soda water

Combine the flour and salt. Add the eggs, milk, and almost all of the oil. Add the sugar if the pancakes are to have a sweet filling. Beat the ingredients to make a smooth batter, and pour in enough soda water to give it a thick, creamy consistency. Leave to stand for about 10 minutes, then cook the pancakes.
If the batter becomes a little too thick while standing, thin it with a little soda water or milk. Because this batter already contains oil, you may find that you have to oil the skillet only for the first pancake.

Szentgyörgyhegyi palacsinta
Pancakes with walnuts and raisins

⅔ cup/150 ml milk
4 sachets of vanilla sugar
1 cup/120 g ground walnuts
½ tsp grated lemon rind
2 tbsp raisins
12 sweet pancakes
Butter for the dish

For the custard:

2 tbsp flour
5 eggs, separated
2 cups/500 ml milk
Scant 1 cup/100 g confectioners' sugar

Bring the milk to the boil with the sugar, then add the walnuts and continue to boil. Add the lemon rind and the raisins.

Spread the walnut cream over 11 pancakes. Roll the pancakes up, and cut them into 1¼ inch/3 cm long pieces. Grease an ovenproof dish with butter, and line the bottom with the remaining pancake. Place the rolled up pancakes in the dish.

Beat the flour and egg yolks with a scant ½ cup/100 ml of milk until smooth, then add half the confectioners' sugar and whisk until fluffy. Bring to a boil with the remaining milk, stirring continuously. Pour the custard over the pancakes, and bake in a preheated (400 °F/200 °C) oven until set. Beat the egg whites with the remaining confectioners' sugar until stiff. Spread the beaten egg whites over the custard, and return to a warm oven until golden.

Rántott sonkás palacsinta
Breaded pancakes with a ham filling

5 oz/150 g ham on the bone
2½ tbsp/40 g butter
5 tbsp flour
¾ cup/200 ml milk
Salt
Pinch of pepper
½ tsp ground paprika
8 unsweetened pancakes

For the coating:

¾ cup/100 g flour
3 cups/150 g fresh breadcrumbs
2 eggs
1¼ cups/300 ml oil for deep-frying

Grind the ham in a meat grinder. Melt the butter, and stir in the flour. Add the milk, and bring to the boil, stirring continuously, to make a thick sauce. Season with salt, pepper, and ground paprika, then stir in the ham. Spread the ham mixture over the pancakes, and fold each one into a square. Sift the flour and breadcrumbs onto separate plates. Beat the eggs in a deep bowl. Dip the folded pancake in the flour, then in the egg, and finally press both sides in the breadcrumbs. Cook in plenty of hot oil until golden on both sides.

Serve as an appetizer or as a snack, accompanied by seasoned mayonnaise (see page 301).

Popular pancakes

Almás palacsinta: Grated apple is added to the pancake batter.

Diós palacsinta: Rolled-up pancakes with a nut cream filling.

Gesztenyés palacsinta csokoládéöntettel: Chocolate-covered pancakes with a chestnut filling.

Lekváros palacsinta: With an apricot jam filling and dusted with confectioners' sugar.

Kakaós palacsinta: Pancakes sprinkled with a mixture of confectioners' sugar and cocoa powder.

Mágnáspalacsinta: Prepared as *Csúsztatott palacsinta* (see page 85). The pancakes are spread with walnut cream and apricot jam instead of chocolate.

Rakott palacsinta: Place nine pancakes on top of each other in a heatproof dish, alternating each one with a layer of ground walnuts, quark (smooth cottage cheese), marmalade, and grated chocolate. Finally, top with beaten egg whites and bake until golden.

Sonkás mágnáspalacsinta: Prepared as *Mágnáspalacsinta,* but with a ham filling. The whole thing is topped with sour cream and baked.

Szentgyörgyhegyi palacsinta: Pancakes with a nut cream filling are rolled up, topped with a mixture of beaten eggs and milk, and baked.

Túrós palacsinta: Rolled-up pancakes with a quark (smooth cottage cheese) filling, topped with sour cream and baked.

Kapros túrós palacsinta
Pancakes with a dill and
quark filling

1 cup/250 g quark (smooth cottage cheese)
Pinch of salt
2 eggs, separated
3 tbsp sugar
Bunch of fresh dill
8–10 unsweetened pancakes
Sour cream

Push the quark through a strainer.
Add a pinch of salt to the egg whites and beat until stiff.
Combine the egg yolks with the sugar, and add to the quark.
Finely chop the dill, and stir into the quark mixture. Finally, carefully spoon the beaten egg whites into the mixture. Spoon the filling onto the pancakes, and roll them up.
Top with a dollop of soured cream, and serve warm as a main course or dessert.

Mákos palacsinta
Pancakes with a poppy seed
filling

¾ cup/120 g ground poppy seeds
⅔ cup/80 g confectioners' sugar
2 sachets of vanilla sugar
Scant ½ cup/100 ml milk
2 tbsp raisins (optional)
8–10 sweetened pancakes

Combine the poppy seeds, and the confectioners' and vanilla sugars. Pour over the hot milk, and stir well. Add the raisins, if using. Spread the mixture over the pancakes, and roll them up or fold into squares. Serve warm as a main course or dessert.

Csúsztatott palacsinta
Pancake stack
(Photograph right)

3 eggs, separated
⅔ cup/80 g confectioners' sugar
1 sachet of vanilla sugar
2½ tbsp/40 g butter
Scant ½ cup/200 ml milk
Scant ½ cup/100 ml light cream
1⅓ cups/150 g flour
3½ tbsp/50 g butter for frying
About ⅓ cup/80 g grated chocolate/chocolate flakes

Beat the egg yolks with 2½ tbsp (40 g) confectioners' sugar, the vanilla sugar, and the butter until light and fluffy. Stirring continuously, add the milk and the cream. Gradually add the flour, and stir to a smooth consistency.

Beat the egg whites with the remaining confectioners' sugar until stiff, and carefully fold into the batter.
Butter a round, flat, ovenproof dish and a skillet of about the same diameter, and cook a pancake of about ¼ inch/5 mm thickness in the skillet on one side only. Next, place the pancake, uncooked side up, in the dish, and top with a generous amount of grated chocolate. Cook the remaining pancakes in the same way, continuing to top and stack them as above except for the last one, which is cooked on both sides and then placed on top of the stack. Bake in a preheated (300 °F/ 150 °C) oven until the chocolate has melted, but is still creamy. Serve hot, and slice like a cake.

GINGERBREAD

Lots of traditional fairs are always held in areas where cattle are bred. But what would these events be without the brightly colored cakes and cookies available there for visitors to take home with them? Perhaps that is why gingerbread-baking is such a tradition in Debrecen. The "guild" of gingerbread-making was once one of the widest spread and most important trades in Hungary, and remained so until white refined sugar became more generally available. In the course of time, confectioners devised increasingly intricate delicacies for the sweet-toothed, and thereby gradually dispersed the traditional gingerbread-makers.

Well, most of them. Gingerbread, or honey cake, is still popular – whether as little round sugar-glazed cakes that are available in a number of different flavors and with or without fillings, or simple gingerbread figures with decorated edges.

However, the highly decorated, brightly colored figures made of *mézeskalács* (honey cake) have been the traditional gift for at least 100 years, since the popularity of the traditional gingerbread dolls fell into decline.

1 Making a traditional gingerbread heart: the dough is rolled out thinly and pressed into a wooden mold.
2 The dough is carefully removed from the mold.

3 The beautiful, highly intricate design is revealed.
4 The hearts are placed on the baking sheet and baked in an oven.

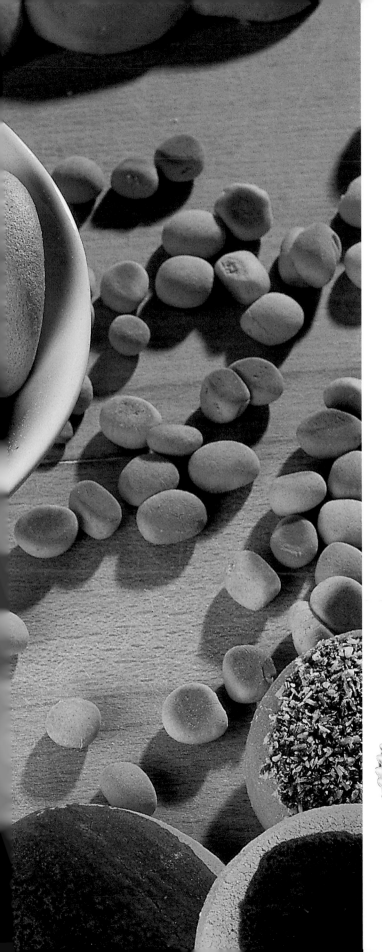

When choosing a token of affection for a loved one, many men will choose a gingerbread heart in preference to flowers. Although often considered to be somewhat "kitschy," a gingerbread heart radiates a certain appeal that many women are unable to resist. To quote the Hungarian writer Kálmán Mikszáth (1849–1910), "The art of gingerbread-baking … is not watched over by Mercury, but by Amour. It is full of love, full of fun. No, the gingerbread-baker is not a tradesman, but a veritable poet."

No two gingerbread hearts are the same. Each one is baked by a master baker, using traditional molds and colors, to his own taste and liking. The hearts are colored in red, and the edges decorated with a fanciful sugar glaze. Large hearts will have a small mirror or picture of a pair of sweethearts at the center, both surrounded by the usual sugar glaze adornment. The picture will be accompanied by a verse or saying, and this is often what decides the prospective buyer in his choice. It is surrounded by brightly colored sugar flowers in white, blue, pink, green, or yellow. It is not only gingerbread figures that are typically found on Hungarian markets: so too are slippers, bound with a ribbon and sold in pairs, as well as small swaddled figures, horses, and Hussars.

Top: Hearts are decorated with the most fantastic designs.
Left: Different types of gingerbread.
Below: Typical Hungarian gingerbread figures.

The inventor of soda water

The Benedictine teacher Ányos Jedlik (1802–95), once professor of physics at the University of Pest, was the first person to construct a dynamo and an electric engine. However, Jedlik omitted to publish these ideas. In 1829 he presented something completely different: the soda bottle. The gas is introduced into the bottle from the bottom, through a vertical tube, thereby keeping carbon loss to a minimum. His invention is still widely used today.

Top: This 100-year-old photograph shows two men who, having done a good day's work, are now spending the evening in the village inn over wine and tobacco.

In many small villages, the soda man still uses a horse-drawn vehicle.

Carrying the soda bottles, which are made from very thick, tough glass, requires considerable strength.

Glass bottles are increasingly being replaced by lighter plastic ones.

SPRITZER WINE

A foreign visitor once noted with surprise that wine at the court of the Hungarian king Matthias Corvinus (1440–90) was taken without water, which was not the case in 15th-century Europe. Conversely, today's visitors to Hungary are amazed at the popularity of wine mixed with soda water. Anyone who tries it will find that this "spritzer" is ideal for quenching thirst, and also goes well with the country's spicy specialties. Soda water (carbonated drinking water) is available in every household and inn. Many families make their own, using a special bottle with a pressurized top, through which carbon is injected from small cartridges into the water. In some regions, soda water is still brought by the soda man, who moves from street to street, attracting attention with his call of *szódás-szódás*. Plastic bottles, which are considerably lighter, are gradually replacing the old bottles that are made of heavy glass. Traditional, richly decorated soda bottles are popular decorative items.

Wines from the Lower Plains

Vines grown on the sandy soil of the Lower Plains produce predominantly table and country wines, including several good quality ones. The character of the wine is marked less by the location and processing methods, and more by the variety, from which they also get their names. Sweet and semidry white wines with low acidity and light red wines dominate. The dry table wines from this region are ideal for "spritzers."

The main types of wine from the Lower Plains are:
Cabernet: excellent red wine from the Hajós region
Ezerjó: green-white in color; fine acidity
Kadarka: ruby red, aromatic wine with a spicy scent; the best red wine for "spritzers"
Ködvidinka: light white table wine
Olaszrizling: green-yellow, sometimes golden in color, scent similar to mignonette; pleasantly bitter aroma; fine acidity

Ratios

There are different names for mixed drinks, depending on the ratio of wine and soda water. The imagination knows no bounds!

Conventional mixes:

fröccs or *nagyfröccs* – "spritzer"
2 parts wine to 1 part soda water

kisfröccs – "little spritzer"
Equal quantities wine and soda water

hosszúlépés – "big step"
1 part wine to 2 parts soda water

Some other mixes are no longer available everywhere:

házmester – "janitor"
3 parts wine to 2 parts soda water
(Now also the name for rum-based mixes)

viceházmester – "deputy janitor"
2 parts wine to 3 parts soda water

háziúr – "house owner"
4 parts wine to 1 part soda water

lakófröccs – "lodger's spritzer"
1 part wine to 4 parts soda water

Krúdy-fröccs – "Krudy spritzer"
9 parts wine to 1 part soda water
This drink is named after the writer Gyula Krúdy (1878–1933), who invented it. Following his example, some people ask for just a few splashes of soda water in 10 fl oz (300 ml) wine.

A variety of old soda water bottles

One clever and one silly bird
DUCK AND GOOSE

Although the term "silly goose" is derogatory, in Hungary they are considered to be clever creatures, since they can feed a whole family for several days, providing such delicacies as roasts, soups, stuffed liver, and goose drippings (the latter being good both for cooking purposes and as a spread).

By contrast, Hungarian chefs do not rate the duck very highly. They consider them to be "silly" creatures, since they provide too much meat for one, and not enough for two (regardless of the fact that this is the case only with young, tender birds). It is also said that the tasty liver cannot compete with the wonderful delicacies obtained from well-hung goose livers.

Hungary has a centuries-old tradition of breeding geese and ducks, and especially of fattening geese, which are famed for

their delicious livers. Hungary's "goose region" in the southern part of the Great Plains reaches from Kiskunhalas in the west to Orosháza in the east. It has the ideal natural conditions for such discerning fowl: sandy soil and lots of sun. For over 100 years, a number of slaughterhouses and factories in the region have concentrated on breeding and fattening geese. An understanding of the right conditions and the art of fattening is passed down from generation to generation.

Small family concerns merely keep a few geese for their own consumption. Commercially available stuffed livers (*libamáj*) come from large companies who specialize in their production.

Once the goslings have left the hatching house, it takes about another eight weeks for them to grow into tender-fleshed "roasting geese." At this stage, some of them go on to be fattened, as it takes more than a natural appetite to produce a nice, fat goose with the highly prized colossal liver. About two weeks before slaughtering, the fattened geese are given

substantially more feed than they require, which is literally forced into them. In former times this was done manually, but today it is done using electric equipment. The process is actually extremely gentle, and lasts only a few moments, but animal-lovers still regard it as a form of torture.

The Romans loved a delicious stuffed liver, and chose to fatten their geese with chestnuts or figs.

Hundreds of geese on an isolated farm.

It is said that their most experienced gourmets could tell from the taste of the liver what the bird had been fed on, and supposedly even whether the figs were dried or fresh.

Hungarian geese are not fed on such exotic delicacies. Their menu consists predominantly of maize, which increases their cholesterol level. Excess fat is stored in the liver, which, with the appropriate diet, can swell to a weight of three pounds. A good goose liver is wonderfully tender, and the maize gives it a yellow color.

Every breeder has his own secret recipe. One will soak the dried maize in water for at least twelve hours, another will steam it, and yet another swears by grinding it. A small amount of animal or vegetable fat is added to the maize, as this not only increases the calorie content, but also helps the goose to swallow it. The addition of salt has a favorable effect on the composition of the digestive juices, and also makes the maize meal more acceptable to the geese.

The bigger and whiter the liver is, the better it tastes.

Below: The goose livers are subjected to rigorous quality controls before being processed.

Hungarian goose liver products are one of the country's main exports.

Finally, the feed is seasoned with a choice of spices that is based on the breeder's own preference and expertise. Yellow aluminium oxide, finely diced hot peppers or ground pepper are just a few of the almost endless possibilities. However, artificial additives, antibiotics, and other substances which the body is unable to digest are strictly taboo. Not only do the breeders believe these are superfluous, but they are also banned by law.

With the exception of French goose livers, which are generally held to be the best in the world, Hungarian goose livers do not really have any serious international competitors. The only other significant contender is Israel – whose success is due in no small part to the efforts of Hungarian immigrants.

For a time, Cuba was also fairly successful in this field thanks to Hungarian specialists who showed their Cuban colleagues how to breed geese as part of a socialist aid program.

Fried goose liver is also delicious cold, but only if the liver is of good quality. The best livers are large, weighing at least 1¾ pounds (800 grams), well hung, and light yellow, almost white in color. Raw fattened livers are very delicate and must be treated with care so that the surface stays light. Liver fried by an expert is an appetizing roast brown on the outside and soft on the inside, and although it will dissolve on the tongue, it can still be cut into wafer-thin slices.

Opinions differ when it comes to the seasoning. Some feel it is a sin to add anything other than salt, others happily place garlic or onions, and maybe cloves beside the liver while it is being cooked. But there is one golden rule: less is definitely more, and the natural flavor of the liver must never be overpowered.

Tepertő
Cracklings
(Photograph below)

Goose skin	
Raw goose fat	
Small amount of milk	
Salt	

Remove the fat from the skin, and clean the skin thoroughly. Cut the skin and the fat into fairly small, evenly sized pieces, then slit the skin. Place in the bottom of a wide pot, and pour over enough water to just cover. Cover with a lid, and simmer until the fat rises to the top of the water. Then remove the lid and continue to cook until the cracklings floating on the top are a nice golden brown. Gently tilt the pot from side to side occasionally. Remove from the hob, and carefully drizzle some milk over the top (carefully; the fat will splash). Then replace the lid, and place to one side for a few minutes. Finally, drain off the fat, and, using a spoon, press on the cracklings in a strainer to remove as much fat as possible. Season with salt.

The melted fat is yellow, slightly coarse, and quite runny. The crispy, golden brown cracklings are delicious either hot or cold. Hot cracklings are served with preserved vegetables. Cold cracklings are delicious with baby onions, tomatoes, and bell peppers. Roast goose is often garnished with warm cracklings.

Vadas libamell
Breast of goose cooked like venison
(Photograph on opposite page, top left)

1 goose breast (1¾ lbs–2¼ lbs/ 800–1000 g)	
Scant 2 oz/50 g smoked bacon	
3½ tbsp/50 g goose fat	
1 tbsp flour	
2 tsp sugar	
Mustard	
Vinegar (optional)	
⅔ cup/150 ml sour cream	

For the marinade:

3½ oz/100 g carrots	
3½ oz/100 g parsley roots	
1 small onion	
2 bay leaves	
2 juniper berries	
5–8 peppercorns	
Salt	
1–2 tbsp vinegar	

Before cooking:
To make the marinade, peel and slice the carrots and parsley roots. Peel the onions and slice into rings. Blanch the vegetables and the seasonings in a little water, then season with vinegar and leave to cool. Remove the skin from the goose breast, and pour over the marinade. Place in the refrigerator for 2–3 days, turning twice daily.
Preparation:
Remove the meat from the marinade, and drain well. Remove the seasoning, and strain the marinade. Cut the smoked bacon into thin slices, and use to lard the meat. Finally, spread the goose fat over the breast. Place in a pot and roast in the oven (400 °F/200 °C) for 30–60 minutes, adding a little water if necessary. Then place the vegetables used in the marinade beside the meat, and add a little of the marinade liquid. Cover, and braise until done. Remove the meat. To make the sauce, reduce the cooking juices. Sprinkle flour over the vegetables and sweat briefly.

Then add some of the cold marinade and cook for 5 minutes. Take another pot and brown the sugar in it. Pour over a little water, and add to the sauce. Season to taste with mustard and vinegar (if preferred), and finally stir in the sour cream. Cut the goose breast into ½ inch/12 mm slices, and pour over the sauce. Serve immediately, with dumplings.

Gombás libamáj
Goose liver with mushrooms
(Photograph opposite page, top right)

14 oz/400 g goose liver	
Milk	
½ a small onion	
7 oz/200 g mushrooms	
Bunch of parsley	
3½ tbsp goose fat	
1 clove of garlic, crushed	
2 tbsp flour	
Scant ½ cup/100 ml light cream	
Scant ½ cup/100 ml dry white wine	
Pinch of pepper	
Salt	

It is a good idea to soak the liver in milk for about 30–60 minutes, then pat dry with paper towels. Remove the membrane and the veins from the liver, and cut it into dice. Peel and grate the onion, and cut the cleaned mushrooms into thin slices. Finely chop the parsley. Melt some goose fat and sauté the onions briefly. Add the crushed garlic and the chopped parsley. Cover with a lid and simmer until the liquid has evaporated. Then add the diced liver and stir-fry carefully. Sprinkle over the flour, and brown lightly. Stir in the cream and the white wine, then

cover with a lid and cook for a few more minutes. Season lightly just before arranging on a dish, and serve with rice.

Kacsapecsenye
Roast duck
(Photograph on opposite page, bottom)

1 oven-ready duck (about 6½ lbs/ 3 kg)	
Salt	
1–2 apples (optional)	
1–2 quinces (optional)	
1 tsp marjoram (optional)	

Wash the duck inside and outside, and pat dry with paper towels. Tie the drumsticks and wings with kitchen yarn so that the duck retains its shape while cooking. Rub salt on the inside and outside. Insert 1 or 2 whole apples or quinces into the cavity, or sprinkle the marjoram inside. Secure the opening with wooden picks. Roast in a preheated oven (350 °F/180 °C) for 2–2½ hours, adding a little hot water around the sides every 10–15 minutes. Baste the duck with the cooking juices and turn frequently so that it cooks evenly.
When cooked, leave the duck to "rest" in a warm place for 10 minutes, and then either serve whole, or carve.
A delicious accompaniment is sliced new potatoes, boiled in their skins, and turned in the hot roasting juices. Rice with mushrooms or red cabbage with apples also goes very well with this dish. Dried prunes, stewed in wine, are a pleasantly light, sweet accompaniment.

Left: *Tepertő* (cracklings)
Opposite page, from left to right: *Vadas libamell* (breast of goose cooked like venison), *Kacsapecsenye* (roast duck), *Gombás libamáj* (goose liver with mushrooms)

Savanyú nyúlgerinc
Saddle of hare in a piquant sauce

2½ lbs/1.2 kg saddle of hare
5 oz/150 g smoked bacon
2 lemons
1 large onion
Salt
2½ tbsp butter
2 cups/500 ml marrow stock
1¼ cups/300 ml sour cream
1 tbsp sugar
Mustard

Skin the saddle of hare. Cut the bacon into thin slices. Squeeze the juice from half of one lemon, and cut the remaining lemons and the peeled onion into slices. Lard the meat with plenty of bacon, then season with salt and brush with the melted butter. Place in a pot, and cover with the slices of lemon and onion. Pour over the marrow stock and simmer, gradually adding the sour cream. Finally, season with sugar, lemon juice, and mustard.

Dumplings are the best accompaniment for saddle of hare, especially cooked in this style.

Delicacies from field and forest
GAME

In Hungary, the bag consists mainly of hare and wild rabbit. Young animals are very tasty, but there are several excellent recipes for the flesh of older animals. If there are large numbers of deer, they need to be culled as otherwise they do too much damage to buds and trees. The hunting season starts in May. Hunters not only pursue a hobby or passion, but also practice good husbandry.

Őzgerinc vörösborban
Saddle of venison in red wine

1¼ cups/300 ml red wine
5 juniper berries
1 tsp rosemary
1 tsp thyme
1 small leek
2¼ lbs/1 kg saddle of venison (boneless)
1 tbsp oil
Scant ½ cup/100 ml light cream
2 tbsp flour
1 tbsp blackcurrant jelly
4 large potatoes

To make the marinade, combine the red wine with the crushed juniper berries, rosemary, thyme, and the finely chopped leek. Place the meat in the marinade and cover, then leave in the refrigerator for 1 day, turning frequently. Remove from the marinade and drain well. Reserve the marinade. Oil a roasting pan, and place the meat inside. Roast in a preheated oven (400 °F/200 °C) for 30–45 minutes. Carve the cooked roast into slices. To make the sauce, strain the marinade into the roasting juices. Combine the cream and the flour with the blackcurrant jelly, and use to bind the bubbling juices. Pour the sauce over the decoratively arranged venison slices. Serve with baked potatoes and brussels sprouts.

Szalonnás fürj
Larded quail

8 quails
1 small onion
1 clove of garlic
3½ oz/100 g mushrooms
Bunch of parsley
3½ oz/100 g smoked bacon
Salt
Scant ½ cup/100 ml sour cream
Scant ½ cup/100 ml light cream
1 tsp flour

Cut the oven-ready birds into halves. Peel and finely chop the onion and garlic, then wash and finely chop the mushrooms and parsley. Cut the bacon into small dice, and fry in a large skillet until the fat begins to run. Add the onion and the garlic, and sauté until translucent. Add the mushrooms and the parsley, and season with salt, then simmer until the liquid has evaporated. Then place the quail on top of the vegetables, pour over about ⅔ cup/150 ml of water, and season with salt. Simmer for 10–15 minutes, replacing the evaporated liquid as necessary. Remove the quail when they are cooked, and keep warm. Combine the creams with the flour, and use to bind the bubbling juices. Stir continuously until the sauce is thick, then place the birds in the sauce. Bring to the boil again briefly, then serve immediately. Potato croquettes go well with this dish.

Tejfölös fácánleves
Pheasant soup with soured cream

1 pheasant (about 1¾ lbs/800 g)
Salt
1 large carrot
1 medium parsley root
1 tender kohlrabi
2 tbsp butter
3 tbsp flour
Pinch of pepper
Large bunch of parsley
Scant ½ cup/100 ml sour cream

Halve the prepared pheasant, and boil in salted water (about 1½ hours). Pour off the stock, and retain. Remove the flesh from the bones, and cut into small pieces. Finely chop the vegetables, and sauté in the butter with a little salt. Once the cooking juices have evaporated, stir in the flour, and then add the stock. Place the meat in the stock, and season with pepper. Simmer gently until the vegetables are cooked. Finely chop the parsley, and add to the hot soup with the sour cream just before serving.

Fogolypecsenye szalonnában
Roast partridge with bacon

4 partridges
Salt
1 tsp marjoram
Generous 8 oz/250 g streaky smoked bacon
4 tbsp oil

Sprinkle salt and marjoram over the inside and outside of the prepared partridges. Cut all except 4 slices of the bacon into strips, and use to lard the breasts. Then wrap a slice of bacon around each bird, and truss them. Place in an oiled pot, pour over a little water, and roast in a preheated oven (425 °F/220 °C) for 20–30 minutes, basting frequently with the juices. Remove the bacon when the meat is cooked, and keep warm. Place the birds in a roasting pan, and return to the oven until crisp. Arrange on a bed of rice, and garnish with the bacon slices.

The pheasant hunting season lasts from October to January. As a general rule, one pheasant is sufficient for two people.

A touch of romance
FISHING

As old records tell us, Hungary's rivers and lakes used to be full of life, and it is even said that the rivers were once two-thirds water and one-third fish. One consequence of this abundance is a variety of highly imaginative fish recipes. A 15th-century Italian humanist was amazed: "Even fasting here is a feast." Just 200 years ago the Tisza was full of fish, and apparently all you had to do was dip a bucket in the water to catch your next meal.

Fishing idyll on the river Körös. Fishing is a popular pastime, and for the Hungarians it is not only a sport, but also a form of relaxation.

Above: A carp has bitten.
Right: Fish you have caught yourself definitely taste the best.

But now it is not just the stocks in Hungarian waters that have dwindled, so has the number of varieties. One variety that is no longer found in Hungary's rivers is the beluga, a member of the sturgeon family. This magnificent water-dweller can reach a length of 26 feet (8 meters). From the Black Sea, the beluga used to swim up the Danube and its tributaries to spawn. In 1957, south of Budapest near Pécs, a specimen measuring over 6½ feet (2 meters) was caught, and before then they were still caught much farther up the river. There is a particular section of the Danube near Budapest, where the current is fairly weak and where thermal springs bubble along the riverbed, which was one of the beluga's favorite haunts. That part of the city is still known as Vizafogó ("place where beluga are caught"), but none seems to have been caught since 1908.

No bones in this soup

When young Károly Sipos opened his first restaurant in a Budapest suburb in 1910, he tempted his guests with a "boneless" fish soup. Any diner who found even a single bone in his or her soup would receive a bottle of champagne as compensation. Word quickly spread, and the restaurant soon became a popular destination. However, the practice ceased when, to the innkeeper's surprise, increasing numbers of diners were demanding the bubbly consolation prize. Sipos finally realized that the resourceful diners were bringing in their own bones, and smuggling them into his soup.

Remove the scales, scraping from the tail toward the head.

Use a knife to cut along the center of the back.

Carefully remove the fillet from the central bone, and remove any small bones.

Finally, score the fillet to prevent it from curling during cooking.

Nowadays, fish is of secondary importance in the Hungarian diet, probably the result of changes in people's eating habits; there is certainly no lack of freshwater fish. The fish come not just from breeders, but also from clubs of keen anglers who, whatever the season, are happy to spend their free time with a rod in their hands. After all, it's a well-known fact that fish you have caught yourself taste the best! Not only do these anglers share a certain amount of sporting ambition, but also a desire for rest and relaxation, combined with a dash of romance. To many a stressed city dweller, nothing is more relaxing than to stand in silent waters, with a fishing rod in hand, thoughts slipping and sliding like the fish in the water; and later to fry the catch over a campfire or make a kettle of fish soup; then to share this meal and a glass or two of wine with a neighbor, discussing God and the world; and finally to sleep a deep, restful sleep under canvas or in a cabin.

Enthusiastic anglers can indulge their passion in rivers, ponds, and natural or artificial lakes. The dead tributaries of the Lower Plains, created in the 19th century, are considered a veritable fishing paradise. In order to control the devastating floods that regularly engulfed the Lower Plains, and at the same time to acquire more farmland, the highly meandering river courses were gradually brought under control. This was done by separating off numerous oxbows, which subsequently became dead tributaries.

At the top of the popularity scale of Hungary's fish is the carp. In general, the flesh of fish that are able to swim freely in natural waters is more popular than that of their specially bred counterparts, which are found in countless lakes and ponds. This is why the "wild" scaly carp is considered to be more valuable, whereas the pond-bred mirror carp is generally thought to be more fatty.

The delicious flesh of the catfish is also a favorite of gourmets and anglers alike, and Hungary's waters can contain some huge specimens. The largest one ever caught by an angler weighed about 220 pounds (100 kg). But what is that compared with the Tisza catfish noted by an academic named István Gáti in his "History of Nature" at the end of the 18th century, which supposedly swallowed whole geese. It is even said that a catfish once grabbed the leg of an unfortunate horse, dragging it into the depths of the river. And on several occasions, bolder, or perhaps cheekier, specimens at the top of the Tisza or in the Szamos have even pulled clothing from the hands of unsuspecting housewives doing their laundry there.

Fish traps are set close to the riverbank, and the contents checked daily. Once a fish has swum into the funnel-shaped opening, there is no way out.

Background right: Anglers from Szeged fishing in the rivers Tisza and Maros.

The dragnet is another method of catching fish. It is suspended between two boats, dragged along the river, and finally drawn around to form a closed circle.

Fillet of sturgeon is considered to be a true delicacy.

No two the same
FISH SOUP

Even though Hungary is not a "nation of fishermen" the native fish soup, which is made only from freshwater varieties, is one of the country's most popular dishes, and is even considered to be a national specialty.

There are numerous regional versions of this bright-red delicacy. Some are made with lots of different varieties of fish, others with only one. In some areas, the cook starts with an oil and onion base, similar to that for *pörkölt*, which is then pushed through a strainer, topped up with water, and large pieces of fish added. For thicker soups, a basic broth is made from less epicurean small fish. In the area around Baja, broad strips of pasta are added. If the soup is simply cooked "the fisherman's way," the ingredients are just placed in a large pot, or kettle, so minimum effort is required.

But however it is cooked, bright red ground paprika is ubiquitous in Hungarian fish soup. It was not until the end of the 18th century that paprika was widely grown in Hungary, and it follows that this must have been when it became common practice to add it to fish soup. Sweet or semisweet paprika can safely be used for most Hungarian specialties without suffering any loss of flavor. However, this is not the case with fish soup. Although it need not be hot enough to bring tears to the eyes, at least medium hot paprika should be used to give it the right flavor. Fresh green or dried red paprika pods can be served separately for the benefit of those who prefer spicier food, adding this to suit their own tastes. And, of course, fresh white bread is also required, as this will "put out the fire." Fish soup is traditionally followed by a farinaceous dish: quark pasta.

Not only does each area have its own particular recipe, it also has its own master chef, whose reputation will have transcended the region's borders. All year round, numerous well-attended cooking competitions are held all over Hungary, at which both professional and amateur cooks have the opportunity to show just what they can do. Their entries are judged by a very strict jury, and subsequently tried by all of the participants and visitors.

Fish soup cooked the fisherman's way

1 From top to bottom: zander, pike, eel, tench, trout, roach, river perch, carp.
2 The fish are gutted and cleaned, then cut into pieces, and placed in the kettle.
3 The onions are sliced and added to the fish.
4 Chopped tomatoes and sliced bell peppers are placed on top.

5 Water is poured over the contents of the kettle, which are then briefly brought to the boil.
6 A tablespoon of ground paprika is added. Rather than stirring the contents, the kettle is gently tilted from side to side.
7 The soup is left to bubble away for about 1 hour.
8 The bright red soup tastes best when still very hot.

Fish soup competitions, such as this one in Gyomaendrőd on the Körös, are held all over Hungary.

Halászlé vegyes halból

Fish soup made from different varieties of fish

About 3½ lbs/1.5 kg fish (e.g. carp, catfish, and perch)	
Salt	
1 bell pepper (capsicum)	
1 tomato	
2 medium onions	
1 tbsp rose paprika	
1–2 hot peppers (optional)	
Fresh white bread to serve	

Scale and gut the fish, retaining the milt and roe. Remove the bones, and wash. Cut into bite-size pieces, and season with salt. Chop the bell pepper and tomato into small pieces, and slice the onion. Place the fish heads, large bones, and the fins in a pot with the onions, and add enough water to cover. Bring to a boil, add the rose paprika, and simmer gently for 1 hour. Strain the broth, and place in a pot together with the pieces of fish. Add the roe, milt, and the chopped tomato and bell pepper, and cook over a fairly high heat for about 20 minutes. Do not stir the soup; simply tilt it gently from side to side.

The cooked soup is often garnished with sliced green bell pepper before serving. Fresh or dried hot peppers are always served separately to let the diners season their soup according to their own taste. This soup is always served with freshly baked white bread.

The soup is just as tasty if the broth is made with smaller, less grand fish. It can also be made from just a single variety, but the use of several different ones makes it more aromatic.

Dorozsmai molnárponty
Carp à la Dorozsma
(Top of photograph)

1¼ lbs/600 g carp fillet	
3½ oz/100 g smoked bacon	
Salt	
1 large onion	
3 bell peppers (capsicum)	
2 large tomatoes	
9 oz/250 g mushrooms	
4 tbsp flour	
3½ tbsp oil	
1 tsp ground paprika	
¾ cup/200 ml sour cream	
10 oz/300 g large square pasta pieces (see page 38)	

Cut the fish fillets into 1½–2 inch/4–5 cm pieces. Cut the bacon into thin slices, and use a larding needle to lard the pieces of fish. Season and leave to rest for a few minutes. Peel and finely chop the onion. Seed the bell peppers and cut into thin rings. Skin the tomatoes and the mushrooms, and cut into thin slices. Coat the pieces of fish in flour. Sauté in hot oil until crispy on both sides, then remove. Fry the onions in the cooking juices, then remove from the heat and sprinkle over the ground paprika. Pour over a little water and add the vegetables. Simmer until cooked, then add the sour cream and bring to the boil again. Place the pieces of fish in the sauce and simmer for about 15 minutes, gently tilting the pot from side to side occasionally. Meanwhile, cook the pasta. Carefully remove the fish from the sauce. Add the hot pasta to the vegetables. Place in a heatproof dish, and arrange the pieces of fish on top. Heat through in a preheated oven (300 °F/150 °C).
Garnish with sliced tomatoes and bell peppers.

Kemencés harcsa
Oven-baked catfish
(Bottom right of photograph)

1¾ lbs/800 g catfish fillets	
Salt	
1¾ lbs/800 g potatoes	
2½ tbsp butter	
1 large onion	
1¼ cups/300 ml sour cream	
½ tsp ground paprika (semisweet)	

Cut the fillets into fairly small pieces and season with salt. Cut the boiled potatoes into very thin slices. Butter an enamel or other heatproof dish, and arrange the potatoes over the bottom. Season with salt, and place the pieces of fish on top. Grate the onion and combine with the sour cream and ground paprika. Spread this mixture over the fish. Bake in a preheated oven (300 °F/150 °C) for 40–50 minutes until the potatoes are cooked.

Csuka tejfölös tormával
Pike in horseradish sauce
(Left of photograph)

1 pike (about 2½ lbs/1.2 kg)	
1 large carrot	
1 large parsley root	
1 medium onion	
1 tbsp lemon juice	
1¼ cups/300 ml sour cream	
3 tbsp flour	
3½ oz/100 g grated horseradish	
Salt	
Pinch of white pepper	
3½ tbsp/50 g butter	

Remove the scales from the pike, then gut, fillet, and cut into small pieces. Peel and slice the carrot, parsnip, and onion. Add the lemon juice and the vegetables to 4 cups/1 liter of water, and bring to a boil. Place the pieces of fish in the boiling water, and cook

Clockwise from the top: *Dorozsmai molnárponty* (carp à la Dorozsma), *Kemencés harcsa* (oven-baked catfish), and *Csuka teifölös tormával* (pike in horseradish sauce)

over medium heat for about 15 minutes. Combine the sour cream and the flour in a skillet, then add the grated horseradish and a little stock, and bring to a boil. Season to taste with salt and white pepper, and finally add the butter. Remove the fish from the stock using a slotted spoon, and drain. Arrange on a serving dish, and pour over the hot horseradish sauce. Serve with rice or boiled potatoes.

Pontyszeletek hagymás káposztával
Carp fillets with sauerkraut

1¾ lbs/800 g carp fillet
Salt
4 tbsp flour
4 oz/120 g bacon
2 tbsp oil
1¾ lbs/800 g sauerkraut
1 large onion
Scant ½ cup/100 ml dry white wine
¼ tsp pepper

Season the fillet with salt, and turn in the flour. Finely chop the bacon and cook in the hot oil until the fat begins to run, then remove the cracklings. Quickly sauté both sides of the fillet, and set aside. Rinse and drain the sauerkraut. Peel and slice the onion, and briefly fry the rings in half the bacon fat. Add the sauerkraut. Pour over the wine and season with pepper. Cover with a lid and simmer for 20 minutes, stirring occasionally. Grease a flat heatproof or enamel dish with the remainder of the bacon fat. Place the fish in the dish and cover with the sauerkraut. Bake in a preheated oven (400 °F/200 °C) for about 20 minutes.

Harcsapörkölt
Catfish pörkölt

1 catfish (about 3¼ lbs/1.5 kg)
Salt
1 large onion
1 large tomato
2–3 bell peppers (capsicum)
4 tbsp oil
1 tsp ground paprika (semisweet)

Remove the scales from the fish, gut, and clean. Cut off the head and the tail, place in water, and bring to a boil. Fillet the fish and season on both sides with salt. Peel the onion and cut into thin rings. Cut the tomato and the seeded bell peppers into small pieces. Sauté the onion in hot oil until golden, then remove from the heat and sprinkle over the ground paprika. Add the chopped tomatoes and bell peppers, and stir well. Strain the fish stock over the vegetables. Cover everything with a lid, and simmer. Add the fish fillets as soon as the broth starts to thicken, and cook over an even heat for about another 20 minutes. Serve with pasta or boiled potatoes.

Sült csuka
Fried pike

1 pike (about 3¼ lbs/1.5 kg)
Salt
3½ oz/100 g smoked bacon
4 tbsp oil

Remove the scales from the fish, gut, and clean. Season with salt and pat dry. Cut the bacon into thin slices and lard both sides of the fish. Heat the oil in an enamel dish and place the fish in the dish. Bake in a preheated oven (350° F/180 °C) for about 45 minutes, until crispy. Serve with potatoes and parsley.

QUARK AND CHEESE

Quark is a smooth cottage cheese that is usually made from cow's milk, and more rarely from ewe's or goat's milk. It is available with different fat contents. Low-fat Hungarian quark (*sovány*) contains 5% fat, the most frequently used *félzsíros* has 15%, and the creamy *zsíros* is 35% fat.

Housewives used to make their own quark. First, the fresh milk, which might have been skimmed, was poured into a clay jug and left in a warm place. Once it had turned sour (usually after a day), it was moved to a warmer place, generally the oven, to intensify the curdling process. This also helped to separate the sour-tasting whey more quickly. The curdled milk was then poured into a sack so the whey could drip out. Nowadays, quark is made in large factories from pasteurized milk. The curdling process is not left to chance, but brought about by the addition of lactic acid bacteria. Quark is healthy and tasty, and, because it has a mild flavor, also highly versatile.

Túrós csusza
Quark pasta

Pasta dough (made from 14 oz/ 400 g flour and 3 eggs)
3½ oz/100 g smoked bacon
4 tsp/20 g butter
1¾ cups/400 g creamy quark
¾ cup/200 ml sour cream

Prepare the pasta dough (see page 38). Tear into pieces of about 1½–2 inches (4–5 cm) in length and cook in boiling salted water. Cut the bacon into small pieces and fry in the hot butter until the fat begins to run. Remove the cracklings from the pan and keep warm. Reserving some of the fried bacon as a garnish, stir the pasta in the rest. Add half the quark and the sour cream, and combine well. Heat through again, and pour into a warm dish. Spread over the remainder of the quark. Heat the remaining sour cream and pour over. Sprinkle over the reserved bacon pieces, then the cracklings, and serve immediately.

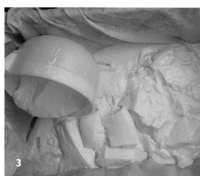

1 Pasteurized milk is poured into the quark bowl.
2 A few drops of rennet are added to whole milk.
3 Once the milk has set, the mass is divided into portions.
4 The broken curds are wrapped in a damp cloth.

5 The whey takes between six and eight hours to drain away.
6 The contents of the cloth are returned to a bowl and stirred.
7 This gives the quark the desired creamy consistency.
8 The quark is measured into jars and offered for sale.

Dairy cattle and their products

For a long time, just about the only type of cattle kept by Hungarian dairy farmers was the brown and white Schecke. A cross between the robust Hungarian gray and the Simmentaler, it was imported for its superb milk yield. The highly popular Holstein Friesians and Jersey cattle were imported in the 1970s, again for their high milk yield, as these breeds are better able to meet the industrial requirements for milk processing. They are more suitable for

Milk pitcher

mechanical milking, and Jersey milk's high fat content makes it suitable for a variety of purposes.

In time, the Hungarian Schecke was crossed with the Holstein Friesian and the Jersey, and this resulted in the Hungarifries, a breed that exemplifies the best qualities of each parent.

Butter

Is a type of fat obtained from dairy milk that consists of 80% milk fat, plus water and usually common salt. Butter is the best fat for baking, since it has an unbeatable flavor and lends substance. Despite this, however, margarine is becoming increasingly popular in Hungarian kitchens.

Cream

Is obtained from the milk by separation or centrifuge. Whipping cream contains at least 30% fat. When heated, the proteins, which form most of the foam when the cream is whipped, curdle. It is then left to mature in a cool place for at least two days, and during this time the butter oil crystallizes into tiny fat globules. Cream whips best if it is chilled first.

Sour cream

Similar to crème fraîche. This is made from milk which has been acidified by the addition of lactic acid or other bacteria, also known as "starters." Sour cream is used to bind soups and sauces, and is essential in creating the flavors of countless Hungarian meat and farinaceous specialties.

Cheeses

The following cheeses are specialties from all over Hungary.

1 **Bakony:** A soft cheese, made from cow's milk, with a white rind

2 **Parenyica:** Lightly smoked rolled cheese, usually made from ewe's milk, but also made from cow's milk; surrounded by an edible cheese twine

3 **Pálpusztai:** Melting cheese, made from cow's milk in the Romadur tradition; has a piquant flavor and strong aroma

4 **Márványsajt:** Blue cheese, made from cow's milk, with a high fat content

5 **Sonkás:** Ham-flavored cheese

6 **Oázis:** Lightly smoked cheese

7 **Pannonia:** Hard cheese with large holes, made from cow's milk

8 **Gauda:** Mild cheese made from cow's milk

9 **Ilmici:** Semihard cheese made from cow's milk

10 **Trappista:** Semihard cheese, made from cow's milk, with a slightly sour flavor

11 **Óvári:** Semihard rindless cheese; made from cow's milk

12 **Köményes:** Rindless caraway-flavored cheese with a low fat content; made from cow's milk

13 **Lajta:** Semihard cheese, made from cow's milk; has a light orange rind

14 **Palóc gomolya:** Finely pored white cheese, made from goat's milk

15 **Pálpusztai:** Melting cheese, made in the Romadur tradition from cow's milk, with a piquant flavor and strong aroma

16 **Vajas márványsajt:** Spreadable cheese, made from blue cheese and butter

17 **Kaskaval:** Semihard cheese, made from ewe's milk

18 **Karaván:** Semihard smoked cheese with a dark brown rind; made from cow's milk

19 **Anikó:** Soft cheese, made from cow's milk

The apricot tree originally came from China, and arrived in Europe via Asia Minor.

Seductive cherry

The sweet cherries of the Lower Plains caused an international furore as long ago as the 16th century, when Hungarian aristocrats, hoping to win themselves a leading position at court, presented the first specimens to the Habsburg king of Hungary.
The Germersdorfer Riese variety, which came from Germany and is the preferred choice for cultivation in Hungary, is the one the consumer desires the most. These large, heart-shaped "crunchy" fruits are a lovely red color, and taste wonderful.

APRICOT CULTIVATION

A wealth of historical evidence confirms that apricots have been cultivated in Hungary's Lower Plain for centuries. While they were still in power, the Turks possessed huge apricot plantations, but their flowering gardens withered and died during the course of Hungary's tumultuous history, and it was not until the 19th century that apricot cultivation was resumed in the Lower Plain. At that time, the area was in grave danger of becoming a desert, and the intensity of the sandstorms that occurred between the Danube and the Tisza almost matched that of Central Asia. Apricot trees were ideal for binding the wind-borne sand, since they like a sandy soil and are well able to survive heat and dryness.

The most (and best) apricots grow in the region around Kecskemét. Most Hungarians automatically think of this area when they hear the word *barack* – although some think of the wonderfully aromatic fruit, and others of the no less aromatic apricot schnapps.

It is just a shame that the apricot season is so short – although this could also be the reason why apricot jam and schnapps were invented in the first place!

Barackos gombóc
(Apricot dumplings)

Barackos gombóc
Apricot dumplings
(Photograph top right)

For the dough:

2¼ lbs/1 kg potatoes
3 cups/350 g flour
2 tbsp/30 g butter
Pinch of salt

Generous 1 lb/500 g apricots
½ tsp ground cinnamon
1¾ cup/100 g fresh breadcrumbs
3⅓ tbsp/50 g butter
Cinnamon and confectioners' sugar (optional)

Wash and dry the apricots, and remove the pits. Boil the potatoes in their skins. Peel while still warm and mash them. Leave to cool a little, then add the flour, butter, and salt, and knead to a dough. Roll out to a thickness of ¼ inch/5 mm on a floured surface. Sprinkle over some flour and cut into 2½ inch/6 cm squares. Place an apricot on each square and sprinkle over a little cinnamon. Fold the edges of the dough over the fruit and shape into a dumpling. Place the dumplings in a large pot of boiling water. Once the dumplings have risen to the surface, leave them to simmer for another 4–5 minutes. Meanwhile, melt the butter in another (large) pot, and fry the breadcrumbs in it. Remove the dumplings from the water with a slotted spoon, and drain well, then gently place in the pot with the breadcrumbs. Cover with a lid and leave to stand for 3–4 minutes (this allows the dumplings to firm up). Then coat the dumplings in the breadcrumbs.

Serve immediately, sprinkled with cinnamon and confectioners' sugar if preferred.

1 Dip the washed apricots in boiling water.
2 This makes it easier to remove the skins.
3 Remove the pits from the apricots, and weigh the fruit.

4 Push the fruit through a grinder.
5 Add the sugar.
6 Stir the jam well throughout the entire cooking process.

Apricot jam

Wash the ripe apricots thoroughly. Place in a strainer and dip in boiling water. Remove, then skin the apricots and pit them. Weigh the flesh, then push through a grinder. Boil for 15–20 minutes, stirring continuously. Then add the sugar (about one part sugar to two parts fruit), and continue to cook. Put the hot jam in screw-top jars, and close firmly. Wrap the jars in paper and dry sterilize (see page 300).

7 To test whether the jam is ready, spoon a small amount onto a plate and leave to cool.
8 Wrap the jars in paper, then place in a basket and keep warm.
9 The jam keeps best in screw-top jars.

Packers at work. *Barackpálinka* from Kecskemét is known beyond the country's borders.

Kecskemét's modern, computer-controlled distillery.

The process is observed through a window such as this.

A sample is taken before the end of the distilling process.

No amount of technology is a substitute for the experience and expertise of the distiller.

FRUITY SPIRITS MADE FROM APRICOTS AND CHERRIES

Kecskemét is famous for its *barackpálinka*, or apricot schnapps. Its high quality is due mainly to the apricots used, such as *magyar kajszi* or *magyar legjobb*, which thrive in the region. However, the apricot kernels are ground and added to the liquid during the distillation process, and this is what gives the schnapps its marked flavor.

For the first part of the process, the apricot fruit is stored in large barrels. During this time, the fructose converts naturally into alcohol. The mash is washed and immediately distilled. That is to say, it is heated, and the rising vapors are collected. As they cool, they turn back into liquid. The first distillation produces a distillate with an alcohol content of 8–15% (proof). This distillate is further distilled and refined, which increases the alcohol content and the aroma. The resulting schnapps, or brandy, is transferred into oaken barrels and left there to mature for at least one year, during which time it loses its "bite" and develops the characteristic, brown-yellow color – it is "fit for bottling."

The modern, computer-controlled distillery at Kecskemét still follows traditional methods. However, there is no substitute for the knowledge and expertise of the distiller, who regularly takes samples to check the quality of the spirit and decide on the choice and duration of the subsequent processes. As you would expect, the quality of the fruit varies between harvests, but – unlike with wine production – no differentiation is made between vintages. Instead, attempts are made to maintain the same flavor,

aroma, and quality from one year to the next. The alcohol content is also predetermined. For *fütyülős barack* and *pecsétes barack* it is an impressive 43% proof. The first *barackpálinka* left the Kecskemét Municipal Distillery in 1884, and owes its reputation to the Duke of Windsor (1894–1972), who became Edward VIII in 1936 only to abdicate a few months later before his coronation. He was a frequent visitor to Hungary throughout the 1930s, and, as befitted his well-founded reputation as a bon viveur, became closely acquainted with the nightlife of Budapest. On his first visit to a particular restaurant, he asked his companions to order him a national drink so as not to draw attention to himself. Thus he was introduced to apricot schnapps, which he soon grew to love and made famous abroad.

Barackpálinka gives mixed alcoholic drinks a distinctly Hungarian note.

Puszta-Cocktail

4 parts Tokajer Szamorodni (dry)
3 parts apricot schnapps
1 part Mecsek liqueur
Lemon oil

Measure the ingredients into a cocktail shaker, and mix with the spoon. Spray lemon oil over the top. Mecsek is a spicy, typically Hungarian herb liqueur with a slightly bitter flavor. It gets its unmistakable aroma and name from the herbs of the Mecsek mountains in Transdanubia.

The "Ornamental Palace" of Kecskemét is an office block in the national Hungarian art nouveau style. The brightly colored majolica decorations are reminiscent of the embroideries of the Lower Plain.

Cherry schnapps
(kirsch)

Cherry schnapps from Kecskemét (43% proof), which is made from the Germersdorfer Riese cherry, is another extremely popular variety. It is distilled with the cherry pits, and they are what give it its unique aroma.

Cseresznyepálinka becomes crystal clear if it is left to mature in ash barrels. A few decades ago, it was the done thing to drink kirsch in Hungary, and over the years it became more popular than the apricot and plum brandies.

To wrap around a Hussar and his horse
STRUDEL

Strudel is one of the most famous dishes in Hungarian cuisine, and great skill and patience are required to make the parchment-thin dough. The artistic movements used to stretch and draw the dough across the back of the hands while slowly circling the table are quite a sight, and invariably the strudel bakers will happily "perform" in full view of their customers, or else in a position that enables them to be observed through a window from the street.

The best type of flour for the dough contains high amounts of gluten and starch, and is completely dry, so ideally should be from the previous year's harvest. In Hungary, a slightly coarse flour is available just for this purpose.

There is a particular cookbook, just 100 years old, that tells us how thin the dough should be: "The housewife will know her strudel dough is good enough when she can take a piece of dough the size of a bread roll and work it sufficiently to wrap up a Hussar – and his horse – in strudel."

Rétestészta
Strudel dough

⅓ cup lard	
1¼ lbs/600 g flour	
1 egg	
2 tsp vinegar	
½ tsp salt	
6½ tbsp/100 g butter for brushing	

Melt the lard, then leave to cool to room temperature. Knead together the flour and the lard with the egg, vinegar, and as much lukewarm, lightly salted water (¾–1¼ cups/200–300 ml) as is needed to make a medium-firm dough. Continue to knead the dough, which is quite sticky at first, slamming it down on the worktop from time to time, until the surface becomes shiny and starts to bubble. The dough is ready to use when it no longer sticks to your hands or the work surface. Sprinkle flour over the work surface, then halve the dough and shape each half into a loaf (which must not have any creases or tears anywhere on the surface). Leave the loaves on the work surface and cover with a warm inverted bowl for about 20 minutes. The dough is ready to use when it feels soft, and a light touch with a fingertip leaves a small indentation.

Spread a smooth linen cloth over a large table so that it hangs down the sides, and sprinkle evenly with flour. Using your hands, carefully stretch a piece of dough until it is the size of a plate, then place it on the middle of the table and spread with melted, lukewarm butter. Insert your hands under the dough, and pull it outward on the back of your hands toward the edge of the table, constantly moving around the table.

(Continued on p.117)

Sift the flour into a bowl and combine with the melted lard.

Stir in the egg, vinegar, and salted water.

Mix the ingredients well.

Continue to work the dough, which is quite sticky at first.

Place the dough on the floured worktop and continue to knead.

Gently throw the dough onto the worktop from time to time until it bubbles.

Form the dough into the shape of a loaf, then cover with an inverted bowl and set aside to rest.

Stretch the dough over the backs of your hands.

Cover the table with a white linen cloth. Sprinkle it with flour and place the dough on the cloth.

Use both hands to draw the dough out to the size of the tabletop.

Insert your hands beneath the dough and gently pull it until it is so thin that you can see through it.

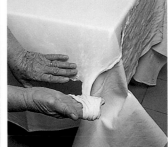

Trim the overhanging, somewhat thicker pieces of dough.

Brush with the melted lard.

Use the tablecloth to fold the dough over.

Brush evenly with a thin layer of butter.

Lift the tablecloth along one of the narrow ends of the dough.

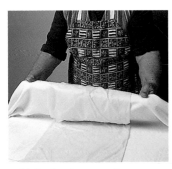

Fold the dough over again.

Spoon a strip of filling onto the dough a hand's width from the edge.

Using the tablecloth, roll the dough over again.

Carefully place the strudels on a greased baking sheet a small distance apart.

Brush the strudels with melted butter.

Place the baking sheet in the preheated oven.

Vargabéles

This dessert was invented by a Klausenburg innkeeper named Varga. His recipes are all easy, especially as the strudel and pasta doughs do not need to be homemade.

14 oz/400 g ribbon pasta
Salt
⅔ cup/150 g butter
4 eggs
2 sachets of vanilla sugar
Scant 1 cup/100 g confectioners' sugar
2 cups/500 g quark
½ tsp grated lemon rind
¾ cup/100 g raisins
2 cups/500 ml sour cream
6 sheets of strudel dough
1 cup/50 g fresh breadcrumbs
Vanilla and confectioners' sugar for sprinkling

Cook the pasta in plenty of salted water. Drain, and toss in about 2½ tbsp/40 g melted butter. Beat the egg yolks with the vanilla and confectioners' sugars until creamy. Pass the quark through a sieve, then stir in the lemon rind, the egg yolk mixture, the raisins, and sour cream. Beat the whites with a pinch of salt until stiff, then carefully combine with the quark mixture. Add the ribbon pasta.

Grease a medium baking sheet with high sides. Place three layers of strudel dough over each other, brushing each layer with plenty of melted butter, and finish with an even layer of breadcrumbs. Spread over the quark mixture and top with the buttered strudel dough. Dot the top layer with a generous amount of butter.

Place in a preheated (medium) oven and bake until crispy (about 30 minutes). Remove from the oven and leave to cool for about 10 minutes. Use a sharp knife to cut into squares of about 4 x 4 inches/10 x 10 cm. Sprinkle with the combined vanilla and confectioners' sugars, and serve hot.

Homemade strudel is something of which any housewife can quite rightly be proud.

Cut off the thick, overhanging pieces of pastry, and knead them together to make a single big piece of dough again at a later stage. Again, leave the dough to rest before working it in the same way. Brush the parchment-thin piece of dough with lukewarm melted butter, and fold it over several times. Spread a strip of filling, the width of a hand, close to the edge of the dough (the filling should be cool; if it is runny, add a few ground walnuts or fine breadcrumbs to thicken). Lift the cloth to roll up the pastry, and cut into slices that will fit onto your baking sheet. Carefully place the pieces of dough, three fingers apart, on the greased baking sheet. Brush with a generous amount of melted butter, and bake in a preheated oven (400 °F/200 °C) until golden. Cool a little, and cut into slices (about 2½ inches/6 cm wide) with a sharp knife. Serve warm, sprinkled with confectioners' sugar if preferred. Proceed in the same way with the second "loaf," and the remaining dough.

Strudel made with commercial dough

Dampen a dish towel and spread out over a smooth work surface. Remove the wrapping from the dough, then spread one layer over the dish towel and brush with plenty of melted shortening or oil. Place a second and third layer on top, brushing each one as the first. Proceed as in the recipe for homemade strudel (see page 114).

Fillings for two rolls:

Kapros túrós rétes
Quark strudel with dill

14 oz/400 g quark
2 eggs, separated
Generous 1 cup/120 g confectioners' sugar
1 tbsp semolina
Bunch of fresh dill

Pass the quark through a sieve, and combine with the egg yolks and the sugar. Add the semolina, the finely chopped dill, and the beaten egg whites. Spread over the strudel dough, then roll into a sausage and bake.

Káposztás rétes
Cabbage strudel

2¼ lbs/1 kg cabbage
Salt
2 tbsp sugar
3½ tbsp oil
Pepper

Chop the cabbage, then sprinkle over the salt and leave to stand for 30 minutes. Brown the sugar in hot oil, then add the pressed cabbage. Sauté, uncovered, until golden, stirring occasionally. Season to taste with pepper. Spread over the strudel dough, then roll into a sausage and bake.

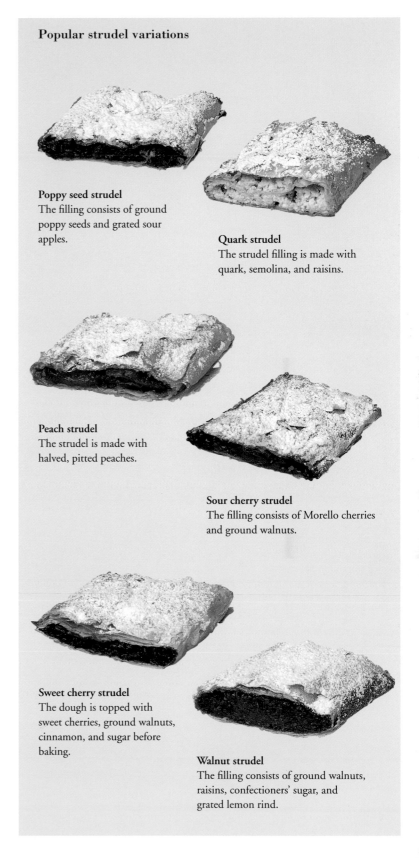

Popular strudel variations

Poppy seed strudel
The filling consists of ground poppy seeds and grated sour apples.

Quark strudel
The strudel filling is made with quark, semolina, and raisins.

Peach strudel
The strudel is made with halved, pitted peaches.

Sour cherry strudel
The filling consists of Morello cherries and ground walnuts.

Sweet cherry strudel
The dough is topped with sweet cherries, ground walnuts, cinnamon, and sugar before baking.

Walnut strudel
The filling consists of ground walnuts, raisins, confectioners' sugar, and grated lemon rind.

FRITTERS, TWISTS, AND DOUGHNUTS

"Carnival doughnuts should be as light as a feather – light enough to melt on the tongue. They should be golden in color, with a 'belt' around the middle, and eaten while still hot …" so said Elek Magyar, an expert on Hungarian gastronomy.

This yeast pastry specialty with the "golden ring" – as the lighter-colored indentation is known – is now available all year round, and not just at carnival time. Although usually eaten cold, they definitely taste better warm, so it is always worth making them yourself. To ensure success, the yeast dough should be prepared in a draft-free room where the temperature is constant (about 68–75 °F/20–24 °C). The flour and other ingredients, as well as the work surface and dish towel used to cover the dough, should all be at room temperature.

Clockwise from top: *Forgácsfánk* (twists), *Farsangi vagy szalagos fánk* (doughnuts), and *Aranygaluska* (fritters)

A noble piece of dough

There are countless stories about how doughnuts first came to be made, and why they became "fashionable." One story tells how the widow of a Viennese baker, one Frau Krapf (the German word for doughnuts is *Krapfen*), found that her bread was not ready in time, and threw a piece of dough in a pot of boiling fat in a fit of temper.

According to a different story, Queen Marie Antoinette of France "ennobled" the doughnut after being introduced to the sweet temptation by a village baker when, traveling incognito, she joined in some riotous carnival celebrations.

Farsangi vagy szalagos fánk
Carnival or "golden ring" doughnuts

2 cups/500 ml milk
1 tbsp superfine sugar
1¼ cakes/20 g fresh compressed yeast
Generous 1 lb/500 g flour
2 egg yolks
5 tbsp confectioners' sugar
3½ tbsp/50 g butter
Liqueur glass of rum
Pinch of salt
At least 4 cups/1 liter oil for deep-frying
Vanilla sugar and confectioners' sugar

Make a dough from 1¼ cups/300 ml milk, the sugar, yeast, and 3 tablespoons of flour (see yeast dough recipe on page 299). Beat the egg yolks with the confectioners' sugar until fluffy, and combine with the risen yeast. Melt and cool the butter, then add to the egg mixture with the remaining flour and the rum. Stir in enough lightly salted, lukewarm milk to make a smooth dough. Knead well (tradition has it that the dough is beaten with a wooden spoon for 20 minutes) until the dough starts to bubble. Sprinkle with flour, then cover with a dish towel and leave in a warm place until it has almost doubled in size. Sprinkle some flour over the work surface, and, with your hands, pat to a thickness of about ½ inch/12 mm. Use an item such as a water glass to cut out rounds. Place these rounds on the work surface, then cover with a cloth and leave to rise for about another 30 minutes. Press a fingertip on the center of each round to make an indentation. Deep-fry in plenty of oil (the doughnuts should have enough room to float). The temperature of the oil should remain constant, and not be too high. Only place a few doughnuts in the oil, as they expand quite considerably while frying. Cover to fry the level side, but leave uncovered when frying the side with the indentation facing upward. Turn and remove with a slotted spoon. Place on paper towels to dry. Sprinkle with a mixture of the vanilla and confectioners' sugars and serve immediately. Serve with thinned, warm apricot jam, into which you dip pieces of the doughnuts.

turn out onto a plate and sprinkle with the vanilla and confectioners' sugars. Serve immediately, accompanied by wine cream or vanilla sauce and warm jam. You will know this recipe is a success if you can break the fritters easily with a fork.

Forgácsfánk
Twists

1 tbsp sugar
5 egg yolks
1 egg
1 tbsp sour cream
1 tbsp rum
Pinch of salt
3 cups/350 g flour
Generous 2 cups/500 ml oil for deep-frying
Vanilla sugar and confectioners' sugar

Combine the sugar, egg yolks, the whole egg, cream, rum, and salt in a bowl. Add the flour and knead to a dough. Halve the dough, then shape each half into a loaf and brush with oil. Cover and leave to rest for 30 minutes. Roll out on a floured work surface to the thickness of a knife blade. Pierce with a fork and divide into strips of 4 x 1½ inches/10 x 3 cm with a dough wheel. Twist each strip over itself as if tying a knot.
Heat the oil. The temperature is right when a piece of dough, dropped into the oil, rises to the top and expands quickly. Place the "twists" in the oil. Reduce the heat when they turn golden, and turn them over.
Remove the cooked "twists" with a slotted spoon. Carefully shake off the excess oil and place on paper towels to dry. Sprinkle with the vanilla and confectioners' sugars, and serve immediately.

Aranygaluska
Fritters

1 cup/250 ml milk
2 sugar cubes
1¼ cakes/20 g fresh compressed yeast
2 eggs
Generous 1 cup/120 g confectioners' sugar
6½ tbsp–⅔ cup/100–150 g butter
Salt
2½ cups/300 g flour
¾ cup/40 g fresh breadcrumbs
2½ tbsp/120 g ground walnuts
½ tsp grated lemon rind
⅓ cup/50 g raisins
1 egg yolk
Vanilla sugar and confectioners' sugar

Stir the sugar in a scant ½ cup/100 ml lukewarm milk until completely dissolved. Crumble in the yeast, and leave in a warm place for 8–10 minutes. Whisk the remaining milk with the eggs, 2 tablespoons of sugar, the same amount of butter, and a pinch of salt. Combine the flour with the yeast and egg mixture in a mixing bowl, then knead and punch well. Cover with a dish towel and leave for about 1 hour until doubled in size.
Grease a deep cake pan (10 cup/2.5 liter capacity) or heatproof dish and sprinkle over the breadcrumbs. Combine the nuts and lemon rind with the raisins and the remaining sugar. Melt the remaining butter and cool to room temperature (it must not be warm). Use a tablespoon, which you dip frequently in the butter, to scoop out equal-size pieces of the dough. Fill the cake pan with alternating layers of dough pieces and nut mixture. Sprinkle the remaining butter over the top layer of dough.
When the pan is two-thirds full, cover with a dish towel and leave in a warm place until the dough fills the pan. Brush with beaten egg yolks, and bake in a preheated (medium) oven for 35–40 minutes.
Leave to cool in the pan, then

BUDAPEST
& SURROUNDING AREA

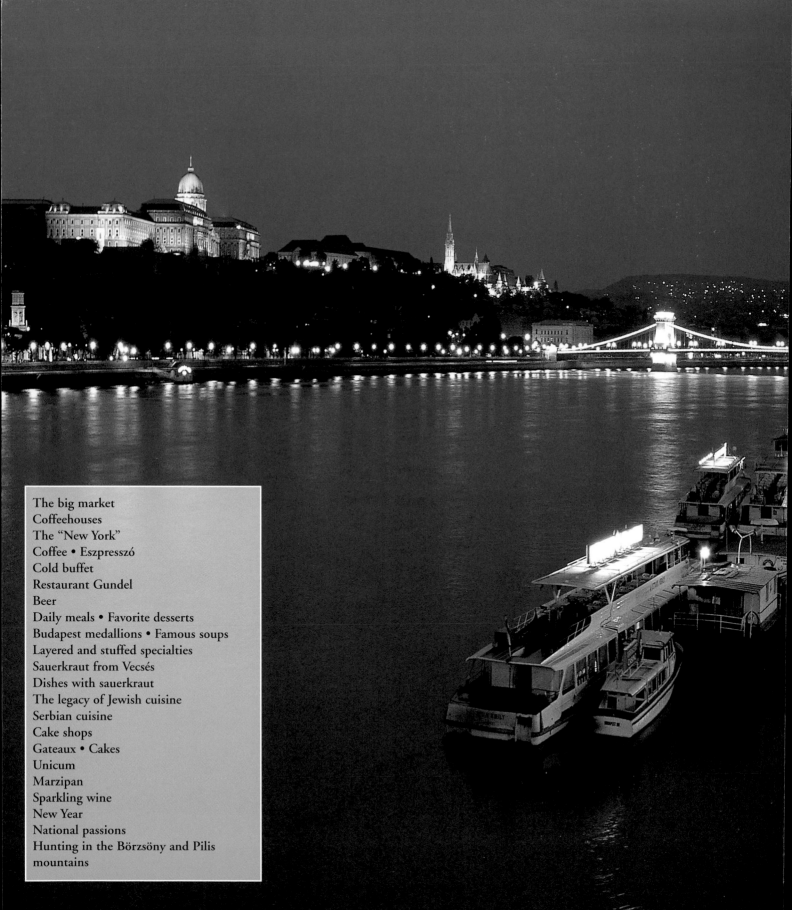

Almost a quarter of the total population of Hungary lives in the Budapest conurbation. The metropolis on the Danube is the heart of the country, its economic and cultural center, and it mirrors Hungary in miniature.

The towns of Buda and Óbuda, both located on the hilly west bank of the Danube, and Pest on the plains to the other side of the river, merged officially to form the capital called Budapest only in 1873. Even so, being a citizen of Buda or Pest is far from the same thing, even today. If one is a native of Pest, it is possible to live in hilly Buda for decades and still be known as a "plainsman."

After this merger and the incorporation of other villages, Budapest quickly developed into a major European city that, with its cosmopolitan attitude, readily accepted anything new, and then transformed it in its own unique way.

The cuisine is like the city – varied and colorful, sometimes strictly traditional, sometimes daringly experimental. Bars, restaurants, and cafés in Budapest are striving to regain the glory of ages past. They have been successful too – it is possible once more to enjoy epicurean delights in splendid surroundings; you just need to know the right places.

The heart of Budapest
THE BIG MARKET

Market Hall No. 1, to give it its official name. Here you can buy everything that Hungarian agriculture has to offer. The varied range of goods, abounding in color, are equally easy both on the eye and on the taste buds. And if your shopping trip has made you peckish, you can immediately satisfy your craving in the market's restaurants and snack bars.

The "big market," as it is called by the inhabitants of Budapest, was opened in 1897, along with four smaller markets. Then goods were transported by railroad straight to its doors, or delivered by barges plying the Danube that were able to berth close to the market. In 1991 it was closed down, and a thorough restoration took place. Since 1996 it has shone forth in its former splendor, to the delight of each and every visitor.

1 The market is not just somewhere to do your shopping, it is also a popular meeting place.
2 Hungarian and international delicacies packed in tubes.

1 You will regret not spending some time here.
2 The choice of fruit and vegetables is overwhelming and enticing whatever the season.

The central market is also worth viewing from the outside.

The market has also been called an "iron cathedral" due to its shape and metal construction.

Numerous butcher's stalls await you with a wealth of produce.

Daylight floods the interior of the market through the massive windows.

COFFEEHOUSES

In the first half of the 20th century Budapest, like Vienna, was a city of coffeehouses. Nowadays, it is a futile exercise to seek the once famous institutions; instead there are only fast-food outlets, banks, or stores. Only a connoisseur's eye would still be able to detect their traces – unusually large display windows, lavish interior decorations, and generously proportioned, inviting doors.

If you discount the Turkish coffee shops that were available to Muslims only at the time of the Ottoman domination of Buda, the first coffeehouse opened in the area of present-day Budapest at the beginning of the 18th century. On the Pest side, close to the Danube, somewhere between the present-day Elisabeth and Freedom bridges, a certain Blasius, a Serb who lived in the city, founded a café that soon had countless imitators. Coffeehouses flourished with the industrial age, when the up-and-coming middle classes gradually turned them into an important social institution. A Hungarian coffeehouse was also the birthplace of the 1848 revolution, eventually ending in the Hungarian War of Liberation. On 14 March 1848 news spread from the Café Pilvax that revolution had broken out in Vienna. The next morning, in the same café, the young poet Sándor Petőfi (1823–49) read aloud for the first time his national anthem, "Arise Magyars, your homeland calls!…"

During the first half of the 20th century many literary figures spent a large part of their time in coffeehouses. Their stories describe the atmosphere of the coffeehouses so accurately, it is easy to relate to them. Many readers believe that, on entering a famous coffeehouse for the first time, they would be able to identify it immediately from the detailed descriptions.

The coffee houses were spacious and lavishly furnished. Their huge glass windows ensured a good view in and out, so that life in the café seemed to be a more leisurely continuation of bustling street life. Service was attentive and unassuming, the coffee houses never closed, and you could sit for hours over just one cup of coffee, leafing through newspapers, or playing cards, chess, or even, in some places, billiards. Many coffee-houses served hot food at lunch and dinner, and sometimes there were musical or artistic diversions too. These premises, whether elegant or modest, offered like-minded persons a pleasant environment in which to meet informally; radiating a secure, homely atmosphere, they also ensured that even people of limited means had a social salon.

Right: Regular patrons at the Café Central, 1910.

A legendary coffeehouse
THE "NEW YORK"

At the end of the 19th century the New York Life Insurance Company extended its business interests to Hungary, and commissioned the famous architect Alajos Hauszmann (1847–1926) to build flagship premises in Budapest. A four-story, eclectic building was constructed, with striking architecture emphasized by a tower that rises from the center of the frontage. A spacious café opened on the ground floor, sumptuously furnished with marble, bronze, silk, velvet, sculptures, and frescoes in the Art-Nouveau style of the turn of the century.

The proud building, which has in the meantime needed renovation, has withstood the vagaries of time and the Café New York still welcomes guests from all over the world. They come to experience a delicious lunch or dinner in the part of the café that is used as a restaurant, or to chat at the café's little marble tables, relaxing after a sightseeing trip or recovering from a shopping spree. Indeed, they come to savor a little of the atmosphere of a bygone era.

At one time in its history the New York was a hive of activity around the clock. From the day it opened, the cream of the Hungarian literary and artistic worlds met here. Soon the same people would meet at the same table every time, and there was a core of regular patrons which changed depending on the time of day. On a whim, the dramatist Ferenc Molnár (1878–1952), with the active approval of his friends, threw the keys to the café into the Danube, so that it should never close its doors again.

"The New York … attracted aristocrats, the bourgeois, and artists alike. … No-one could resist its magic. Here everyone knew everyone else," wrote the Pest author Jenő Heltai. Numerous world-famous careers started in the New York. When the Hungarian movie industry was still in its infancy, a movie producer once asked a fellow regular whether he knew of anyone he could turn into a movie director. The friend pointed to a young, cigar-smoking journalist: "Young Korda. Try him …" Thus began the world-famous career of the man who became Sir Alexander Korda (1893–1956), to whom the British cinema owes so much. Other regulars in their youth were Michael Curtiz (1888–1961), subsequently Hollywood's star director, whose works include the cult classic *Casablanca*, and the king of operetta Imre Kálmán (1882–1953), composer of the immortal works *The Czardas Princess* and *Countess Maritza*.

Despite their size and open-plan design, the spacious cafés and restaurants radiate a cosy, intimate atmosphere.

A postcard from 1900 showing the Café New York.

The list of celebrities goes on and on, and to it can be added the names of those guests who were already famous when they visited the renowned coffeehouse and immortalized themselves in the guest book – Josephine Baker, Emil Jannings, Thomas Mann, Jacques Picard, Maurice Ravel, Johann Strauss, and Enrico Toscanini. Despite having survived the ravages of time, the valuable book disappeared after the last refurbishment.

In addition to famous guests, the café's book also chronicled memories of the ever-changing tenants and head waiters, some of whom rendered outstanding service to Hungarian literature and its representatives, more so than many a worthy literary society! The chronicle also recorded the minor and major works to the building, and the terrible period after the siege of Budapest in 1944, when molasses and potatoes were sold from the building. The brief period as an *eszpresszó* is also documented, as is its temporary misuse as a sports equipment shop. Finally the coffeehouse was condemned as a "breeding ground for bourgeois thought" and closed down. But it is supposed to have reopened its doors as early as 1954, under the name of Café Hungaria. Soon the writers and journalists returned too, not just because this coffeehouse had since its inception been synonymous with Hungarian spiritual life, but also because the Budapest publishing house, with its numerous editorial departments, was located in the same building, until the upper floors were vacated only a couple of years ago. Since 1990 the legendary café has once again been known by the name "New York."

Left: Most visitors feel drawn by the nostalgic charm of the interior and the spirit of the past.

The beloved drink of the Turks
COFFEE

The actual national drink of Hungary is coffee – a strong mocha with a high level of caffeine, a kind of Italian espresso, which is called *kávé, presszókávé,* or *fekete* (strong black coffee). Without doubt it was the Turkish conquerors who brought coffee to Europe. According to reliable sources, the first delivery reached Buda in 1579, addressed to a Turkish merchant by the name of Behrám. Initially the Hungarians called the drink *fekete leves* (black soup). The term *kávé* appears for the first time in the mid 17th century, in an epic by Miklós Zrínyi (1620–64).

Be that as it may, the Hungarians still were not used to the taste of coffee, even after 150 years of Turkish domination, because it frequently brought with it unpleasant side effects. In accordance with Oriental custom, the Turks would not discuss money matters at table, or indeed any unpleasant matter. At the end of the meal, however, when coffee was served, they had no compunction about simultaneously producing the list of taxes to be collected. When faced with trouble, Hungarians even today say, "The black soup (i.e. the worst) is yet to come."

In any case, before World War II only middle-class families could afford coffee. Today, coffee is the essential daily drink in Hungary. It is usually prepared in espresso machines, but the use of filter machines is on the increase. Coffee is drunk very strong, "neat" or heavily sweetened, and sometimes diluted with milk or cream.

Opposite, top: Espresso machines for personal use.
Opposite, bottom: The coffee glasses of the 1960s are increasingly being replaced by china cups.

Coffee-drinking Turks in front of the Hungarian town of Pécs.

The espresso machine

The espresso machine alternately forces hot water and steam through the ground coffee under high pressure. The water releases the flavor, and the steam forces the drink into the cups within 30–40 seconds. Most modern machines only use boiling water, so they are faster than their predecessors. An espresso machine clad in Herend porcelain (above) was for many years regarded as the epitome of elegance.

ESZPRESSÓ

When the owner of the Pest coffeehouse Spolarich imported the first Pavoni espresso machine from Italy to Hungary in 1924, it heralded the dawn of a new era in the catering trade. Coffee could be made stronger and more quickly with the new machine. Furthermore, the equipment itself was decorative. Preparation of coffee thus emerged from the secrecy of the kitchen into public areas, and a simple piece of kitchen equipment was transformed into a cult object, around which lovers of the hot drink gathered time and again. After World War II the venerable coffeehouse was superseded within a short time by the *eszpresszó*, known as *presszó* for short. These establishments spread like wildfire and, unlike the coffeehouse, also spread into rural areas. As life in general became poorer and simpler, the *eszpressó* also became mediocre – small rooms with unattractive interiors, not quite fresh sandwiches and cakes from the central kitchen behind the counter, uncomfortable chairs at tiny tables packed close together, coats thrown over the backs of chairs or hung on packed coat pegs. Yet places like these, though far from inviting, became an important meeting place for an entire generation, and are now remembered with nostalgia. Cigarette smoke blended with the wonderful aroma of fresh coffee, and if the lever on the coffee machine was pulled down, the hiss of steam cut through the murmur of customers' voices. The waitress was the center of attention, courted by men who liked to whisper sweet nothings in her ear. If you wanted a stimulating mocha rather than a weak coffee, you slipped some loose change under the bill – this was the practice even in the days when the following reminder hung resplendent on the wall: "Class-conscious workers do not give tips and do not accept any!"

Some *eszpressós* also organized live music, with customers often patronizing the café because of a particular musician. The pianist György Cziffra (1921–94) played in such places before he became world famous.

Over the decades the décor, choice of drinks, and food on offer in the *eszpressós* has changed; only the coffee machines have retained their pivotal role. In the second half of the 1990s, the younger generation increasingly lost interest in this institution, and more and more Budapest *eszpressós* have been forced to close.

People still meet friends in the *eszpressós* of today, but there is no longer any dancing.

Left: Cinderella by day, at night a princess. During the 1960s not only were the customers quick-change artists, many *eszpressós* were too.

COLD BUFFET

Formal receptions are the same the world over. The elegantly or flimsily dressed ladies and gentlemen storm the long buffet table as though they are starving, even though the choice of food and its arrangement hardly differs throughout the world. There are, however, some specialties typical of Hungarian buffets.

All recipes serve 10

Hideg csabai karaj
Cold Csaba chop

2½ lbs/1.2 kg loin of pork (boned)
6½ tbsp/100 g butter
7 oz/200 g Csaba or other spicy chili sausage
Salt, 1–2 cloves of garlic

To garnish:
1 head of lettuce
Diced aspic
Pickled vegetables

Using a long, sharp knife, make a cut lengthwise in the pork to form a pocket. Use a wooden spoon to widen the cavity. Spread the butter thinly over the sausage and insert it into the cavity. Rub the loin of pork with salt, and tie it up with kitchen string. Place the pork in a roasting pan and add sliced garlic to taste with a little melted butter or hot water. Roast in a preheated (medium) oven for 1½ hours, basting frequently with the juices, turning the meat so that it is crisp and golden brown all over. Leave the pork to cool, then place it in the refrigerator. When cold, slice thinly. Arrange the lettuce leaves on a plate and layer the sliced pork loin on top. Scatter diced aspic over the meat, and serve with pickled vegetables.

Főtt füstölt marhanyelv
Cured tongue

2½ lb/1.2 kg cured tongue

To garnish:
1 head of lettuce
2 cups/250 g grated horseradish
Diced aspic (optional)

Soak the tongue in water for about 2 hours to prevent it being too salty. Change the water frequently and give the tongue a final rinse. Place it in a large saucepan of cold water and bring to the boil. Change the water and cook the tongue until tender (about 2½ hours). Drain and transfer it to a large bowl of cold water to cool. When cold, remove the membrane and refrigerate the tongue. To serve, slice it evenly, starting from the thick end. Arrange the lettuce on a serving plate. Layer the sliced tongue on top. Garnish with dots of grated horseradish and diced aspic if preferred.

Hideg sült libamáj
Cold roasted goose liver

1¾ lbs/800 g roasted goose liver
Salad leaves
Prepared liquid aspic (optional)
Diced aspic (optional)

Heat a sharp knife in hot water. Carefully slice the cold, roasted goose liver (see page 299) into equal slices. Arrange the salad leaves on a serving dish. Layer the sliced liver on the salad leaves, and coat with aspic if preferred. The dish may also be garnished with diced aspic.

Kaszinótojás
Eggs Casino

10 eggs
⅔ cup/150 g butter
2 tbsp mustard
Salt or anchovy paste to taste
¼ tsp white pepper

Above: The buffet awaits the onslaught of guests.

To garnish:
1 head of iceberg lettuce
Vinaigrette dressing
2 oz/50 g tongue
Bunch of fresh parsley (optional)

Hard boil the eggs, shell them and cut in half lengthwise. Scoop out the yolks, and push them through a fine sieve. Mix them to a smooth paste with the butter, mustard, salt or anchovy paste, and pepper. Transfer the mixture to a pastry bag fitted with a star-shaped tip, and pipe it into the whites. Arrange the shredded iceberg lettuce on a serving dish and drizzle over the vinaigrette. Arrange the hard-boiled eggs on the salad. Either simply place them on top of the salad, or put the halves back together in such a way that the filling is still visible. Garnish the dish with thinly sliced tongue or chopped fresh parsley. Serve well chilled.

Károlyi-saláta
Károlyi salad

1 lb/500 g waxy potatoes
5 eggs
7 oz/200 g green bell peppers
Salt

Clockwise, from top left: *Csekonics-saláta* (Csekonics salad), *Károlyi-saláta* (Károlyi salad), *Gundel-saláta* (Gundel salad), *Hideg sült libamáj* (Cold roast goose liver), *Hideg csabai karaj* (Cold Csaba chop), *Kaszinótojás* (Eggs Casino), *Fôtt füstölt marhanyelv* (Cured tongue).

7 oz/ 200 g cucumber	
1 lb/500 g firm tomatoes	
4 heads of lettuce	
2 cups/500 ml seasoned mayonnaise	

Cook the potatoes until just tender, drain, and leave to cool. Boil the eggs until hard, then transfer to a bowl of cold water to cool. Peel and slice the potatoes. Shell the eggs and slice them thinly too. Remove the stalks, seeds, and membranes from the bell peppers, keeping the peppers whole. Slice them into thin rings then sprinkle over salt and leave to drain for about 30 minutes. Peel the cucumbers, slice them thinly. Skin the tomatoes, seed them, slice them thickly. Reserve a few leaves for garnish, then tear the remaining lettuce leaves into small pieces. Put the sliced potatoes, eggs, peppers, cucumber, and tomatoes in a large bowl. Season to taste with salt, then add the seasoned mayonnaise (see page 301). Mix all the ingredients together carefully, ensuring that they remain whole and are coated with a thin layer of dressing. Arrange the lettuce leaves on a serving dish, and pile the salad on top.
Serve chilled.

Gundel-saláta
Gundel salad

5 oz/150 g cucumber
Salt, ¼ tsp white pepper
2 tbsp white wine vinegar
10 oz/300 g tomatoes
3½ oz/100 g bell peppers
5 oz/150 g button mushrooms
3½ oz/100 g runner beans
Juice of 1 lemon
12 oz/350 g asparagus tips
½ tsp sugar
1 small lettuce

For the dressing:

3 tbsp olive oil
½ tsp sugar
½ tsp salt
½ tsp white pepper
2 tbsp tomato paste
Bunch of parsley

Peel and slice the cucumber thinly. Combine it with ½ teaspoon of salt, leave to degorge. After 15 minutes, squeeze out the liquid, season the cucumber with white pepper and vinegar. Skin the tomatoes and dice finely. Remove the seeds and membranes from the bell peppers, and dice them small. Slice the mushrooms. Top and tail the beans, then slice them diagonally. Bring ⅔ cup/150 ml water to the boil with a pinch of salt and half the lemon juice. Add the sliced mushrooms and simmer for 3 minutes, then strain them and leave to drain.
In another saucepan of boiling water, simmer the runner beans until *al dente*. Strain them and leave to drain. Simmer the asparagus tips in water, with a pinch of salt and the sugar, until just tender. Drain and leave to cool. To make the dressing, whisk together the olive oil, sugar, salt, pepper, tomato paste, finely chopped parsley, and remaining lemon juice, then refrigerate. Combine all the vegetables, except the mushrooms and lettuce, with the dressing. Arrange the lettuce leaves on a serving dish. Pile the salad on top and scatter over the mushrooms. Refrigerate for 30 minutes before serving to let the flavors blend.

Fortuitous encounters
RESTAURANT GUNDEL

The life story of the founding father of the famous Gundel dynasty is almost like a fairy tale. In 1857, at the age of 13, Johann Gundel left his family home in the Bavarian town of Ansbach, southern Germany, because he didn't see eye to eye with his stepfather. He set off to find a distant relative, whom he knew of only by hearsay, and who supposedly ran an inn in Pest, Hungary. On the way he made friends with Eduard Sacher (1830–92), who at this time was an apprentice in the delicatessen of his father, Franz Sacher. As a 16-year-old apprentice chef in the household of Count Metternich, Franz Sacher had created the famous Sachertorte that is named after him. Eduard Sacher secured a place as a trainee for his new friend too, thus laying the foundation for what was to come. After some time in Vienna, Johann Gundel continued his journey to Pest, where he received a warm welcome from his relatives. He combined helping to serve in the family's simple inn with training as a waiter, thus continuing his education. Soon Gundel was working his way up through the better restaurants. Only just 25 years old, he was already well regarded by and popular with both guests and colleagues. He married and bought his first restaurant. The business flourished, and soon he took out a lease on the smartest hotel in town, the István Főherceg. The hotel quickly acquired a good reputation for its reliable, imaginative cuisine, comfort,

friendly service, and attentive approach to regular guests. Its success also stemmed from the fact that Johann Gundel realized the importance of refining Hungarian cuisine, and adapting the style of bourgeois Viennese cuisine to suit the times, thus bringing his hotel up to a European standard.

Johann Gundel (1844–1915)

Opposite: View of the dining–room in the famous traditional restaurant Gundel, in the Városliget, or City Park.

Specialties created by Károly Gundel

Töltött uborka
Stuffed gherkins

Wipe 14 oz/400 g mushrooms, then dice them finely and reserve. Dice half an onion very finely and sweat it in oil. Add the mushrooms to the onion. Season the mixture with salt and pepper. Bring the mushroom juice to a boil and reduce it, stirring all the time. Leave it to cool. Then add enough mayonnaise to make a creamy paste and mix well. Season to taste with a few drops of Worcestershire sauce and a squeeze of lemon juice, and refrigerate. Cut 8 medium-size gherkins pickled in brine in half lengthwise and scoop out the seeds. Fill one half of each gherkin with the onion and mushroom mixture, then sandwich together with the other half. Arrange the stuffed gherkins on a bed of lettuce. Just before serving, coat them completely in seasoned mayonnaise. Place 3 slices of tomato on top of each gherkin, and sprinkle with freshly chopped parsley. Garnish with more salad leaves, hard-boiled eggs, and diced aspic. Serve as an hors d'oeuvre.

Mustáros sült paprika
Roast bell peppers with mustard

Cut the stalks off 8 green bell peppers without damaging the fruit and core (so that no oil later penetrates the peppers during frying). Wash and dry them thoroughly. Deep-fry the bell peppers, two at a time, in plenty of hot oil, turning occasionally. As soon as the skin blisters, take the peppers out of the oil. Skin the peppers while they are still warm. Leave the oil to cool. Blend 8 teaspoons of mustard to a smooth paste with lemon juice, confectioners' sugar, pepper, and chopped tarragon. Gradually add enough of the cold oil, stirring all the time, to form a thick dressing. Season the dressing to taste; it should be piquant, but not hot. Dip the bell peppers in the dressing, then arrange them on a serving dish lined with lettuce leaves, and pour over the remaining dressing. Refrigerate for 1–2 hours. Especially good with roast meat.

Feszty-bélszín
Roast sirloin of beef à la Feszty

Árpád Feszty (1856–1914) was an important artist.

Cut a well-hung sirloin of beef (1¾–2 lbs/800–900 g) into thick slices weighing about 7 oz/200 g each. Do not beat them out! Spread mustard over the slices of beef, then dip them in oil and sprinkle over a little pepper. Place them side by side on a plate and cover. Refrigerate for 3–4 days. Sprinkle a mixture of salt and paprika over the slices of beef. Make several incisions across each steak, taking care not to cut all the way through. Insert a piece of smoked bacon and a layer of onion in each cut (peel off layers from one large onion; do not slice it). Roll the steaks up and secure with kitchen string. Broil until medium rare, basting them occasionally with oil. Arrange on croutons and serve with the accompaniment of your choice.

Károly Gundel

Under Károly Gundel (1883–1956), the son of and successor to Johann Gundel, the house cuisine was enriched by French influences. Károly not only learned from his father, he also trained at the famous Ritz and Adlon hotels. In 1910 he leased a garden inn in the Városliget, the loveliest open space in Budapest, with the zoo, and turned it into the "Gundel."

He became world famous not only because of his talent and expert skills, which he continued to develop throughout his life, but also for his passionate love of his trade. Every day he drove to market to buy the best ingredients for the kitchen himself. Afterward he would deal with administrative matters and with the staff, and at lunchtimes and in the evenings he would devote himself to the guests in the restaurant.

Károly Gundel published tales of his experiences in the catering trade, and recipes for his house specialties – both his own creations and masterpieces by his colleagues. Adapted to modern tastes, his recipes are still followed today.

József Marchal

József Marchal (1832–1914), a bright star in the firmament of Hungarian gastronomy, was born Joseph Maréchal in France. In his youth he cooked for Emperor Napoleon III, and later served at the court of the Russian Tsars. Finally, Prince Pál Esterházy made the French master chef "*chef de cuisine*" at the "National Casino," the most exclusive club in Pest, in 1863.

Marchal revolutionized Hungarian cuisine. He still used the traditional seasonings and ingredients of the national cuisine, but every dish showed a French influence.

His art was recognized in his lifetime. In 1867, he was granted the highest honor, that of preparing the celebratory lunch on the occasion of the coronation of Emperor Franz Joseph I of Austria as King of Hungary.

Today many Hungarian menus simply write "liver à la Marchal" as "Marsall liver," which is not a spelling mistake, but a sign that his name has been completely adopted into the language, because that is how the Hungarian word for "field marshal" (French *maréchal*) is spelled.

The cutlery is decorated with the house monogram.

The dishes are a treat for taste buds and the eye.

The restaurant values well-trained staff.

The design of the serving dishes is simple, yet elegant.

Living tradition

The name Gundel still stands for stylish dishes, comfort, and elegance. This was evident at the State reception which the Hungarian Prime Minister gave in 1993 to honor Queen Elizabeth II and Prince Philip.

The guests were served a truly royal meal, which combined trends from Hungarian and western European cuisine. Furthermore, every dish was presented in the shape of a crown. Apart from this little refinement, everyone can expect the same first-class cuisine at Gundel.

Ingredients for veal braid à la Queen Elizabeth.

To make the filling for the veal braid, combine the rice and vegetables in a skillet.

Stuff the morel mushrooms with finely diced roasted goose liver.

Coat the veal loin in the herb mixture and braid the strips together.

Wrap the veal braids around a steel pipe and secure the ends with wooden picks.

Arrange the roast veal on a plate, and fill with the rice and vegetable mixture.

Fonott borjúszűz Queen Elizabeth módra
Veal Braid à la Queen Elizabeth
(Photograph)

⅓ cup/60 g long-grain rice
⅓ cup/60 g wild rice
Salt
1 red bell pepper (capsicum)
1 green bell pepper (capsicum)
4 small mushrooms
3 tbsp oil
Pepper
1 tbsp chopped parsley
2¾ oz/80 g roasted goose liver
4 large morel mushrooms
2 loins of veal (about 1¼ lbs/600 g)
3 tbsp oil
3 tbsp finely chopped herbs (basil, rosemary, marjoram)
1 cup/200 g mashed potato
1 egg
Oil for brushing
7 oz/200 g latticed potatoes

Boil the two types of rice in separate pans of salted water until tender. Drain and set aside. Finely dice the seeded bell peppers and the mushrooms. Sweat the vegetables in the oil until soft and the peppers are slightly translucent. Season the mixture with salt, pepper, and the parsley, then add the cooked rice. Finely chop the roasted goose liver (see page 299). Blanch the morels and stuff them with the goose liver. Cut each loin of veal in half lengthwise. Then make two cuts lengthwise in each half to form three strips. Leave one end uncut. Season the veal with salt, roll it in the mixed herbs, then braid the strips together. Wrap each of the 4 braids around a steel pipe, 2¼ inches/6 cm in diameter, and secure the ends with wooden picks or meat skewers. Brush a skillet or griddle with oil and roast the meat on it, turning the steel pipe from time to time, until crisp. Carefully remove the roast veal from the pipe. Place each veal braid on a plate and carefully extract the wooden pick or skewer. Fill the center of the circle with the rice and vegetable mixture, and place a stuffed morel mushroom on top. Beat the egg into the mashed potato. Fill a pastry bag with the potato mixture and pipe five stars around the top of each crown. Garnish the stars with latticed potatoes.

The royal menu consisted of:

Füstölt lazac fehér spárga koronán
(Smoked salmon on a crown of white asparagus)
Arrange steamed asparagus stalks in a starburst pattern on a plate. Place a slice of smoked salmon on top, and finish with a quail egg stuffed with caviar.

Galambeszencia
(Consommé of pigeon)
Simmer the meat from a pigeon and a chicken in water, together with carrots, onion, leeks, and parsley. Boil the resulting stock until very reduced. Strain through fine cheesecloth, and flavor with dry sherry.

Fonott borjúszűz
Queen Elizabeth módra
(Veal braid, see above)

Tavaszi eperkorona
(Coronet of early strawberries)
Fill pastry crowns with strawberries and cream, and decorate with strawberry ice cream in the shape of strawberries.

Opposite, top: The veal braids are roasted on the stove top. The pipe gives them the crown shape.
Opposite, bottom: The filling is garnished with a stuffed morel mushroom, surrounded by lattice potatoes.

The steel pipe has to be turned frequently during roasting.

In Hungary beer is served in three differently sized glasses.

The art of traditional brewing from Pest
BEER

Background above: The Hungarians love pale beer, especially *pils*, which is served with a head of white foam.

The Hungarians enjoy drinking beer, and lots of it. On May Day, it is preferred above all other drinks. Domestic beer production is hardly dependent on imports, because most of the ingredients flourish in the country itself. In addition to the traditional Hungarian brands which are also familiar beyond the borders of Hungary, numerous well-known foreign brands are brewed under license, including products by the firms Holsten and Heineken. Furthermore, the number of micro-breweries has been on the increase for the last 20 years, enriching the market with their specialties. And new bars (*söröző*) are opening all the time.

Despite all this we are constantly being told that Hungary is a nation of wine lovers, not beer drinkers, and that beer is not a typical component of the national cuisine. Yet this is not quite true. The ancient Magyars enjoyed a forerunner of the beer we know today, an alcoholic drink that also underwent fermentation. A lot of brewing went on in the Middle Ages

too, and even the Turkish Conquest could not interrupt the consumption of beer. Fellow beer drinkers meeting together to enjoy their favorite beverage were countered by groups of citizens who abided by strict rules of prohibition.

At any rate, the size of the beer glasses shows that Hungarians, contrary to the "genuine" beer nations, prefer to enjoy the hop-based beverage in small measures. The beer tankard commonly used today (*korsó*) holds two cups (500 ml). For lesser thirsts you can order a *pohár* or a *kiskorsó* (small tankard) holding 1¼ cups (300 ml), and in some places there is also a *pikoló*, which holds only three-quarters of a cup (200 ml). At one time much fun was made of the *pikoló* unit of measurement. It was known as a "nip," in other words, something which could be drunk in one gulp.

Like its Central European siblings, Hungarian beer is also poured with a white frothy head and is best drunk cool. *Pils*, a pale lager-style beer, is top of the popularity stakes, followed by other light-colored beers. Dark beers, on the other hand, are not particularly prized.

The center of Hungarian beer production focuses on the left bank of the Danube, in the Budapest district of Kőbánya, whose name means "quarry." This area on the Pest side was granted to the city by King Béla IV, in the 13th century, so that stone could be quarried for the city walls. For centuries tunnels were driven under the ground to quarry stone. In the 1840s, a brewer discovered the empty shafts which had been forgotten with the passage of time. He discovered that the cool, even temperature and high humidity made them an ideal place to ferment beer. As the local springs also supplied superb water, the most important breweries in the land sprang up around Pest and Buda.

Around this time Anton (Antal) Dreher (1810–63), a member of the Swabian beer-brewing family Dreher, that had ended up in Schwechat near Vienna, settled in Pest. He discovered lager, a bottom-fermented beer that does not have the same bitter taste as *pils*. It is stored for months after the main fermentation and thus acquired the name lager, meaning "store" in German. Kőbánya became the headquarters of the Dreher dynasty, that extended over several generations. In constant competition with other firms which also established themselves in this area, it created a massive brewing empire.

The family has died out, but the Dreher brand name lives on and sales flourish as before. Another equally popular brand from Kőbánya is *Kőbányai világos*, a pale, light, and, moreover, reasonably priced beer.

"Beer is liquid bread" claims a successful advertising slogan.

Beers from throughout Hungary

DAILY MEALS

Like everywhere else in Europe, Hungarians eat three meals a day. In addition, children are given a little snack, *tízórai*, which they eat around ten o'clock *(tíz óra)*, but many adults also fortify themselves with a second breakfast at work.

Breakfast
Of all three meals, breakfast is less traditional than the rest. What is eaten, and when, is determined by the time of day. Fresh bread rolls and pastries, butter, jam, and honey almost always feature on the breakfast table. This selection is supplemented by a choice of cold, sliced meats, cheese, and eggs including omelets. Muesli only became fashionable in the 1990s. People tend to drink tea and coffee with breakfast, but sometimes prefer hot or cold milk and hot chocolate too.

Lunch
Lunch is the main meal of the day and is eaten between noon and two o'clock It usually consists of three courses: to start there is often soup, usually followed by a meat dish with accompaniments (salad or pickled vegetables are obligatory), or a vegetable dish accompanied by meat, or a meat stew. Cake or fruit is served for dessert, sometimes both. Another popular variation on the lunchtime menu is a filling soup – a goulash or bean soup, for example – and a dish based on flour as the main course. This menu is always rounded off with seasonal fruits.

Evening meal
Generally eaten between seven and eight o'clock. Sliced cold meats, salami, prosciutto, cheese, eggs, and seasonal vegetables such as tomatoes, bell peppers, leeks, radishes, and cucumber are customary. Popular evening delicacies are cream cheese or omelets, and, in winter, pork brawn or slices of fried bread rubbed with garlic.

Breakfast (clockwise, from top right): bread rolls and brioche, coffee, omelet with sausage, croissants and specialty bread roll, garnished and flavored Liptau cheese spread, butter, sausages and mustard, and (in the center) cold sliced meats.

A typical lunch for the cold season (counterclockwise from bottom left): *Gombaleves* (Mushroom soup), *Sertéscsülök pékné módra* (Ham shank boulangère), *Nyers céklasaláta* (Beet salad), and *Madártej* ("Bird's milk" with meringue dumplings).

Sample winter menu
(Photograph above)

Appetizer:
Gombaleves
(Mushroom soup)
A soup made from mushrooms and caramelized onions, thickened with flour and sour cream, and seasoned with paprika. Mushroom soup is often served with little dumplings as a garnish.

Main course:
Sertéscsülök pékné módra
(Ham shank boulangère)
First sauté the ham shank in a roasting pan, then roast in the oven with potatoes and onions.

Nyers céklasaláta
(Beet salad)
Season finely grated beets to taste with salt and vinegar. Leave to marinate for one day, then add grated horseradish, and confectioners' sugar if preferred, and refrigerate for a couple of hours.

Dessert:
Madártej
("Bird's milk" with meringue dumplings)
Bring the milk to the boil with a vanilla bean, and poach "dumplings" made from stiffly beaten egg white in it. As soon as the dumplings are cooked, remove them. Make a custard with the milk, egg yolk, and confectioners' sugar, and serve with the dumplings.

Sample summer menu

Appetizer:
Spárgaleves
Asparagus soup
First make a stock using veal bones, onions, carrots, and parsnip. Then remove the bones and vegetables. Add asparagus chopped into small pieces to the stock, and cook until tender. Thicken the soup with a white *roux* and milk, and enrich it with sugar and egg yolk.

Main course:
Zöldborsós csirke
(Chicken with peas)
Seal chicken portions in oil, and saute them in their own juices until almost cooked. Then add peas and a splash of stock, and cook until tender. Thicken the juices with a *roux*, and season to taste with salt and finely chopped parsley. Serve with rice as an accompaniment.

Dessert:
Sárgabarackos lepény à la nagyi
(Apricot cake à la grandmère)
Beat together flour, baking powder, confectioners' sugar, butter, and stiffly beaten egg whites to form a batter. Top this with halved and pitted apricots, then sprinkle over sugar and chopped walnuts, if liked, and bake.

FAVORITE DESSERTS

The following desserts are among the best that Hungarian national cuisine has to offer and would be recommended with pride by any Hungarian.

Somlói galuska
Schomlau dumplings
Serves 8–10
(Photograph right)

This specialty was created in the 1960s at the Restaurant Gundel.

1 plain jelly roll (made with 3 eggs)
1 chocolate jelly roll (made with 3 eggs)
1 hazelnut jelly roll (made with 3 eggs)

For the vanilla custard:

1/2 vanilla bean
2 cups/500 ml milk
4 egg yolks
2/3 cup/80 g confectioners' sugar
4 tbsp flour
2 tsp powdered gelatin

For the rum syrup:

3/4 cup/150 g superfine sugar
2 tsp grated orange zest
1 tsp grated lemon zest
Scant 1/2 cup/100 ml rum (40 % proof)

For the filling and topping:

2/3 cup/100 g raisins
3/4 cup/100 g walnuts
3 1/2 tbsp apricot jam
2 tbsp cocoa powder
1 2/3 cups/400 ml heavy cream

For the chocolate sauce:

5 oz/150 g couverture
Scant 1 cup/100 g confectioners' sugar
Scant 1/2 cup/100 ml rum

Bake the jelly roll bases (see page 298) or buy them. To make the custard: slit the vanilla bean in half lengthwise, and bring it to the boil with the milk. Cover and leave to infuse for 10 minutes, then remove the vanilla bean. Whisk the egg yolks and confectioners' sugar until foaming, then gradually beat in the flour. Strain the vanilla-flavored milk through a fine sieve. Stir it into the egg mixture and cook in a bowl over hot water, whisking all the time, until a custard forms. Slake the gelatin with a splash of cold water, then dissolve it in a bowl over hot water and stir thoroughly into the warm custard. To make the rum syrup: place the sugar and the orange and lemon zest in a saucepan with 3/4 cup/200 ml water and bring to the boil. Simmer until a light syrup forms. Leave the syrup to cool, then add the rum. Pour one-third of the syrup over the plain jelly roll base, then spread half the custard on top. To make the filling: halve the raisins, coarsely chop the walnuts, and sprinkle half of each over the jelly roll base. Place the chocolate jelly roll base on top, and cover this with one-third of the rum syrup, the remaining custard, raisins, and walnuts. Place the hazelnut jelly roll base on top. Drizzle over the remaining rum syrup, spread the warmed apricot jam on top, and dust with the cocoa powder. Carefully wrap this "gateau" in aluminum foil (be careful with the top layer!), then refrigerate for at least 10 hours. Using a tablespoon, carefully scoop out 3–4 spoonfuls ("dumplings") and arrange them on a plate. Spoon the stiffly whipped cream into a pastry bag and pipe rosettes of cream on top of the dumplings. Dissolve the couverture and confectioners' sugar in 2/3 cup/150 ml warm water, over a low heat until a sauce forms. Stir in the rum and pour the sauce over the cream rosettes in a thin stream.

Stíriai metélt
Styrian noodles

The Hungarian word *Stíria* is an old name that is no longer used for this part of Hungary. No-one knows why the noodles are so called. At any rate, they are no longer made in present-day Styria.

Generous 1 lb/500 g quark or smooth cottage cheese
1 2/3 cups/200 g flour
4 eggs
Salt
3/4 cup/200 ml sour cream
6 tbsp/90 g butter
2 tbsp sugar
2 tsp vanilla sugar
1/3 cup/40 g raisins
1/2 tsp grated lemon zest
1/3 cup/20 g fresh white breadcrumbs
1/3 cup/50 g confectioners' sugar

Push the quark through a sieve and beat it together with the flour, 1 egg, a pinch of salt, and 1 tablespoon of sour cream. Knead the mixture to form a dough. Roll out the dough on a floured work surface until it is 1/4 inch/5 mm thick, then cut it into 1/2 inch/12 mm long strips. Bring a large saucepan of water to a boil, and add a pinch of salt, then add the noodles. Try cooking 2–3 strips first, to check the dough. If the dough is too stiff, add a splash of sour cream; if it is too soft, add a little flour. Simmer the noodles until they rise to the surface, then strain off the water, and leave them to drain. Beat together 1/3 cup/80 g butter, the sugar, vanilla sugar, 3 egg yolks, and the remaining sour cream. Add the noodles, raisins, and lemon zest. Whisk the egg whites until very stiff, then carefully fold them into the mixture. Butter a small baking sheet or a square flameproof dish, and scatter over the breadcrumbs. Transfer the mixture to the baking sheet or dish, smooth off the top, and bake in a preheated (medium) oven for 30–40 minutes. Take the cake out of the oven and let it cool a little, then cut it into large squares. Serve warm, dusted with confectioners' sugar.

Túrógombóc
Quark dumplings
(Photograph right)

Generous 1 lb/500 g quark (20% fat) or smooth cottage cheese
Salt
2 eggs
3/4 cup/130 g semolina
1 tbsp sugar (optional)
Flour
1 cup/60 g white breadcrumbs
3 1/2 tbsp/50 g butter
3/4 cup/200 ml sour cream
Confectioners' sugar

Mix together the quark, a pinch of salt, the eggs, semolina, and sugar (optional). Leave the mixture to rest for at least an hour, but preferably half a day, in the refrigerator. Dust your hands with flour, and shape the mixture into 12 large dumplings. Three-quarters fill a very large saucepan with water, and bring it to a boil, then add the dumplings. Simmer the dumplings for at least 15 minutes. To check whether the dumplings are cooked, remove one from the pan and cut it in half. While the dumplings are cooking, sauté the breadcrumbs in the butter, until golden brown. Take the dumplings out of the pan using a slotted spoon, and place them on a warmed plate. Sprinkle the sautéed breadcrumbs over them, and drizzle a splash of sour cream on top. Serve with slightly warmed sour cream and confectioners' sugar. The dumplings swell

during cooking and become soft
and light. Serve immediately,
otherwise they harden.

Gundel-palacsinta
Gundel pancakes
(Photograph below)

8 pancakes
For the filling:
Scant ½ cup/100 ml milk
3 tbsp sugar
¾ cup/100 g ground walnuts
2 tsp candied orange peel
¼ cup/40 g raisins
2 tbsp rum

For the chocolate sauce:
1¼ cups/300 ml milk
⅔ cup/120 g sugar
2 tsp vanilla sugar
3½ oz/100 g coverture
2 egg yolks
2 tbsp cocoa powder
2 tbsp flour
2 tbsp rum
4 tsp/20 g butter

Make the pancakes (see page 83)
and keep them warm. To make
the filling: bring the milk and
sugar to the boil, then add the
nuts. Simmer the mixture,
stirring all the time, until it
thickens and a custard forms. Add
the candied orange peel, raisins,
and rum. Fill the pancakes with
the custard. Fold the pancakes
over twice, into a fan shape, and
arrange them on a serving dish.
Keep them warm. To make the
sauce: mix together ⅘ cup/200 ml
of the milk with the sugar, and
vanilla sugar. Bring to a boil and
melt the chocolate in the hot
milk. Whisk together the
remaining cold milk, egg yolks,
cocoa powder, and flour until
foaming, then add it to the
chocolate mixture, stirring all the
time. Bring the sauce to the boil
again, then remove from the heat
and add the rum and softened
butter. Pour the chocolate sauce
over the pancakes and serve
immediately. This specialty is
often flamed, although this was
not specified in Károly Gundel's
original recipe. To flame the
pancakes, drizzle 1–2 tablespoons
of high-proof rum over the
pancakes, and ignite carefully.

Clockwise, from top: *Gundel-palacsinta* (Gundel pancakes), *Somlói
galuska* (Schomlau dumplings), and *Túrógombóc* (Cream cheese
dumplings).

BUDAPEST MEDALLIONS

This truly Hungarian composition with choice ingredients was created for the restaurant in the Hungarian Pavilion at the 1958 World Exhibition in Brussels, Belgium.

Bélszín Budapest-módra
Fillet of beef Budapest

1 large onion	
¼ cup/60 g butter	
½ tsp sweet paprika	
10 oz/300 g veal bones	
Salt	
Pepper	
7 oz/200 g goose liver	
3½ oz/100 g smoked ham, or bacon	
2 large bell peppers (capsicum)	
7 oz/200g button mushrooms	
1 large tomato	
1 cup/150 g peas	
1¾ lbs/800 g fillet of beef	
⅓ cup/80 ml oil	

To make the stock: dice the onion finely. Melt the butter in a saucepan, and sweat the onion in it until translucent. Take the saucepan off the heat and sprinkle paprika over the onion. Add the veal bones, and enough cold water to cover them. Add a pinch of salt and bring to the boil. Cover, and simmer for about 40 minutes. Strain the stock through a fine sieve, season to taste with salt and pepper, and reserve it, keeping warm.

To make the ragout, dice the goose liver and the smoked ham (or bacon) very finely (maximum ¼ inch/5 mm dice). Seed and finely dice the bell peppers. Finely dice the mushrooms. Skin and finely dice the tomatoes. Saute the ham in a skillet until crisp. Deglaze the pan with stock, then add the peppers, tomatoes, mushroom, and goose liver. Cook over a high heat, stirring all the time, until the vegetables are browned. Add the peas and continue cooking until all the vegetables are tender.

Cut the fillet of beef into slices ¾ inch/2 cm thick, and flatten them out using the heel of your hand (or beat them very gently with a meat mallet). Heat the oil in a skillet and sauté the beef on both sides until the center of the beef is medium rare. Arrange half of the ragout on a warmed serving dish, and place the fillets of beef on top. Place one tablespoon of ragout on each of the fillets. Serve the medallions with rice, French fries, or sautéed latticed potatoes.

To make the stock, first sweat the onions in the butter, then sprinkle over paprika.

To make the ragout, saute the ham until crisp, then add the stock. Brown the diced peppers and tomatoes, as well as …

… the diced liver and mushrooms for a few minutes.

Finally add the peas.

Toss the contents of the skillet and saute until tender.

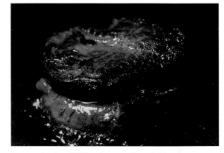

Saute the beef fillets in another skillet.

FAMOUS SOUPS

Many soups are associated with the name of a famous person or an ethnic group. Thus János Gundel created *Palócleves* soup for the birthday of Kálmán Mikszáth (1847–1910). It was named after the Palócs, a sub-ethnic group which is native to the mountainous north of Hungary. Mikszáth, who came from the same area, romanticized the life of these "good highlanders" in his first successful novel.

The actor Ede Újházy (1844–1915), himself a gourmet, created a chicken soup à la Újházy for which he used only roosters, according to the memoirs of the author Endre Nagy: "Old roosters were required …, such as those whose tough tendons were proof of the spice of passionate love scenes. They had to boil for three days and three nights, before they combined with the stock and vegetables, above all with the "legendary" celeriac. The master paid particular attention to coxcombs, and other powerful organs of the rooster, in whose hereditary effect he passionately believed. And it was deemed a sign of the greatest consideration if he served someone one of these components." Perhaps this description explains why Ede Újházy's dinner guests, who consisted of men only, prized this soup so highly …

Above, left: *Marhahúsleves velőscsonttal* (Beef broth with marrowbone dumplings)
Above, right: *Jókai bableves* (Bean soup à la Jókai)

Marhahúsleves velőscsonttal
Beef broth with marrowbone dumplings

The author Gyula Krúdy (1878–1933) immortalized this soup in many stories.

1 piece of marrowbone (9 oz/250 g)
1½ lbs/700 g beef (leg, chuck, or shin)
9 oz/250 g beef bones
10 peppercorns
1 tbsp salt
1 medium onion
1 clove of garlic
2 medium carrots
2 medium parsley root
1 small celeriac
1 small kohlrabi
1 piece of savoy cabbage (or 1–2 cauliflower florets)
2 mushrooms (optional)
1 bell pepper (capsicum) (optional)
1 small tomato (optional)
1 bouillon cube
Soup garnish, e.g. noodles
Sliced white bread
Salt
Paprika

Dip each end of the marrowbone in salt, so that as little of the bone marrow as possible oozes out during cooking. Put the meat, beef bones, marrowbone, and peppercorns in a large pan of salted water. Bring to the boil slowly over a low heat, then simmer. Peel the vegetables. Cut the carrots and parsnips into strips. Add all the vegetables to the stock when the meat has been cooking for about 2 hours. Continue cooking the meat for another 1–2 hours, until tender. Bring a second saucepan of water to the boil, then dissolve the bouillon cube in it and cook the chosen soup garnish. When the soup is ready, leave it to stand for a few minutes. Then strain it into a warmed soup tureen, reserving the marrowbone and beef. Strain the garnish and serve separately. Toast the bread. Scoop out the hot bone marrow, and spread it on the toast, then sprinkle over salt and paprika. Slice the beef, and serve with grated horseradish and mustard.

Jókai bableves
Bean soup à la Jókai

This soup was named for the Hungarian novelist Mór Jókai (1825–1904).

1⅓ cups/250 g red kidney beans
10 oz/300 g smoked ham shank (boned)
1–2 bay leaves
1 large carrot
1 large parsley root
½ small celeriac
7 oz/200 g Frankfurter sausage
4 tsp/20 g butter
4 tbsp flour
1 small onion
1 clove of garlic
1 heaped tsp sweet paprika
1–3 tsp vinegar
¾ cup/200 ml sour cream
Bunch of parsley

Soak the beans overnight, and also the ham shank, so that the dish will not be too salty. Drain and rinse the beans. Put the beans, ham, and bay leaves in a saucepan with 6 cups/1.5 liters cold water, and bring to the boil over a low heat. Peel the carrots, parsnip, and celeriac, then dice them finely. After 30–40 minutes, add the vegetables to the saucepan with the sausage. Remove the ham shank and sausage from the soup. Melt the butter, then add the flour, stirring all the time, and sweat it until the flour turns pale gold. Take the pan off the heat. Stir in the diced onion, crushed garlic, and paprika. Stir the *roux* into the soup to thicken it, and bring the soup to a boil again. Dice the ham shank, and slice the sausage. Season the soup to taste with vinegar. Add the sour cream to the soup and bring it to the boil again, then add the ham and sausage. Sprinkle chopped parsley over the soup and serve immediately. Sometimes plucked pasta (see page 39) are added to the soup toward the end of cooking.

LAYERED AND STUFFED SPECIALTIES

Layered dishes are very popular, because they allow plenty of scope for the imagination. The same applies, at least in part, to the fame and popularity of filled specialties.

Rakott krumpli
Potato layer
(Photograph above)

2_ lbs/1.2 kg potatoes
5 oz/150 g bacon
4 hard–boiled eggs
7 oz/200 g Debrecen or other spicy sausage, suitable for baking
Butter for the dish
1¼ cups/300 ml sour cream
2 tbsp/30 g fine white breadcrumbs, optional

Cook the potatoes in their skins in boiling salted water until just tender. Drain and leave to cool until just warm, then peel and slice them. Dice the bacon finely. Sauté it in a skillet, without any oil, until it is crisp and golden. Slice the eggs and sausage. Butter an ovenproof dish, and cover the bottom with a layer of sliced potato. Add a layer of sliced egg and sausage and pour over a generous splash of sour cream. Then add a layer of crispy bacon, with the juices from the skillet.

Continue layering the remaining ingredients in the same way until they are all used, reserving a little of the bacon, pan juices, and sour cream. Finish with a layer of potato. Pour the remaining sour cream over the potato, and top with the bacon pieces and pan juices. Sprinkle the breadcrumbs on top, if used. Bake the potato layer in a preheated (medium) oven for 40 minutes, until the top is crisp and golden brown. Serve with seasonal salad or pickled vegetables. An alternative version of this dish omits the bacon; melted butter is used instead.

Töltött karfiol
Stuffed cauliflower
(Photograph below)

1 large, firm cauliflower (minus leaves weighing about 2¼ lbs/1 kg)
Salt
9 oz/250 g boiled ham
1¼ cups/300 ml sour cream
¼ cup/60 g butter
3 tbsp flour
½ cup/50 g grated parmesan
½ tsp pepper

Wash the cauliflower and remove the leaves. Bring a large saucepan of salted water to a boil, then add the cauliflower and cook until it is just tender. Drain, reserving the liquid. Slice the cauliflower in half horizontally, just above the center. Make a slight hollow in the bottom half. Grind or finely dice the ham and combine it with half of the sour cream. Fill the bottom half of the cauliflower with the meat mixture, and use the top half as a lid. Use a small nut of butter to butter an ovenproof dish, and place the cauliflower in it. Melt the remaining butter in a skillet. Add the flour and cook it, stirring all the time, until it foams and turns pale golden. Add enough of the cauliflower liquid to form a smooth sauce, and bring to the boil. Fold in the remaining sour cream and parmesan. Season to taste with pepper and pour the sauce over the cauliflower. Bake in a preheated (medium) oven for about 30 minutes until the sauce bubbles and turns golden brown.

Töltött karalábé
Stuffed kohlrabi
(Photograph above)

8 new season's kohlrabi
Salt
2 bunches of parsley
2 bunches of dill (optional)
3½ cups/400 g ground pork
1 egg
¼ cup/60 g dry white
breadcrumbs
4–5 young kohlrabi leaves
(optional)
Scant ½ cup/100 ml hot stock
2½ tbsp/40 g butter
4 tbsp flour
Scant ½ cup/100 ml milk
½ tsp pepper (optional)

Peel the kohlrabi. Bring a saucepan of lightly salted water to the boil, then add the kohlrabi and cook until just tender. Drain the kohlrabi. Scoop out the centers. Mix together the ground pork, egg, breadcrumbs, and half of the finely chopped parsley and dill if used. Stuff the kohlrabi with the pork mixture. Use a nut of butter to butter a lidded flameproof dish, and place the kohlrabi in it. Any leftover pork mixture can be shaped into small balls and placed in the dish around the kohlrabi. Finely dice the flesh from the center of the kohlrabi. If used, the kohlrabi leaves should be cut into strips, then blanched and drained. The chopped kohlrabi, and blanched leaves if used, may then be scattered over the stuffed kohlrabi and the pork meatballs. Pour the hot stock into the dish and cover with the lid. Place the dish on the stove, over a low heat, and poach the kohlrabi until they are tender and the pork mixture is cooked. Melt the butter in a skillet. Add the flour, stirring all the time, and cook until the flour foams and turns golden. Add the milk, and pepper to taste. Continue cooking until a *roux* forms. Arrange the stuffed kohlrabi and meatballs on a warmed serving dish. Thicken the liquid from the cooked kohlrabi with the *roux* and bring to the boil. Pour the sauce over the kohlrabi and meatballs. Garnish with the remaining parsley and dill. Serve with rice.

It is absolutely essential to use tender new kohlrabi for this recipe, and it should therefore be prepared in spring or early summer. Smaller portions can also be served as an appetizer.

Töltött borjúszegy
(Photograph above)

1¾ lbs/800 g breast of veal, boned
Salt
1 cup/120 g dry white
breadcrumbs
¾ cup/200 ml milk
2 bunches of parsley
¼ cup/60 g butter
½ small onion
5 oz/150 g mushrooms (optional)
2 eggs
⅛ tsp pepper
Scant ½ cup/100 ml dry white
wine

For the Sauce:
1 tbsp tomato paste
2 tbsp flour
Salt
Pepper

Ask your butcher to prepare the breast of veal so that it can be stuffed. Rub salt all over the meat. Finely chop the parsley and reserve some for the sauce. Melt 2 teaspoons/10 g butter in a skillet and sauté the onion in it briefly. Add the thinly sliced mushrooms, if used, and sauté them for 5 minutes with the onion. Take the skillet off the heat, then add the breadcrumbs, eggs, and parsley. Mix everything together thoroughly and season with salt and pepper. Pack the mixture loosely into the cavity in the veal. Shape any remaining stuffing into dumplings. Close the cavity with meat skewers, or sew it up with kitchen thread. Preheat the oven to 400 °F/200 °C. Place the veal and dumplings in a deep roasting pan. Melt the remaining butter and pour it over the meat. Add the white wine too. Roast the veal for about 1 hour, until crisp. Remove the veal from the pan, reserving the juices, and leave the meat to rest for 5–10 minutes before removing the skewers or thread. Cut the meat into ½ inch/12 mm thick slices, and serve with or without the sauce. To make the sauce: skim the fat from the pan juices. Stir the tomato paste and flour into the pan juices, blending thoroughly. Deglaze the pan with 3½ tbsp water, and season to taste with salt and pepper. Finally add the reserved parsley. Serve the sauce separately. This dish may be served with various potato and vegetables dishes as accompaniments, or rice. You can use loin of pork instead of breast of veal.

SAUERKRAUT FROM VECSÉS

Every Hungarian immediately associates top-quality sauerkraut with the little town of Vecsés, to the southeast of the Budapest conurbation. Hungarian researchers have discovered that cabbage has been grown here since the end of the 18th century. In 1786 the lord of the manor moved some 50 Swabian families from the surrounding, overpopulated villages, so that they could cultivate the land. Toward the end of the 19th century, as the capital city became more of a metropolis and fewer citizens of Budapest found the time to make for themselves the sauerkraut that is so important to Hungarian cuisine, demand in the market places grew. Sauerkraut from Vecsés exceeded even homemade pickled cabbage in freshness and flavor, and was soon a coveted product not just in the capital, but throughout the land – a state of affairs which continues to this day.

Four hundred Swabian-Hungarian families in Vecsés earn their living from the production of sauerkraut, and also vegetables pickled in vinegar. Most have their own fields where the various varieties of white cabbage are cultivated. Even if the early varieties are ready in August, the main harvest period covers October and November. Pickling takes place according to strictly traditional methods in a room which is hardly larger than a good-sized garage. Every year a family will process 22,000–110,000 pounds (10,000–50,000 kilograms) of cabbage.

Chopped and whole leaves are pickled in different ways. Chopped cabbage is layered in wooden barrels, then salted and spiced – with bay leaves, peppercorns, chiles, and sometimes with caraway too. The cabbage is packed down well, so it gives off as much juice as possible, to cover it completely. The barrels are finally closed with a wooden disc, weighted down with stones, and placed in a room with an even temperature. After about two weeks of lactic acid fermentation, the result is a cabbage which is still "crisp," but

1 First the outer leaves are removed with a knife.
2 Then the stalk is extracted using a drill.
3 Large, rotating blades cut the cabbage into thin strips.

4 The baskets with the shredded cabbage are emptied into large barrels made from acacia wood or oak.
5 In the barrels the cabbage is seasoned with salt, peppercorns, and chiles, and sometimes also with caraway.
6 The barrels are covered with a wooden disc, then weighted down with basalt blocks.

Finely chopped white cabbage, before it is turned into sauerkraut.

Background above: The women of Vecsés still sell their excellent sauerkraut straight from the barrel.

which has a pleasantly sour flavor.

True skill, however, lies in pickling whole leaves. A special variety of cabbage is grown for this purpose, with sturdy, wide, and not too dense, heads, and thin leaves. The expert selection process takes place while the cabbage is still in the field, because not all are suitable. Those which are suitable for pickling whole are harvested differently. Not only is the solid head cut off, but the wide open outer leaves too, to protect the precious harvest during transportation and preparation. The heads of cabbage have to be prepared for the actual fermentation process. First the stalk is removed and the resulting cavity filled with salt. A few days later, the protective outer leaves are removed. The heads of cabbage are layered carefully in barrels that are filled with cold water. Six to eight weeks later, the fermented cabbages and their leaves are ready for consumption.

Opposite: Production of chopped sauerkraut has taken place according to the same method for generations. Nowadays, though, it is easier to remove the stalk. The drill is no longer hand-powered, but runs on electricity.

Sour pickled vegetables

Hungary's winter menu is rich in spicy meat dishes that would be more difficult to digest, and less tasty, without sour pickled vegetables. If you shop at a market stall during the cold winter months, you will be offered pickled cucumbers, peppers, beets, melons, tomatoes, and a colorful variety of mixed vegetables in various pickling liquors. Summer is a different matter altogether, for it's the season of fresh salads and vegetables. The sole exception is sour pickled gherkins that are preserved by the action of natural lactic acid fermentation, without the use of vinegar, and which are intended for immediate consumption.

The choice of sour pickles is great. The vegetables are either chopped or left whole. Some jars contain one variety, others a mixture. The vegetables are always raw when they are put in the jars, and are arranged attractively. The jar is filled with water mixed with vinegar, salt, sometimes a little sugar, and spices, such as horseradish, peppercorns, bay leaves, caraway, or dill.

Comfort on cold winter days

DISHES BASED ON SAUERKRAUT

Kolozsvári rakott káposzta
(Layered cabbage
Klausenburg-style)

According to an old Hungarian proverb, sauerkraut is "like fur, it needs to be lined, as well as trimmed."

Székelygulyás (Székely goulash with "coxcombs")

Székelygulyás
Székely goulash

The name of the dish is not derived from the Székler, a Hungarian ethnic group in Transylvania, nor is it goulash. Instead, in 1846, a county archivist by the name of József Székely is supposed to have dropped into his local inn in Budapest, the "Arany Ökör," just before closing time, and found there was nothing to eat in the kitchen except a little *pörkölt* and cooked sauerkraut. At his request, the leftovers were heated up together. He was so delighted with the "dish" that henceforth he and his friends often ordered cabbage "à la Székely." The poet, Sándor Petőfi, is supposed to have finally christened it *Székelygulyás*.

1¼ lbs/600 g pork (leg or shoulder)
5 oz/150 g bacon
1 large onion
1 heaped tsp sweet paprika
2¼ lbs/1 kg sauerkraut
3 tbsp flour
1 cup/250 ml sour cream
"Coxcombs" made from slices of bacon to garnish

Dice the pork into ¾ inch/2 cm pieces. Dice the bacon finely. Sauté the bacon in a skillet, without any oil, until crisp. Remove the bacon from the skillet, reserving the juices. Sauté the finely diced onion in the bacon juices, then take the skillet off the heat and add the paprika and pork. Put the skillet on the heat again, then cover and sauté the meat for 30 minutes. Rinse the sauerkraut under cold, running water. Drain and add it to

the skillet. Add enough water to just cover the sauerkraut and meat. Bring to the boil and simmer until the meat is tender. The liquid should not boil dry. Slake the flour with a splash of water, and blend to a smooth paste. Stir in ¾ cup/200 ml sour cream. Thicken the juices with the flour and cream mixture. Arrange the pork and cabbage on a warmed serving dish. Pour the remaining sour cream over the cabbage, and garnish with "coxcombs" (see page 299).
If you use smoked meat, or a spicy sausage like Debrecen, it will have a stronger flavor. Because smoked meat is salty, and quite tough, it should be soaked beforehand, then parboiled. Add the sausage or smoked meat to the cabbage at the same time as the water.

Korhelyleves
Night owl soup

10 oz/300 g smoked ham shank (or 14 oz/400 g smoked pork ribs)
10 oz/300 g sauerkraut
2½ tbsp/40 g butter
1 large onion
2 tsp sweet paprika
4 cups/1 liter sauerkraut pickling liquor
⅛ tsp pepper
3 tbsp flour
¾ cup/200 ml sour cream
5 oz/150 g Debrecen or other spicy sausage, sliced
Salt

Boil the meat until tender (see page 301, Smoked Meat Stock). Rinse the sauerkraut under cold, running water, then drain and

Korhelyleves
(Night owl soup)

chop. Melt half the butter in a saucepan, and sauté the finely diced onion in it until golden brown. Take the pan off the heat and stir in the paprika, 1–2 tbsp of water, and the sauerkraut. Blend the sauerkraut liquor with some of the smoked meat stock to produce an acidic stock that is not too salty. Pour it over the sauerkraut. Dice the smoked meat and add it to the pan. Bring to a boil, and season with pepper. Melt the remaining butter in a saucepan, add the flour and cook, stirring all the time, until the flour foams and turns golden. Blend the *roux* into the stew, and stir well until the sauce thickens. Add the sour cream, and bring the stew to the boil again. Finally add the sliced sausage. Add a little

salt if necessary. This soup should be served after an all-night party, around dawn, because it is supposed to prevent a hangover.

Kolozsvári rakott káposzta
Layered cabbage Klausenburg-style

2¼ lb/1 kg sauerkraut
½ cup/130 g butter
10 tbsp/150 g long-grain rice
1 medium onion
1½ tsp sweet paprika
4½ cups/500 g ground pork
Salt, ½ tsp pepper
5 oz/150 g Debrecen or other spicy sausage
2 hard-boiled eggs (optional)
1⅔ cups/400 ml sour cream

Rinse the sauerkraut under cold,

running water. Melt 2 tbsp/30 g butter in a saucepan, then add the sauerkraut, and braise until soft. If necessary, add a splash of water or smoked meat stock. Melt a nut of butter in a skillet and add the rice. Sauté until translucent, then add enough water to cover, and cook the rice until *al dente*. Melt 2½ tablespoons/40 g butter in a skillet, and sauté the onion until translucent. Take the skillet off the heat, add 1 tsp of paprika and the ground pork. Season to taste with salt and pepper, then return the skillet to the heat. Cover the skillet and sauté the meat, stirring frequently, until the liquid has evaporated. Remove the skin from the sausage and slice it. Shell the hard-boiled eggs and slice them. Butter an ovenproof dish

with 3½ tbsp/50 g butter, and line the bottom with one-third of the sauerkraut. Pour some of the sour cream over the cabbage, then spread over half of the ground pork mixture, sliced egg, sausage, and rice. Add another layer of cabbage and sour cream, and the remaining pork, sausage, egg, and rice. Finish with a layer of sauerkraut. Melt 2 tsp/10 g butter in a saucepan, and blend in the remaining sour cream and paprika. Pour the mixture over the sauerkraut. Bake the layered sauerkraut in a preheated oven (350 °F/180 °C) for 30–40 minutes, until golden brown. This dish is often prepared from leftover pork *pörkölt* (see page 31), with the *pörkölt* gravy being poured over the layered cabbage.

THE LEGACY OF JEWISH CUISINE

Until World War II, countless followers of the Jewish faith lived in Hungary. Some of them were strict observers of the religious laws pertaining to food, others did not follow them so closely. But even Jews who no longer observed the laws on food preparation did not entirely forget their traditional dishes, some of which have become enshrined in Hungarian cuisine.

The best-known dish is *sólet*, bean stew, which was probably introduced by Galician Jews who settled in Hungary. The origin of this name is still unknown today. Some believe it is related to the French word *chaud* (warm); others link it to the Yiddish word that indicates the end of the ceremony on the eve of the Sabbath and yet others believe the name is of Hebraic origin.

The laws of Moses prescribe that on the seventh day, which is dedicated to God, no work should be done, which also precludes lighting a fire. This made *sólet* a popular Sabbath meal – the beans were soaked on Thursday. On Friday all the ingredients were placed in a clay or iron pot, which was tightly closed, and taken to the baker, who put the pots in his oven where the dish cooked slowly until the next day, when it was tender and flavorful.

Sólet probably found its way into Hungarian cuisine through mixed-race marriages. Non-Jewish intellectuals possibly also had a hand in its migration, because they enjoyed frequenting the Jewish restaurants in Budapest. Initially the dish was

Flódni

prepared in the traditional manner. In time, the smoked beef brisket or smoked goose leg, as well as the stuffed goose neck, have been replaced by smoked pork. Another Jewish specialty that is very popular with Hungarians is matzo dumplings, that are used as a soup garnish for beef or chicken broth. *Matzo* is the Jewish name for a type of unleavened bread. The soup garnish is prepared from matzo flour which nowadays is available from any Hungarian food store.

Flódni
(Photograph left)

For the pastry:

¾ cup/200 g goosefat	
3 cups/350 g flour	
1 egg	
1 egg yolk	
Pinch of salt	
1 tbsp confectioners' sugar	
Juice of 1 lemon	

For the filling:

2¼ lb/1 kg apples	
2–3 tbsp sugar	
½ tsp cinnamon	
⅔ cup/100 g ground poppy seeds	
Scant 1 cup/100 g confectioners' sugar	
⅛ tsp grated lemon rind	
¾ cup/100 g ground walnuts	
Scant 1 cup/100 g confectioners' sugar	
3–4 tbsp/60-80 g apricot jam	

For glazing:

1 egg, beaten	

Rub the goosefat into the flour, then add the egg, egg yolk, salt, confectioners' sugar, and lemon juice, and knead together well. Leave the dough to rest for 8–10 hours in the refrigerator. In the meantime, prepare the fillings. Peel and grate the apples. Put them in a saucepan, without any liquid, and cook them until soft. Leave to cool. Combine the poppy seeds, confectioners' sugar, and lemon zest. Combine the walnuts and confectioners' sugar. Divide the pastry into 5 portions and roll each one out into a rectangle. The rectangles should be of equal size. Place a rectangle of pastry on a baking sheet, then spread it with stewed apple and sprinkle sugar and cinnamon on top. Place a pastry rectangle on top, and spread this with the poppy seed mixture. Add another layer of pastry, and cover with the nut filling. Add another layer of pastry, and brush it with a thin layer of warmed apricot jam. Top it with a final layer of pastry, and brush this with the beaten egg. Leave the cake to rest for 2 hours. Bake in a preheated oven (425 °F/ 220 °C) for 15 minutes. Leave to cool on the baking sheet, then cut into rectangular slices.

Sólet füstölt libahússal és töltött libanyakkal

Sólet with smoked goose leg and stuffed goose neck
(Photograph left and below)

3 cups/600 g navy beans	
1¼ lbs/600 g smoked goose leg	
½ cup/120 g goosefat	
2 large onions	
2 cloves of garlic	
1 heaped tsp paprika	
4 eggs	

For the stuffed goose neck:

Skin from 1 goose's neck	
1⅓ cups/200 g flour	
3½ tbsp/50 g goosefat	
1 tsp sweet paprika	
½ tsp pepper	
Salt	

Soak the beans in cold water (at least 8–10 hours). Soak the goose leg.

Melt the goosefat in a flameproof casserole dish. Add the thinly sliced onions, and sauté until translucent (do not let them brown). Take the casserole off the heat, then add the crushed garlic and paprika, and fill with cold water. Drain the beans and rinse them under cold, running water. Add them to the pan with the goose leg. Put the casserole on the heat again, and bring to a boil. Cover the casserole and place it in the oven. Braise the beans and goose leg for 1½ hours.

Next stuff the goose neck. Fasten the skin at one end. Combine the flour, butter, paprika, pepper, and salt. Stuff the skin with this mixture and tie up the other end. Wash the egg shells very thoroughly, and put the eggs in the stew, with the goose neck, halfway through cooking. Top up the liquid so that the beans remain covered.

Take the goose leg and stuffed goose neck out of the bean stew, and slice them. Cut the hard-boiled eggs into quarters. Season the bean stew to taste with salt. Serve the bean stew with the sliced goose leg, goose neck, and hard-boiled eggs arranged on top

Ricset

Ritschet

Ingredients as for sólet	
1 cup/100 g barley porridge	

Prepare as for sólet, but mix the beans with barley porridge before cooking.

Zsidó tojás

Jewish eggs

5 eggs	
1 small onion	
1 tbsp butter	
½ tsp pepper	
1 tsp mustard (optional)	
Salt	

Boil the eggs until hard, then shell them and mash them with a fork. Combine the eggs, finely grated onion, butter, pepper, mustard if used, and salt.
This is a hearty spread for bread or *barches*.

This excellent kosher plum brandy matures in barrels for three to twelve years.

Barches is a bread which is shaped into a rounded or long plait and sprinkled with poppy seeds. Originally it was baked for the Sabbath or other Jewish festivals.

Sólet füstölt libahússal és töltött libanyakkal (Scholet with smoked goose drumstick and stuffed goose neck)

A splendidly decorated Serbian church in Pest.

SERBIAN CUISINE

Many Hungarian place names start with the syllable "Rác," and the surname Rácz is still common. The generic term *rác*, which has already died out, means "Serb, Serbian." Time and again, over the centuries, Serbs fled to Hungary before enemy troops. Some of them settled in the country where they established settlements, mainly along the Danube. At the start of the 18th century almost half of Buda, at that time independent, was inhabited by Serbs. The "City of Serbs" lay to the north of Mount Gellért, roughly where Tabán Park is located today. The Serbs produced a spicy red wine, the "Serb vermouth," from the kadarka and pinot noir grapes which at that time flourished on the heights above Buda. It was also popular with their neighbors from Pest and Obuda.

It is still possible to identify the Balkan Serb origins of dishes – tomatoes and bell peppers predominate, and one frequently finds smoked bacon too, but you will search in vain for paprika.

Rácponty
Serbian-style carp
(Photograph right)

1¾ lbs/800 g potatoes
Salt
1¾ lbs/800 g carp fillet
3½ oz/100 g smoked bacon, sliced
5 tbsp flour
1 tsp paprika
6½ tbsp/100 g butter
4–5 green bell peppers
2 large tomatoes
2 large onions
¾ cup/200 ml sour cream
1–2 bacon "coxcombs" (optional)

Cook the potatoes in their skins in a saucepan of boiling, salted water until just tender. Drain and leave to cool. Peel and slice the potatoes.

Make incisions every 1–1½ inches/3–4 cm along the sides of the carp fillet, and divide it into 4 even-size pieces. Lard the carp fillet with the slices of bacon, and season to taste with salt.

Mix the flour and ½ teaspoon paprika together. Toss the pieces of fish in the flour. Melt the butter in a skillet, and seal the carp fillet for about 1 minute on each side. Seed the bell peppers and slice them into rings.

Brush the bottom of an ovenproof dish with a little of the melted butter. Cover it with a layer of sliced potatoes. Season the potatoes with salt, then place the carp fillet on top and follow with even layers of peppers, sliced tomatoes and sliced onions. Mix together the sour cream and remaining butter from the skillet and pour it over the carp and vegetables. Bake in a preheated oven (350 °F/180 °C) for 35–40 minutes.

Serve the carp straight from the oven. Garnish with bacon "coxcombs" (see page 299) if desired.

Rácponty (Serbian-style carp) is Hungary's most popular specialty from
Serbian cuisine.

Rác töltött paprika
Stuffed bell peppers Serbian-style

8 medium-size bell peppers	
Salt	
5 oz/150 g bacon	
2 medium tomatoes	
¾ cup/100 g dry white breadcrumbs	
1 large onion	
4½ cups/500 g ground pork	
1 egg, beaten	
3 cloves of garlic	
½ tsp pepper	
Butter for the dish	
1¼ cups/300 ml sour cream	

Cut the bell peppers in half
lengthwise. Seed them and
sprinkle the insides lightly with
salt. Cut the bacon into strips and
slice the tomatoes. Mix together
the breadcrumbs, ground pork,
grated onion, beaten egg, crushed
garlic, pepper, and salt. Use to
stuff the pepper halves. Butter an
ovenproof dish and lay the stuffed
peppers in it. Place a strip of
bacon and a slice of tomato on
top of each bell pepper. Finally
pour over the sour cream and
place in a preheated oven
(300 °F/150 °C).
After 5 minutes increase the
temperature to 350 °F/180 °C and
bake for 30 minutes. Then
increase the temperature to 425 °F/
220 °C, so that the stuffed bell
peppers are baking on a high heat
for the last 15 minutes. Serve
straight from the oven,
accompanied by mashed potato.

Kelkáposztás rácpaprikás
Serb *paprikasch* with savoy
cabbage

1¼ lbs/600 g round steak, sliced	
Salt	
1¾ lbs/800 g savoy cabbage	
1¾ lbs/800 g potatoes	
7 oz/200 g tomatoes	
10 oz/300 g bell peppers	
1 medium onion	
2½ tbsp/40 g butter	

Beat the slices of beef out thinly,
and sprinkle lightly with salt.
Remove the stalk from the
cabbage and discard, then slice
the cabbage. Peel and dice the
potatoes. Slice the tomatoes. Seed
and slice the bell peppers. Melt
the butter in a saucepan. Add the
finely diced onion, and sweat
until golden.
Seal the beef in the butter, then
add sufficient water to cover and
stew the beef for about 30
minutes, until semi-cooked.
Add the bell peppers, tomatoes,
and cabbage. Cover the pan and
continue cooking. After 10
minutes add the potatoes, and a
splash more water, if necessary,
and cook for another 20–30
minutes, or until the meat and
vegetables are tender. Thicken the
cooking liquid, and serve it as
gravy to accompany the meat and
vegetables.

Sweet enticement
CAKE SHOPS

Hungarians who travel around the world may marvel at beautiful scenery and splendid cities, but sooner or later they will miss one thing terribly, and in many places not find it – a really good cake shop. These exist in large numbers in Hungary: big and small, elegant and modest, the kind that are recommended in travel guides and awarded many stars, and the kind that are known only to the locals.

The cake shop is a legacy of the Austro-Hungarian dual monarchy and it has resisted every change in gastronomic trends for the last 200 years. They still await their patrons with cakes, gâteaux, and pastries of the most varied sort. They also offer a wide variety of drinks, and the more stylish establishments sell candy and chocolates. The highlight of the winter months is chestnut purée and the main summer attraction is ice cream. The ice cream stand, or in some places the ice cream machine, is as much a part of the basic equipment as the cake counter. Unless the cake shop is very sparsely furnished, the atmosphere tends to be rather nostalgic and cozy.

Only some of the patrons will take a seat in a Hungarian cake shop; many fortify themselves standing up, or choose cakes and pastries from the plentiful choice to take out.

Small cake shops pack tarts and cakes in simple cardboard boxes or on cardboard trays, wrapped in wax paper. Big, famous establishments, however, place a lot of emphasis on packaging, which is as individual as their cakes. It is often so striking and imaginative that decades later many customers still recall an elegant cake box, a colorful, curled ribbon that surrounded a smart package, or a decorative wooden handle which served to carry the delicacy …

The Gerbeaud cake shop around 1890.

This is what the citizens of Budapest like best: a piece of layered sponge cake (see page 164) and a cup of freshly brewed, strong coffee.

The rich imagination of an establishment, however, is not just restricted to packaging. Small cake shops, in particular, can thank their original produce for their many years in business, because a really good baker and confectioner knows how to give basic recipes a special, individual touch. Of course, he keeps his recipes strictly secret. This secrecy also extends to the Hungarian Museum for the Catering Trade. Family recipes are handed over to the Museum only on the strict understanding that they are not made public for the next 30 years, not even for research purposes.

Left: Cake shops attract custom with delicious cakes, elegant gâteaux, and aromatic coffee.

Ruszwurm

In the castle district of Budapest there is a small, much-frequented cake shop: the renowned Café Ruszwurm. It was opened in 1827, and you can still admire the original Empire furnishings today. At the same time it is no small wonder that the café survived intact the occupations of 1849 and 1944, which caused great damage. At one time Ruszwurm supplied the aristocracy in the castle and the surrounding area, who not only placed orders, but also liked to visit the café in person. The Austrian Empress Elisabeth (1837–98) is supposed to have been a customer. The cakes and pastries were packed in beautiful boxes for the customers to take away. They were decorated with views of Buda Castle, the nearby Church of St Matthias, or portraits of the royal family.

Gerbeaud

The famous Gerbeaud, on Vörösmarty Square, in the heart of Budapest city center, enjoys a legendary reputation. The first coffee house to try and outdo its Parisian counterparts in splendor and pomp was opened on this site in 1861. In 1870 Henrik Kugler's flourishing cake shop moved to its present

Because they are easy to prepare, *zserbószelet* (Gerbeaud slices) are popular to make at home.

location. Hungary can thank his family for numerous elegant cakes and pastries. His name lives on today in the popular chocolate confection *Kugler*.

Gerbeaud's logo embellishes many a cake or pastry.

A bust of Ilona Gerbeaud graces a room in the Café. It was created by the sculptor György Zala.

In 1884 Henrik Kugler handed over the business to a worthy successor, the gifted Swiss pastry chef Emil Gerbeaud, whose name has been borne by the establishment since then. There were a few years when the cake shop traded under the name "Vörösmarty," because there was a legal dispute about use of the old business sign.

Gerbeaud was very critical and demanded the utmost perfection from his employees. Under his guidance, the establishment became a meeting place for wealthy and influential citizens of Budapest. The splendid furnishings, the superb cakes and pastries, and the friendly service were its trademarks. Female staff were employed on strict conditions: they had to be courteous, cultivated, beautiful, and, moreover, of good character.

The owners who came and went always took care not only to maintain the establishment's good reputation, but also to preserve the original furnishings. Hence Gerbeaud still looks as it did in the founding years – luxuriously furnished, elegant, yet comfortable. And with a little luck it is still possible today to sit at one of the little marble tables with the turned pedestals which Emil Gerbeaud ordered from the Paris World Fair in 1900.

One of the establishment's specialties is Esterházy gâteau, which was created around 100 years ago. It consists of pale yellow buttercream between layers of almond sponge, coated with white frosting, decorated with chocolate and candied fruits, while the sides are coated with flaked almonds. Another specialty is wine cream cake, made from jelly roll sponge with a sabayon custard filling.

Mignons, the little tartlets made by Kugler, conquered the entire country, although the "Red Cross version" is sold almost exclusively in Gerbeaud. It is not just special because of the cross made of red fruits, gleaming through the glaze, which gives it its name, but also because of the marzipan filling flavored with apricot schnapps.

Gerbeaud slices, coated with chocolate frosting and made from layers of plain pastry filled with jam, crushed nuts, and pieces of apple, are a prime example of the establishment's gastronomic scope. Because they are easy to prepare, they have found a place in the repertoire of home bakers, and are especially popular at weddings.

The "little Gerbeaud" is also one of the café's traditions. This is not a cake, but a little cake shop, close by, which sells the same produce as its brother café – but cheaper.

Right: The only opportunity to revel in Gerbeaud's atmosphere in enjoyable silence comes early in the morning.

Classic Hungarian cakes and pastries

Taste in cakes and pastries changes as often as taste in fashion, yet there are perennial classics, some of which are familiar outside Hungary.

Indiáner
(Indian's/Moor's heads)
Balls of jelly roll, sliced in half and filled with whipped cream, with the sponge ends dipped in chocolate.

At the start of the 19th century the Hungarian count Ferdinand Pálffy was Director of the Vienna Theater. Because the repertoire, mainly consisting of classical pieces, was not very popular with the public, the Count engaged an Indian magician, who at that time was fêted throughout Europe, to liven up the proceedings. As the citizens of Vienna still came only sporadically, Pálffy had his Hungarian cook create a novel pastry, which was distributed throughout the theater, and which was intended to remind the audience of the magician. It was a brilliant idea; the theater was packed night after night, and the *Indiáner* was firmly established in the culinary repertoire.

Rákóczi-túrós
(Baked cheesecake Rákóczi)
Squares of baked cheesecake on a plain pastry base, decorated with a lattice of meringue and apricot jam.

Created by János Rákóczi in 1958 for the Hungarian restaurant at the Brussels World Fair. This cheesecake is also a popular home bake. The cheesecake has no connection with the Hungarian Counts Rákóczi.

Krémes
(Custard slices)
A thick layer of vanilla custard sandwiched between two squares of flaky pastry, then dusted with vanilla sugar. Custard slices have been available for more than 100 years. For a long time they were regarded as the cheapest pastry, but this is not the only reason custard slices are so popular …

Franciakrémes
(French custard slices)
A layer each of smooth vanilla custard and whipped cream between two thin squares of puff pastry. The top layer of pastry is coated in coffee-flavored frosting.

Right: The little Café Ruszwurm offers the best cakes and pastries in stylish surroundings.

162

Rigó Jancsi
Chocolate-flavored jelly roll is sandwiched together with a chocolate custard and cream mixture, and coated in chocolate frosting.

This cream cake perpetuates the name of a virtuoso Hungarian gipsy violinist. Jancsi Rigó was a master of his art, who was known less for his violin playing, than for the scandal attached to him. At the wane of the 19th century he was playing in a Paris restaurant where the Belgian Count Chimay was dining with his young, beautiful wife, the daughter of an American millionaire. Rigó's violin playing and his passionate gaze entranced the Countess who, giving way to a sudden impulse, put her diamond ring on the musician's finger. This was the start of a passionate romance which shocked aristocratic Parisian society when it became public knowledge. The Countess left her husband and two young children, and followed Rigó throughout the world ...

Countess Chimay

Képviselőfánk
(Cream puffs)
Light choux pastry filled with delicate vanilla custard.

Gesztenye
(Sweet chestnuts)
A delicate sweet chestnut-flavored mixture, in the shape of chestnuts, dipped in chocolate.

Lúdlábtorta
(Chocolate cream gâteau)
Chocolate jelly roll sponge base filled with a mixture of chocolate-flavored custard enriched with cream and pieces of cherries soaked in brandy, the top coated in chocolate frosting.

Puncstorta
(Punch cake)
The filling between the two layers of jelly roll sponge consists of a mixture of crumbled jelly roll, mixed with chopped fruit and nuts, soaked in rum and sugar syrup. Underneath the pink sugar frosting there is a thin layer of strawberry jam.

Krumpli
(Marzipan balls)
Choux pastry balls filled with chocolate buttercream, wrapped in marzipan, and dredged in cocoa powder.

Stefánia-torta
(Stephanie gâteau)
As for Dobos cake (see page 164), but without the caramel layer. Instead it is dusted with cocoa powder, and sometimes the sides are decorated with cream rosettes.

Sarokház
(Corner house)
A portion of chocolate cake smothered in whipped cream.

1 The ingredients for the batter: eggs, flour, confectioners' sugar, vanilla sugar, lemons.
2 Beat together the egg yolks and sugar. Then fold in the stiffly beaten egg whites and flour.
3 Divide the batter into 6 equal portions and make thin, evenly sized sponge bases.

4 The ingredients for the buttercream and glaze: sugar, lemon, rum, butter, cocoa powder.
5 Beat the butter and cocoa powder together, then add the sugar syrup and flavorings.
6 Spread about one-fifth of the buttercream over a sponge base.

7 Cover with another layer of sponge. Continue …
8 … until 5 layers are sandwiched together. Spread the buttercream around the sides of the cake.
9 Decorate the sides of the cake with cookie crumbs, or slivered almonds.

10 Melt the sugar in a saucepan with the lemon juice and …
11 … boil until the sugar caramelizes, stirring all the time.
12 Quickly spread the caramel glaze over the sixth sponge layer.

Dobos cake

This famous cake consists of six thin, individually baked jelly roll bases, filled with chocolate buttercream, coated with a caramel glaze on top, and the sides decorated with crumbled sweet cookie crumbs.

It was created toward the end of the 19th century by József C. Dobos, a Budapest master chef and owner of a delicatessen store. The cake was a sensation in Budapest and soon beyond the borders of Hungary too, because it contained a novel ingredient – buttercream. Orders came from all over, and thus the "Dobos," packed in attractive wooden boxes which the master baker had personally designed, began its triumphal march across Europe.

József Dobos, whose ancestors were famous cooks, was passionately in love with his profession. He was very creative and inventive, because he thought it important that his delicatessen should always be able to offer his rich and extravagant clientele something new. In 1885 he had his own pavilion at the first General National Exhibition in Budapest.

His cakes and pastries were a sensation and started a genuine Dobos fever. The Austrian Emperor Franz Joseph I and his wife Elisabeth also honored the pavilion with a visit. They sampled the sweet attractions and were very taken with them, to the general delight of their subjects. Thereafter, the citizens of Budapest demanded Dobos cake in every cake shop. Other master pastry chefs tried in vain to discover the recipe. There were numerous imitations, which came nowhere near the standard of the original. When

Empress Elisabeth (Sisi) enjoyed great popularity in Hungary.

József Dobos retired in 1906, he passed the recipe on to the Budapest Trade Association, thus making the recipe for his famous creation common property.

All the scandals and struggles surrounding attempts to divine the famous recipe made such a lasting impression on the public that a century later it provided sufficient material for an operetta.

The name of the cake itself even has a strange legacy. Because the brown caramel layer looks like the skin of a drum (*dob* in Hungarian), many believed, and still believe today, that the name of the cake is derived from this, and therefore call the caramel glaze *dob*, or drum.

Dobos-torta háziasan

Homemade dobos cake
(Photograph)

This is not the original recipe.
Every housewife has her own
version. The pale brown, smooth
caramel glaze is very important.

For the batter:

6 eggs, separated	
1⅓ cups/150 g confectioners' sugar	
1 tsp vanilla sugar	
Lemon juice	
1 cup/120 g flour	
½ tsp grated lemon zest	

For the custard cream:

½ cup/100 g sugar
⅔ cup/150 g butter
⅓ cup/40 g cocoa powder
1 tbsp rum, 1 tsp vanilla sugar

For the glaze:

¾ cup/150 g sugar
1 tsp lemon juice

József C. Dobos was one of the
best-known Hungarian cooks and
master pastry chefs of his day.

To decorate:

Crushed cookies (optional)
Slivered almonds (optional)
Ground hazelnuts (optional)
Ground almonds (optional)

To make the batter, whisk together the egg yolks and half of the confectioners' sugar until frothy. Add the vanilla sugar, a few dashes of lemon juice, and 2 tbsp of water. Beat the egg whites with the remaining sugar until stiff. Fold the egg whites, flour, and lemon zest into the egg yolk mixture. Spread a sheet of baking parchment on a baking sheet. Draw 6 rounds on the parchment, using a cake pan as a template. Divide the batter equally between the rounds, and spread it out evenly to form thin cake bases. Bake the bases in a preheated oven (400 °F/ 200 °C) for 10 minutes or until the edges start to brown. Lift them off the baking parchment straightaway, using a broad-bladed spatula and cool on a wire rack. To make the custard, bring 3½ tbsp water and the sugar to a boil, then leave it to cool a little. Add the butter and cocoa powder, stirring all the time, to prevent any lumps forming. Continue beating until the custard is completely cold, then fold in the rum and vanilla sugar.

Set aside the best base for glazing. Place the sugar and lemon juice in a saucepan. Cook them on a medium heat, stirring all the time, until the sugar caramelizes, then quickly pour over the sponge base. Smooth out the caramel over the base. Using a well-buttered knife, cut the glazed base into 16 equal portions. Sandwich the other bases together with the custard. Spread the remaining buttercream around the edge of the cake, finally place the glazed sponge layer on top. The sides of the cake can be decorated with cookie crumbs, slivered almonds, ground hazelnuts, or ground almonds. Refrigerate the cake until just before serving.

The glazed sponge layer is divided into 16
equal segments which are positioned on top
of the finished cake.

Whisk the egg whites with the sugar until stiff.

Carefully fold the egg whites into the yolk mixture.

Sift the flour into the mixture and fold it in carefully.

Diótorta (Walnut gâteau)

Finally fold in the ground nuts.

Pour the batter into a springform pan and bake.

To make the cream, combine the remaining nuts with the milk and flour.

Finally mix in the vanilla sugar and rum.

GÂTEAUX

Gâteaux are reserved mainly for celebratory occasions such as birthdays, weddings, and baptisms. Even the less elaborate versions usually appear on the table only on Sundays.

Diótorta
Walnut gâteau
(Photograph)

8 oz/225 g walnuts

For the batter:
6 eggs, separated
1 cup/120 g confectioners' sugar
1 cup/110 g flour
3½ tbsp rum

For the cream:
1¼ cups/300 ml milk
6 tbsp flour
1⅓ cups/150 g confectioners' sugar
2 cups/300 g butter
3½ tbsp rum
2 tsps vanilla sugar

Grind the nuts, reserving some for decoration. Whisk together the egg yolks and one-third of the confectioners' sugar until frothy. Whisk together the egg whites and remaining sugar until stiff. Fold the flour, rum, egg whites, and 3 tbsp/ 40 g ground walnuts into the egg yolk mixture. Line the base of a springform pan with baking parchment, pour the batter into it. Bake in a preheated (350 °F/180 °C) oven for 30–35 minutes. Leave to cool in the pan, then remove, and slice into three layers. To make the cream: put the flour in a bowl and slake it with the milk. Place the bowl over a saucepan of hot water and heat it, stirring all the time, until the flour and milk thicken. Leave the custard to cool. Cream together the confectioners' sugar and butter. Add it to the custard with the remaining nuts, rum, and vanilla sugar. Continue beating until the cream is smooth. Spread over the bottom layer of cake, place a layer of sponge on top, add another layer of cream and finish with a layer of sponge. Spread the cream all over the gâteau and decorate with the ground nuts and reserved whole walnuts. Leave to set in the refrigerator for 24 hours.

Fillings for sponge cakes
Bake sponge cakes using the recipe for jelly roll (see page 298) and spread them with the cream filling of your choice.

Kávékrém
Coffee cream

Scant ½ cup/100 ml strong coffee
¾ cup/200 ml milk
3 tbsp flour
1⅓ cups/150 g confectioners' sugar
2 tsp vanilla sugar
½ cup/120 g butter, softened

Place the coffee, milk, flour, confectioners' sugar, and vanilla sugar in a saucepan over a low heat, or in a basin over a pan of hot water. Cook, stirring all the time, until a thick custard forms. Stir until the custard is cool, then beat in the softened butter.

Gesztenyekrém
Chestnut cream

7 oz/200 g sweet chestnut purée
⅔ cup/150 g butter
1 cup/100 g confectioners' sugar
2 tsp vanilla sugar, 2 tbsp rum

Press the chestnut purée through a potato ricer. Cream the butter and confectioners' sugar together, then combine with the chestnut purée, vanilla sugar, and rum to form a smooth spread.

Fill the cake with the cream, and spread it over the sides.

If you like, you can pipe decorations on the cake using the remaining cream.

POPULAR HOMEMADE CAKES

The Hungarians have a particular affection for cakes and desserts. Even if rich gâteaux are mostly reserved for high days and holidays, cakes grace the table most days. Every family has its favorite cake, and every housewife has a specialty which is quick to prepare and a guaranteed success. Not only are the recipes passed on from generation to generation, they are also exchanged between friends, and if there is a choice between elaborate store-bought cakes and simple homemade offerings, "Mom's homemade cake" always wins.

Plain pastries have remained popular for over 200 years. The dough is quick to make and can be used in a wide variety of ways – as a base for tarts and flans, in tray bakes, and for cookies.

Meggyes piskóta
Sponge cake with morello cherries
(Photograph below)

Generous 1 lb/500 g morello cherries, pitted
⅔ cup/150 g butter
1⅓ cups/150 g confectioners' sugar
4 eggs, separated
Scant 1⅓ cups/180 g flour
1 tsp baking powder

To decorate:

⅓ cup/50 g confectioners' sugar
2 tsp vanilla sugar

Additional:

Butter and flour for the jelly roll pan

Rinse the cherries and drain them in a sieve. Cream the butter and confectioners' sugar together, then beat in the egg yolks. Sift the flour and baking powder together, then gradually fold into the egg mixture. Whisk the egg whites until stiff, and fold them loosely into the batter.

Butter a jelly roll pan and dust it with flour. Spread the batter over the pan and scatter the cherries on top. Bake in a preheated (400 °F/ 200 °C) oven for 30 minutes. During the first 5 minutes, the oven door should not be opened. Prick the cake with a skewer to test whether it is cooked. Turn off the oven and open the door, then leave the cake in the oven to rest. When the cake has cooled, dust it with a mixture of confectioners' sugar and vanilla sugar, and divide it into squares.

Almás pite
Apple pie
(Photograph above right)

For the dough:

1 cup/250 g butter
3¾ cups/500 g flour
Pinch of salt
½ cup/120 g sugar
1 egg yolk
3½ tbsp/50 ml sour cream

For the topping:

3¼ lbs/1.5 kg cooking apples
½ cup/50 g dry white breadcrumbs
4 tbsp sugar
Generous ⅓ cup/50 g chopped walnuts

Extra:

Butter for the shallow rectangular cake pan
1 egg for glazing, beaten
½ cup/50 g confectioners' sugar for sprinkling

Rub the butter into the flour and salt until it resembles fine breadcrumbs. Add the sugar, egg yolk, and sour cream, and work together to form a smooth dough. Divide the dough in half and refrigerate it for a few hours. To make the topping: peel, core, and grate the apples. Leave the grated apple to rest for 30 minutes, then squeeze out the juice. Roll out one half of the dough and use it to line a cake pan. Scatter the breadcrumbs over the dough, and spread the grated apple on top, then sprinkle over the sugar and chopped walnuts. Roll out the other piece of dough and make a lid for the pie, sealing the edges well with beaten egg or water. Prick the lid all over with a fork. Brush the pastry with half of the beaten egg. Refrigerate the apple pie for 20 minutes, then brush with the remaining beaten egg. If the pie browns too quickly, cover it with a sheet of aluminum foil or baking parchment. Leave the pie to cool in the pan, then cut it into squares. Dust the pie with confectioners' sugar and serve warm.

Női szeszély
(Women's moods)
A thin pastry base topped with apricot jam and cream cheesecake mixture.

Püspökkenyér
(Bishop's bread)
Sponge mixture with candied fruit, raisins, hazelnuts, and almonds.

Lekváros szelet
(Jam layer cake)
Layers of sponge with strawberry preserve.

UNICUM

"That is unique," was supposedly the cry raised by Joseph II, Emperor of Austria and King of Hungary in 1790, when he tasted the pleasant herb mixture prepared by his Court physician, Dr Zwack. The name of the Hungarian tonic bitters known as Zwack Unicum is allegedly derived from this remark.

The Zwack family established its distillery in Pest in 1840. Unicum – the exact composition of which is known only to members of the family – has been made in Hungary ever since, except for a break of about 40 years. After World War II the business became State-owned and the original owners left the country, taking the original recipe with them. While the family produced their herb schnapps in Italy under the name Zwack Unicum, the Budapest distillery continued to produce a beverage with the name Unicum. Although this had a far from unpleasant taste, it was nothing like the original. In 1989 Péter Zwack, a fourth generation member of the family, bought the firm back from the State. Since then, Unicum has once again been distilled in Hungary according to the old traditional recipe.

The popular tonic bitters contains extracts from over 40 different herbs and roots. The active substances are partly released by soaking in water for 30 days, partly by distillation. The harmonious blend of the different flavors to create the unique taste is achieved by the blending ratio as well as the production process. The bitters are matured in oak barrels for at least six months.

The firm's humorous advertising poster which was designed at the beginning of the 20th century, and which many people still remembered decades later, is today a classic of Hungarian poster art. It shows a shipwrecked man, beaming with joy at the sight of a floating bottle of Unicum – tonic bitters as a life saver. Unicum is best drunk like a brandy; at room temperature and served in brandy balloons. Some people prefer it ice cold and drink it from frosted glasses, like vodka. It can also be enjoyed warm, because it is supposed to boost the body's energy reserves. In any case, Unicum is a very good aperitif and digestif.

Background below: The present-day Unicum bottles, available commercially, are sadly much smaller.

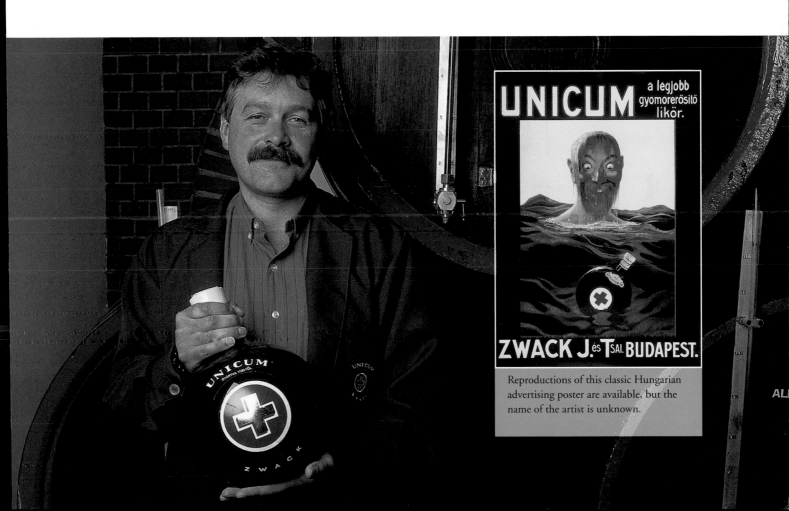

Reproductions of this classic Hungarian advertising poster are available, but the name of the artist is unknown.

More than just a cake decoration
MARZIPAN

At the legendary, splendid wedding banquet of King Matthias Corvinus (1458–90) and Beatrix, daughter of the King of Naples, a chess board was served, with chess pieces made from marzipan. This historically authenticated fact favors the assumption that marzipan, like other refined confectionery, reached Hungary via the Italian pastry chefs in the Princess's retinue.

A century ago, no cookbook was without the exact recipe for marzipan. More or less forgotten for a while, the sweetmeat is now enjoying a revival, though it is no longer made at home.

The ingredients have remained unchanged for centuries: marzipan is a fine mixture of ground almonds and sugar, held together by the almond oil which is released, and worked to form a malleable mass.

Marzipan is popular with pastry chefs and confectioners not only for the delicious taste of the classic ingredients, but also because it is malleable, can be sculpted easily, and colored, and is therefore suitable for edible works of art. The delicate roses and other miniature works of art created by Hungarian marzipan manufacturers are all handmade, as they have always been. Marzipan which is to be used for cake decorations or shaped into figures has a high sugar content, because this makes it easier to shape.

Yet the characteristic flavor of marzipan is most obvious in candy. Classic marzipan candies, which are filled with fruit and coated in chocolate, have a pronounced almond flavor. If the marzipan candy is made from almonds grown on the uplands above Lake Balaton, which have a unique flavor, and contains a piece of dried apricot in the middle that has been soaked in apricot brandy from Kecskemét, then it is a genuine Hungarian specialty, as is a candy which conceals a prune soaked in plum brandy from Szatmár.

One place of pilgrimage for Hungarian marzipan-lovers is a tiny store in a narrow alley in the heart of Budapest. This store sells only produce made by the famous family of confectioners called Szamos who were the first in Hungary, a few decades ago, to start making marzipan again to the original recipe.

1 The almonds are ground and mixed with sugar.
2 The raw mixture is pressed between marble rollers to make it smoother.
3 After the marzipan has been colored, it is kneaded again by hand.
4 To make "flower petals," little marzipan balls are flattened out to make petals, and these are then made up into "flowers."

5 The "flower petals" are modeled so that they look as realistic as possible.
6 The marzipan flowers are placed in a special mold for further work.
7 A spot of yellow marzipan is dabbed in the center of the "flower calyx," which also ...
8 ... acts as holder for the "stamens."

Only marzipan production itself is done by machine.

When the marzipan is transformed into works of art, this is done by hand.

SPARKLING WINE

In the second half of the 19th century a Hungarian called József Törley worked for two French champagne houses. He was employed as a salesman, but he was so enthusiastic about the classic drink that he also learned the production process. One day, his business took him to the wine- producing region of Promontor, near Buda. There, hewn in the chalk, he found a many-tunneled vault from the Middle Ages, which was similar to the champagne cellars in France, and so he decided to produce sparkling wine here himself. He married, and with his wife's dowry he bought a castle near Promontor, with the accompanying estates. He was able to persuade the gifted French winemaker Louis François to leave France and go into business with him, bringing with him the necessary technical expertise. The business flourished, but in 1896 there was a rift between the business partners. Louis François and his younger brother César opened their own champagne house in the immediate vicinity.

The best-known Hungarian brands of sparkling wine still come from the firms of Törley and François. As when the companies were founded, they partly source the young wine from the area surrounding Etyck, which has a microclimate similar to that of the Champagne region of France. However, it is a waste of time to search for the village of Promontor; it is now a suburb of Budapest which goes by the name Budafok.

In addition to sparkling wine produced in the traditional manner, being fermented and matured in the bottle, there are also cheaper sparkling wines that ferment in large tanks, but which are of a very good quality, despite the more basic production method.

Above: Bottle fermentation in one of Törley's vaulted cellars.
Background right: The yeast residue in the bottles is checked with the help of candles.

Pompadour

Hungaria
Grand Cuvée

Hungaria
Extra Dry

Törley
Brut

Claudius Caesar
Sec

Cheerful and relaxed
NEW YEAR

Advent, a time of contemplation, and the Christmas holidays which are usually celebrated within the family, are followed by a night of cheerful company: New Year's Eve. It is a night of boisterous, carefree celebration with family or friends. In Hungary no one would be thought discourteous if he or she turned up at the host's house and brought another six people along, without letting the host know. On the contrary, the more the merrier. But parties are held not just at home; every restaurant does great business, clubs and organizations celebrate in their meeting rooms, and even the State Opera is transformed into a massive ballroom. There is music and dancing everywhere, lots of laughter, and of course plenty to eat and drink.

The hurly-burly on the Great Pest Ring Road lends New Year's Eve in Budapest a unique local flavor. From late afternoon to early the next morning, all parking restrictions are removed and traffic regulations waived. Streets and sidewalks seethe with masked people in party mood who joke with each other and make a dreadful noise with screeching cardboard horns. A relaxed and cheerful mood prevails despite the freezing temperature, and sometimes driving snow.

Sweet and savory for New Year

Sertéskocsonya
Pork brawn. Served with pickled vegetables

Ropogós malacpecsenye
Roast sucking pig

Pezsgős káposzta
Cabbage braised in sparkling wine

Ecetes torma
Grated horseradish seasoned with vinegar

Korhelyleves
Sauerkraut soup (see page 153)

Lencseleves
Lentil soup

Lencsefőzelék
Stewed lentils

Sertéskocsonya (Pork brawn)

Chocolate lucky charms, which are popular gifts.

174

The New Year is welcomed in with paper horns and good cheer.

The revelry, which continues until the early hours of the morning, is interrupted by a moment of silence and remembrance throughout the land. The moment the clock strikes twelve, and before the toast to a happy New Year, the Hungarian national anthem is played on radio and television. Everyone stands and sings the melancholy melody, which at this moment sounds like a prayer: "Send the people of Hungary, God, Happiness, Luck, and Blessings … Grant joy once more to the people who long endured shame."

In Hungary there are special dishes and drinks for New Year – pork brawn and roast sucking pig are always part of New Year celebrations. The latter is usually served with cabbage cooked in dry sparkling wine, or braised cabbage. As in many countries of the world, Hungarians also welcome in the New Year with sparkling wine. The stylish drink is even sold from temporary stalls in the streets. Traditionally, hot weenies with mustard or horseradish, and fresh bread or bread rolls are eaten afterward.

After an eventful New Year's Eve, many try to ward off a hangover with *korhelyleves* (Night owl soup, see page 152). In some places lentil soup is served early in the morning. Certainly lentils in some form should be eaten on the first day of the year, to prevent you running out of money for the rest of the year – or so custom has it.

Left: New Year's Eve at the "New York" coffee house, Budapest, 1935.

NATIONAL PASSIONS

A feature of Hungarian cuisine is meat braised in its own juices, which are then transformed into a delicious sauce through the addition of onions, vegetables, and paprika. The hearty, savory aroma encourages the diner to mop up any sauce remaining on the plate with a piece of white bread. Only the shy use a fork – it increases the sensory experience, and thus pleasure, if you use your fingers to dunk the bread.

Be that as it may, this preference is allowed full rein only in the immediate family circle, because it is regarded as bad manners. Until the 15th century, though, even kings were in the habit of eating with their fingers. Today some restaurants, which specialize in historic cuisine, not only permit you to eat with your fingers, they even encourage it. Thus, for example, they do not serve soup with a spoon, but with a piece of hollowed-out bread crust.

Bread and drippings

Hungary is a nation where wealth has never blessed wide sectors of the population and where, even in the 20th century, every level of society, virtually every generation too, has at least been temporarily acquainted with poverty. In bad times, bread and pork drippings were one of the final pleasures were still within one's means. Many Hungarians remember bread and drippings very well, and have not crossed it off the menu, therefore, even in better times. It tastes so good that even the warnings from doctors and nutritionists, who are always drawing attention to the dangers of a high cholesterol level, have not been able to dent its popularity thus far.

Not all drippings are the same. White, homemade drippings, prepared according to good Hungarian traditions by sautéing bacon, and not by pressing, tastes delicious. Bread and drippings tastes even better if the bread is spread with yellow goose or duck drippings. The greatest pleasure, however, is promised by drippings from roast meat, in which the flavors of meat juices and seasonings mingle. This also includes any golden yellow fat, in which a splendid Hungarian goose liver has been roasted. As far as bread is concerned, however, there is no substitute. It must be fresh, white bread!

A juicy sausage with mustard tastes twice as good if eaten with the fingers.

The taste is intensified by sprinkling the bread and drippings with salt and paprika. Tomatoes and bell peppers are popular accompaniments, but above all different kinds of onions. Vegetables from the onion family even have a healthy side-effect, because they reduce the cholesterol level in the blood. Hungarians also demonstrate their love of bread and drippings to foreign friends and visitors, enjoying it at a wine bar, for example, because wine and spritzers are particularly delicious with this simple snack. Beer, on the other hand, does not go with bread and drippings at all.

On the move

Sooner or later, everyone on a train journey gets hungry. Many Hungarians don't visit the buffet, though, they bring provisions with them from home. The train is still in the station and already they are unpacking their movable feast: hard-boiled eggs, sandwiches, roast chicken drumsticks, pork escalopes in breadcrumbs, fruit, soda, and a thermos flask filled with hot coffee. Even those who are not so well equipped at least carry pretzels or candies with them. The aroma which wafts discreetly around the passengers lets you know whether lemon or garlic sausage is preferred in this part of the country. Both are popular snacks on the move, and more than a century ago people from different social backgrounds were already using them as provisions for the journey, as the author Gyula Krúdy (1878–1933) reported: "During a long train journey, I saw a man who normally made sure he ate at the Emperor's table, eating garlic sausage."

Snacks

The carefully conceived snack foods devised by the big food manufacturers were not the first introduction to the joy of snacking. Old Hungarian farmers also indulged: lightly toasted pumpkin seeds, natural or toasted sunflower seeds, and toasted corn kernels (not popcorn, prepared with oil and salt, which is a modern invention) were their staple snacks, and are just as popular today. True enthusiasts, however, do not buy the shelled seeds, which are sold in stores, but prefer to crunch the shells themselves between their teeth. Another snack which is popular throughout Hungary is boiled baby corn. This rather folksy delicacy may also be enjoyed in more stylish restaurants – with the help of special implements.

Dining in the train: food brought from home is most popular.

Sunflower seeds for nibbling are sold on the streets.

Boiled baby corn is so popular in Hungary that whole plantations of corn are cultivated specially.

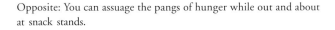
Opposite: You can assuage the pangs of hunger while out and about at snack stands.

HUNTING IN THE BÖRZSÖNY AND PILIS MOUNTAINS

Where the Buda green belt is now being transformed increasingly from a popular local recreation area to an elegant upmarket housing estate, Hungarian kings once rode on horseback to hunt with their greyhounds, noble falcons, or fanged cheetahs.

A little deeper into the forest, it is still possible to encounter the prized game. In the woods on the slopes of the mountains facing each other across the sharp bend in the river, separated only by the water; in the Börzsöny and Pilis mountains – where once Emperor Frederick I Barbarossa (1152–90) hunted too – an observant wanderer may spot wild boar. If he is quiet, and silently observes the powerful and somewhat dangerous animals, nothing can really happen to him. The promising heir to the throne, Prince Emmerich, son of the first Hungarian king Stephan and Gisela, the daughter of the Bavarian Emperor, fared differently. In 1031 his battle with a raging wild boar in the Pilis forest ended in death. Today's hunters, however, are equipped with good firearms, and have an easier time of it than their predecessors, who tried to kill the game with spears and arrows.

Hungarian cuisine has a good reputation for preparation of game. In the olden days cooks used butter rather than pork drippings, and flavored the meat with dill, horseradish, juniper berries, rosemary, sage, and wild marjoram, as well as various types of wild mushroom, rather than paprika.

The wild boar is a loner who joins the herd of wild sows and young animals only in the mating season.

Raspberries

Vast quantities of wonderful raspberries reach the markets from gardens, north of Budapest. Until ready-made fruit juice cornered the market, raspberry juice was a popular soft drink. Production is simple: place the fruit in a large bowl, and crush it with a spoon. Next day transfer the fruit to a clean piece of cheesecloth and squeeze out the juice. Put 4 cups/1 liter of raspberry juice in a saucepan with 2 cups/500 ml water and 5 cups/1 kg sugar and bring to the boil. Pour the hot syrup into bottles and cap them, then dry sterilize them (see page 300). To make a soft drink, dilute at a ratio of 1 part syrup to 3–4 parts soda water.

Tejfölös vadmalacleves
(Young wild boar soup with sour cream)

Tejfölös vadmalacleves
Young wild boar soup with sour cream (Photograph)

1¾ lbs/800 g lean young wild boar meat
1 medium onion
3½ tbsp/50 g butter
4 tbsp flour
1 heaped tsp paprika
Salt
½ tsp pepper
¾ cup–1¼ cups/200–300 ml hot game stock
1 bay leaf
2 egg yolks
¾ cup/200 ml sour cream

Remove any bristles and sinews from the meat, then dice it and place the dice in cold water. Melt the butter in a saucepan. Sauté the grated onion, stirring all the time, until translucent. Sprinkle the flour over the onion, and continue stirring until the flour foams and turns golden. Take the pan off the heat and stir in the paprika. Drain the meat and add it to the pan. Season the meat with salt and pepper. Add the stock and bay leaf. Cover the pan, bring to a boil, and simmer slowly. When the meat is semicooked, add 4 cups/1 liter of water and continue cooking. Finally beat together the egg yolks and sour cream, and use the mixture to thicken the soup.

Gombás vaddisznótokány
Wild boar Tokány with mushroom sauce

1¼ lbs/600 g wild boar (shoulder or leg)
3½ tbsp/50 g butter
1 large onion
1 heaped tsp paprika
Salt
½ tsp pepper
3½ oz/100 g bacon
9 oz/250 g mushrooms (porcini or morels)
3 tbsp flour
¾ cup/200 ml sour cream

Remove any bristles and sinews from the meat and cut it into strips. Melt the butter in a saucepan and sauté the grated onion in it until golden brown. Take off the heat and stir in the paprika, then add the meat and a splash of water. Season to taste with salt and pepper. Put the pan back on the heat, cover and braise. Cut the bacon into thin strips. Sauté the bacon in a skillet until crisp. Add the mushrooms, thinly sliced, then season sparingly with salt and sweat the mushrooms in their own juices. When the wild boar is tender, add the mushroom mixture. Blend together the flour and sour cream, and add it to the meat, stirring all the time. Bring to the boil and simmer the sauce until reduced and thickened.

FELSŐ-
MAGYARORSZÁG

NORTHERN HUNGARY

Northern Hungary offers two delightful and completely contrasting types of scenery: the forested uplands of the north, and the plain which borders them to the south and east, threaded with romantic river meadows. The mountain regions of Mátra and Bükk are richly stocked with game, attracting hunters year after year. The country's anglers are also drawn to Northern Hungary; the Tisza and Bodrog rivers are described as an anglers' paradise. The best trout in the country can be caught in a picturesque mountain stream in the Bükk. At the foot of the uplands lie the vineyards responsible for two world-famous Hungarian products: Tokay and Egri Bull's Blood.

Fruit-farming predominates down on the plain. The produce of the many plum orchards of Szatmár and Bereg is used mainly to make dried prunes, purée or plum brandy. Around Szabolcs, on the other hand, it is the huge plantations of apple orchards that characterize the countryside. The sandy soils of Nyírség, meanwhile, produce the best potatoes in the country.

The easternmost part of the country has barely opened up to tourism. Those who do venture into the small, secluded villages here will not only encounter a friendly welcome, but may also be fortunate enough to sample some rare delicacies.

Favored by Nature
HUNGARY'S APPLE ORCHARD

Apples account for half of Hungary's annual fruit production. The largest apple orchards and plantations are concentrated in three areas: the county of Zala, southwest of Lake Balaton; the sandy soils of the lowlands which lie between the river Tisza and the Danube; and, most importantly, Northern Hungary, especially the northeastern regions of Bodrogköz and Nyírség. The sandy soil of the northeast is not only good for growing rye, an undemanding crop; it also produces seven to nine tons per acre (15–20 tonnes per hectare) of excellent apples. Every village here earns its living from apple-growing, which dominates local agriculture as a result not only of the favorable soil and climate, but of the proximity of large markets within Hungary and in neighboring countries, and the availability of trained labor.

Hardly a domestic garden or allotment is without its apple tree. The great range of varieties grown there is no longer reflected in the markets, however, which are now dominated by the large-scale producers. The leading apple variety on the market is Jonathan, introduced from America 200 years ago. This variety has become the most widely distributed apple in Hungary, and at times accounts for half of the country's production. Beneath the apple's red skin is a delicate flesh which melts in the mouth, and also has an appetizing crunch when bitten into; the country's finest apple juice is produced from Jonathans.

Hungary's most popular apple varieties apart from Jonathan include Golden Delicious, Idared, Jonagold, and Starking. However, the constantly changing tastes of consumers mean that the apple producers of Szabolcs cannot rely on their success with the established varieties. They are constantly trying to improve their production, by grafting or by creating new varieties.

The Hungarian consumer pays scant regard to varieties that are only suitable for immediate consumption or solely for industrial processing; they prefer apples that taste good and store well.

Concentrated apple juice

Concentrated apple juice is one of the export success stories of the Hungarian food trade; 38,500–44,000 tons (35,000–40,000 tonnes) of it are produced annually. Ninety percent of production is exported worldwide. The concentrate is in demand for its pleasant flavor, neither too sweet nor too sharp. The precious aromatic substances it contains are removed during production, and can be re-added to the final product in the desired quantity. The strength of the concentrate depends on the customer's wishes.

Left: Crisp, red apples are a delight to the eye as well as the palate. They are wrapped in tissue paper for transport, to prevent damage to the skins.

Main photograph, opposite: Hardworking fruit pickers take a break and eat freshly picked apples.

Harvesting machines have not yet succeeded in replacing hand-picking.

Apples are harvested from late summer well into the fall.

A large number of seasonal workers earn a living during the harvest.

Local students often help out.

Alma pongyolában
Apple fritters

2 eggs	
2 tsp sugar	
1¼ cups/300 ml milk	
Scant ½ cup/100 ml white wine	
A pinch of salt	
1⅔ cups/200 g flour	
1¼ lbs/600 g sharp-flavored apples	
About 2 cups/500 ml oil for deep-frying	
Ground cinnamon and confectioners' sugar	

Beat together the egg yolks and sugar until frothy. Add the milk, wine, and a pinch of salt. Add the flour little by little, beating constantly, until the mixture has a thick liquid consistency.
Beat the egg whites until stiff, and fold carefully into the batter mixture. Peel and core the apples, and cut into ¼ inch/5 mm thick rings. Heat a generous quantity of oil until bubbling. Dip the apple rings in the batter, then drain off the excess and fry in the oil until golden. Sprinkle with cinnamon and sugar, and serve hot.

Almás rétes
Apple strudel

Strudel pastry	
Generous 2 lbs/1 kg sharp-flavored apples	
½ tsp ground cinnamon	
¾–1 cup/150–200 g sugar	
¾ cup/100 g ground walnuts or breadcrumbs, optional	
Confectioners' sugar, optional	

Use either homemade strudel pastry (see pages 114–117) or use store-bought (see page 117). Peel and core the apples. Slice finely, and sprinkle with cinnamon and sugar. Leave to stand for 20 minutes, then press to extract any excess juice. Scatter the ground walnuts or breadcrumbs onto the pastry to cover a strip of about a hand's width. Place the apples on top of the nuts, and roll up the pastry. Bake as described on page 117. Sprinkle the cooked strudel with confectioners' sugar (optional).

Hungary's fruit harvest consists not only of apples, of course, but pears, too (above). The most important varieties are Arabitka, various Beurré varieties, Clapp's Favorite, and Gyula Guyot and Dahant.

Eating apples

Golden Delicious
Popular variety having a greenish yellow color, often with dark green or brownish mottling. Delicately sweet flavor when fully ripe.

Jonagold
Lovely yellow apple, usually with orange-red blush on the side toward the sun. Flavor has a spicy, aromatic character; ripens early and stores well. Originated as a cross between Jonathan and Golden Delicious.

Idared
Aromatic apple with pleasant acidity. Often acquires a beautiful deep red color when ripe. Of hybrid origin; one of Hungary's most popular apple varieties.

Starking
Lovely velvety red skin, aromatic flesh. Stores well; tastes best in spring.

Jonathan
Hungary's most popular apple variety, originally from America. Delicate fruit flesh beneath a striated yellow and red skin. Very aromatic.

PRESERVING FRUIT

Two traditional methods of fruit preservation continue in Hungary much as they always have done: drying and sterilizing. The reason may well be the incomparable flavor that these two methods give to the fruit; one that freezing, popular as it is, does not achieve.

In the area of Szatmár – where plums and apples abound – the tradition of drying fruit is still widespread. Drying seems a very simple process: the freshly picked and sorted fruit is first spread out in the sun, then transferred to drying sheds, where it loses most of its moisture content. Appearances can be deceptive, however; the length of drying time and temperature are very important. If the fruit is dried too slowly or not long enough, it will become mouldy; if it is dried too quickly, it remains moist inside, and will rot. Dried for too long, the fruit becomes excessively dry and breaks. Dried fruit is best stored hanging in a cool, preferably airy place, in a finely woven cotton or linen bag. Some types of fruit are cut up before drying; apples and pears are sliced, apricots and peaches pitted and usually cut in half. Other types, such as plums and morello cherries, are left whole. Apples and pears may also be peeled. Plums are sometimes pitted and stuffed with a piece of walnut before drying.

Dried fruit is often served stewed in Hungary; it is boiled with cloves, cinnamon sticks, and lemon peel or lemon slices; sugar is sometimes added.

Sterilized fruit is often served as a dessert, or is used to fill a fruit flan. Fruit for preserving must be perfect and not overripe. The containers used are glass preserving jars, sealed with a rubber ring or an airtight screw top; these too must be in perfect condition. The jars, along with the lids and rubber rings, are scrupulously cleaned and rinsed with boiling water before use, and left upside down on a kitchen cloth to drain instead of being wiped dry.

.

Below: Harvesting is done by shaking the branches with long poles. The fruit falls onto a plastic sheet spread out on the ground.

Plums shaken from the tree are dried as prunes, distilled into brandy, or cooked to make purée.

Women sort the plums straight from the plastic sheeting, where they have fallen, into wooden crates. No machinery is used.

The drying process demands a great deal of experience. The resulting prunes must be neither too dry nor too moist.

The prunes are inspected as they dry.

Above: The plums are sorted before drying.

To preserve apricots and peaches in rum

4½–5½ lbs/2–2.5 kg semiripe apricots or peaches (still hard)
Juice of 1 lemon
2½ cups/500 g sugar
3½ tbsp rum (at least 54% vol)
Preservative, as required

Wash and drain the fruit thoroughly. Peel and pit it, and sprinkle with lemon juice. Place the fruit into a 6 lb/2 liter capacity glass preserving jar, sprinkling each layer with sugar. Mix the rum with preservative, if used. Pour the rum over the fruit. Seal the jar well, and place in the sun until the sugar has completely dissolved (about 3–4 days). The top layer may become discolored brown, but this is natural and need cause no concern. The fruit preserved in this way retains its characteristic flavor. If no preservative is used, the fruit should be eaten quickly.
Another method is to add enough rum to fill the jar. This preserves the fruit for longer, but it loses its characteristic fruit flavor.

To preserve cherries and plums

Wash the cherries or common plums in plenty of cold water, then rinse under running water in a colander and drain thoroughly. Remove the stalks, and pits if desired. Prepare the jars, and fill with fruit, tapping the bottom of the jar on the work surface occasionally.

Add enough sugar syrup to cover the fruit completely, leaving a space of about ¾ inch/2 cm at the top of the jar. To make the sugar syrup, take a generous 2 pints/1 liter of water for each 8½ lb/scant 4 kg of fruit, and boil with sugar as follows: 1½ cups/300 g for sweet cherries, 2 cups/400 g for morello cherries, and 2½ cups/500 g for common plums.
A clove or a piece of cinnamon stick can be placed in each jar, if desired. Seal the jars immediately and sterilize by boiling in a preserving pan for 20–30 minutes (see page 300) The temperature for cherries should be 175 °F/80 °C, for common plums, 165 °F/75 °C.

Vörös boros aszalt szilva
Prunes in red wine

7 oz/200 g pitted prunes
1 tsp sugar
Peel of 1 lemon
3 cloves
1 small piece of cinnamon stick
¾ cup/200 ml red wine

Place the prunes, sugar, lemon peel, cloves, cinnamon, and red wine into a saucepan. Cover, then boil for 15–20 minutes. Remove the spices and drain the prunes, then leave to cool. They can be served as an accompaniment to roast meat and taste especially good with roast goose

Prunes
Whether pitted or not, halved or whole, sweet or slightly sharp – but always intense in flavor – prunes eaten raw are a treat. Soaked, they make an excellent accompaniment to meat or a delicious dessert.

A fire is lit in the drying oven. The plums are spread on wooden trays (main photograph) and placed on top of the oven.

Sweet and morello cherries as a filling for fruit tarts and desserts

11 lb/5 kg sweet or morello cherries (only just ripe)
Generous 2 lb/1 kg sugar
Preservative, as required
Scant ½ cup/100 ml rum
1–2 cloves
1 small piece of cinnamon stick

Wash and pit the cherries, and remove the stalks. Place in a bowl with a non-metallic finish, such as plastic, glazed earthenware, or enamel. Add the sugar, preservative, rum, 1–2 cloves, and the cinnamon. Mix well, and cover. Steep for 2 days in the refrigerator, stirring thoroughly with a wooden spoon at least 3 times a day. Then transfer the fruit to the sterilized preserving jars, and pour in the juice. Seal well. The fruit can be stored for a long period; it retains its quality even after the jar has been opened.

Variation

Wash and pit the cherries and remove the stalks. Place in the sterilized jars, layering the fruit with preserving sugar, and including 1–2 cloves and a piece of cinnamon stick in each jar. For 11 lb/5 kg of fruit, allow about 6 cups/1.2 kg preserving sugar for sweet cherries, and 8 cups/1.6 kg for morello cherries. Seal the jars, and sterilize in a preserving pan for 25 minutes at 175 °F/80 °C (see page 300).

Sweet and morello cherries are good for preserving in jars.

Generous fillings; exquisite casings

FILLED PASTA

There is a saying *"Derelye – magyar ember ereje,"* meaning roughly *"Derelye* gives the Hungarian strength." It shows the importance placed on filled pasta *(derelye)* in Hungary.
The common local name for pasta filled with plum purée is *barátfüle*, literally "monk's ears." This dish used to be a popular meal to serve during Lent.

Szilvalekváros derelye (Barátfüle)
Pasta with plum purée filling
(Photograph)

| 3⅓ cups/400 g flour |
| 2 eggs |
| A pinch of salt |
| 9 oz/250 g plum purée |
| 1 egg white |
| 1¾ cups/100 g fresh breadcrumbs |
| 6½ tbsp/100 g butter |
| Ground cinnamon and confectioners' sugar |

Knead the flour, eggs, and salt to a smooth, firm dough. Shape into a ball and leave to rest for 30–60 minutes, covered with a cloth. Handle the dough quickly from this time on, to prevent it from drying out. Roll it out very thinly, and cover one half with a kitchen cloth. Dot the other half with plum purée at regular intervals, 1½ inches/4 cm apart, using a teaspoon. Mix 1–2 teaspoons of water with the egg white, beating with a fork. Brush the dough between the heaps of plum purée with the egg white mixture. Remove the cloth, and fold the other half of the dough over the plum purée. Press down firmly in between the heaps of filling. Cut into separate squares, each containing one heap of filling, using a pasta cutter.
Cook in boiling water in a covered saucepan for 8–10 minutes. Meanwhile, brown the breadcrumbs in the butter until golden. When the pasta squares are cooked, transfer them to a sieve to drain, then add them to the pan of breadcrumbs. Shake the pan carefully to coat the pasta; do not stir.
Serve hot, accompanied by a mixture of sugar and cinnamon.

Túrós derelye
Pasta with quark filling

| 1 portion of pasta dough (see preceding recipe *Szilvalekváros derelye*) |

For the filling:

| 9 oz/250 g quark (smooth cottage cheese) (half fat) |
| 5 tbsp confectioners' sugar |
| ½ tsp vanilla extract |
| ½ tsp grated lemon zest |
| 1 egg yolk |
| 1–2 tbsp semolina as required |

Follow the method described for *Szilvalekváros derelye* (left), simply replacing the plum purée with a quark filling. To make this, stir together all the filling ingredients apart from the semolina. If the resulting mixture is too liquid, blend in 1–2 tablespoons of semolina until the right consistency is reached.

Tüdős táska
Pasta with lung filling
(to serve in a soup)

For the filling:

| 7 oz/200 g calf's lung |
| Salt |
| ½ tsp marjoram |
| 1 bay leaf |
| ½ small onion |
| A bunch of parsley |
| 2 tbsp/30 g lard or white vegetable fat |
| ¼ tsp pepper |
| 1 egg |
| 1 tbsp fine fresh breadcrumbs |

For the dough:

| 2 eggs |
| ¾ cup/100 g flour |

Soak the lung well. Select a sufficiently large saucepan, and bring some water to the boil with the salt, marjoram, and bay leaf. Cook the lung in this. Grind the cooked lung.
Chop the onion and parsley finely. Heat the lard, and fry the onion until translucent. Add the ground lung, parsley, and a generous 3 tablespoons of the cooking liquid. Cook gently together, stirring occasionally, until the liquid has evaporated. Season with salt and pepper. Stir in the beaten egg and breadcrumbs. Cook on a medium heat, stirring constantly, until the mixture sets and acquires a moderately firm consistency.
To make the dough, knead together 1 egg, 1 egg yolk, and the flour until smooth. Cover and rest the dough for 30 minutes. Roll out thinly, then cover one half with a cloth. Dot the remaining half with walnut-size heaps of filling, about 1½ inches/ 4 cm apart. Brush the dough with egg white in between. Remove the cloth, and fold the other half of the dough over the filling. Cut into small squares with a pasta or pastry cutter.
Bring some bone stock or meat soup to a boil, and cook the pasta in it for about 10 minutes.

The dough ingredients: flour, eggs, and salt.

Roll out the dough very thinly.

Dot evenly with plum purée.

Brush the dough in between with egg white.

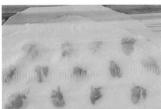

Fold over the other half of the dough to cover the filling.

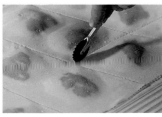

Cut into individual squares of filled pasta.

Cook in boiling salted water for 8-10 minutes.

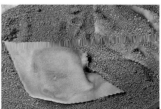

Carefully coat the pasta in breadcrumbs browned in butter.

Sure to keep out the cold
PLUM BRANDY

Hungarians enjoy a good, strong dram. Fruit brandy aids the digestion after a sometimes heavy meal. Taken on a raw day and an empty stomach, the inner glow keeps out the cold: the arteries widen; the blood can be felt coursing warmly to every extremity of the body. And an evening spent amicably drinking good schnapps with friends leaves no hangover, however often the glasses may have been raised.

Ever since the 17th century, plum brandy (*szilvapálinka*) has been distilled in the neighboring regions of Szatmár and Bereg at the easternmost tip of Hungary. The home-distillation of spirits is no longer permitted, but people are allowed to take their own fermented plums to a small local distillery to be distilled. Each person's fruit is kept separate from everyone else's. The product is called *kisüsti* (small vat). The way to distinguish a good, clear *kisüsti szilvapálinka* from an inferior imitation is to rub it on the back of the hand: a genuine *kisüsti* leaves a strong aroma of fruit.

The large Kisvárda distillery has a tradition going back over a hundred years. The products distilled here are made following ancient recipes but using ultramodern technology. Their most famous product, *Szatmári szilva* (Szatmár plum brandy) uses only local fruit. To these the brandy owes both its outstanding flavor and aroma and its exceptionally high alcoholic content.

The brandies of this locality are characterized by the wood aroma that develops during the long period of maturation in wooden casks. This wood contact is also responsible for the marked brownish hue. Some producers swear by the use of oak casks; others prefer mulberry.

Opposite: There is time for a chat while the fruit is distilled.

The plums are first placed in large containers ...

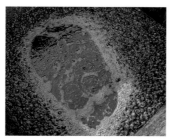

... where, without any additions, they are left to ferment.

Using a bucket, the fermented fruit ...

... is tipped into large copper stills.

The farmer has to supply the wood needed to heat the still.

For the distillation process, a fire is lit beneath the still.

Distillation continues until the brandy reaches the desired alcoholic strength.

Once the farmer is satisfied with the result, the clear plum brandy is run off into containers.

SZESZFŐZŐ ES
FINOMITOHELYISEG

The *kisüsti szilvapálinka* produced in a
small distillery is transferred to bottles of
more convenient size.

Easter eggs and the Easter bunny

Within the Christian tradition, the custom of dyeing eggs red goes back a thousand years. Red symbolizes the blood of Christ; the egg, eternal life. Other colors began to be used only three hundred years ago.

Hungarian Easter eggs are decorated with simple geometric shapes or ornamented with swirls of plants and flowers. Ancient symbols sometimes feature too: the wheel of the sun or the cockscomb, for example. The colorful flowers that adorn so many eggs echo the embroidery on Hungarian national costume. The decoration of Easter eggs is a Hungarian craft in its own right. Wax-resist dyeing is the most popular method: The pattern is painted onto the shell using a quill dipped in molten wax. The egg is dyed, and then warmed slightly to melt off the wax, so that the white, undyed pattern appears.

Engraving, an alternative method, requires the egg to be dyed first. The pattern is then engraved on with a knife. According to how deeply the surface is scratched, a deeper or paler color is revealed.

A simple but effective method is to boil onion skins in water; boiling the eggs in this gives them a lovely dark brown color. They are then rubbed with bacon rind skin to give them a sheen. Pretty, natural patterns in a paler color can be obtained by sticking leaves onto the shells of the eggs before they are boiled. Once the eggs are dyed, the leaves are removed.

Another traditional technique is to decorate blown eggs with tiny metal horseshoes. This requires some dexterity, so is done only by trained craftsmen.

The first chocolate eggs arrived on the market at the beginning of the 19th century. The confectioners decorated these eggs lavishly; some creations featured in the local press. One such was a chocolate egg with the picture – likewise executed in chocolate – of the chain bridge then under construction. Built between 1842 and 1849, this was the first fixed bridge over the Danube uniting Buda and Pest.

The Easter rabbit has rather more recent origins; it probably did not reach Hungary until the 20th century. It comes from a German cultural background, and is first mentioned at the end of the 17th century. Unlike the other Easter customs, which are rural in origin, the Easter bunny spread from the town outward.

Left and far right: After High Mass on Easter Sunday, the priest blesses the food brought by the faithful. Each basket is covered with a fine white cloth. At the top lies the Easter loaf.

Many walnut trees are to be seen in Hungary. They grow to a height of nearly 100 feet/30 meters.

The preference is for thin-shelled walnuts. They are easier to crack by hand.

Walnut trees

Walnut trees are found in great numbers all over Hungary. People value not only the walnuts, but the tree itself: a shade in summer, and a symbol of optimism for the future, for it is said that when people plant a walnut tree, it is their grandchildren who will be able to enjoy its fruit. Walnuts with especially thin shells are the most desired. They are easy to crack by hand, and so ideal for immediate consumption. Ground walnuts often feature in Hungarian cooking, and many families still use their grandmother's old grinder. This type results in less stress and less loss of oil from the nuts as compared with modern electric machines,

POGÁCSA

In Hungarian folk tales, the heroes always take *pogácsa* baked in embers as food for the journey when they set out on their adventures. These are small pastries, which can be savory or sweet, and are preferably eaten hot. Widely different in size and flavor, they have in common their circular shape. The diameter can vary from the dimensions of a thimble to those of a drinking tumbler.

Pogácsa can be any size. However, all the rounds in any one batch should be the same size. They can then be given the same cooking time.

Vajas pogácsa
Butter pogácsa
(Photograph)

Generous 4 cups/500 g flour
I tbsp confectioners' sugar
⅔ cake/10 g compressed yeast
2 egg yolks
I cup/250 g butter
Pinch of salt
Scant ½ cup/100 ml sour cream
I egg for glaze

Sift the flour and sugar. Add the remaining ingredients, and work together to form a smooth dough. Roll out and fold over, so that the dough is four layers thick (see Puff Pastry, page 298). Rest for 20 minutes in a cold place. Repeat the process twice more. Then roll out the pastry to a thickness of just under ¼ inch/ 5 mm, and score the surface. Cut into rounds. Place these on a floured baking pan, brush with beaten egg, and bake in a preheated medium oven for 30–40 minutes until golden.

Túrós pogácsa
Quark pogácsa

10½ oz/300 g quark (smooth cottage cheese)
2½ cups/300 g flour
5 tsp baking powder
1¼ cups/300 g butter
Generous pinch of salt
Lard or white vegetable fat for greasing
I egg yolk for glaze

Pass the quark through a sieve. Sift the flour and baking powder. Knead the butter, salt, flour, and quark to a smooth dough. Rest it in the refrigerator for at least 1½ hours (ideally 2 hours). Preheat the oven. Roll out to just under ¼ inch/5 mm, and fold to four layers of thickness (see Puff Pastry, page 298). Repeat this process four or five times. Then score the top and cut into small rounds. Place on a greased baking sheet. Brush the tops with beaten egg yolk, ensuring that it does not run down the sides. Bake in a preheated hot oven for about 30 minutes.

Pogácsa can be made using a variety of doughs and flavorings, and in different sizes.

The ingredients for butter pogácsa.

Mix all the ingredients together.

Knead the dough until smooth.

Roll out to just under ¼ inch/5 mm thick on a floured surface.

Fold over each end of the rectangle to the middle.

Fold over once more in the middle. Leave the dough to rest.

Then roll out again.

Score the surface in both directions before cutting into rounds.

POTATOES

Potatoes are grown all over Hungary. The main production areas are around the small village of Nógrád in the Börzsöny Range north of Budapest, and in the region of Szabolcs in the northeast of the country, with its sandy soils. Both areas are known for their regional potato recipes. These recipes owe more to the influence of nearby Slovakia, where potatoes are very popular, than to the fact that the ingredients are grown locally.

One of the oldest and most popular methods is to bake the potatoes in their skins. The potatoes are placed in the embers, over a glowing fire, or in an oven. No water or fat is used in the cooking. They are eaten with salt and butter or goose drippings. A baked potato used to be a good substitute for wearing gloves among poor families: children would be given a hot potato by their mothers to put in their pockets and warm their fingers on the long walk to school. Shoemakers' apprentices were also given potatoes by the master craftsman.

The potato came originally from South America. In the last 250 years, it has become one of the staple foods in Europe.

When the potato noodles rise to the surface, this indicates that they are cooked.

They are then coated in fried breadcrumbs.

Prézlis nudli
(Potato noodles in breadcrumbs)

These served not only as hand warmers, but as the morning meal. This practice is the origin of the Hungarian nickname for potatoes, "shoemakers pancakes."

Until quite recently, potato parties used to be held in Buda's inns on the day after Christmas. The custom is said to go back to the time when a severe snowstorm forced people out walking in Buda to take refuge in the nearest inn. The only way of catering for so many unexpected guests was to give them baked potatoes.

Potato dishes

Hagymás tört krumpli:
Mashed
potato with fried onions

Krumplifőzelék:
Boiled, sliced
potato with white sauce made
from a roux and sour cream

Krumplileves:
Potato soup with
paprika and celeriac

Sült újkrumpli:
New potatoes,
fried whole or in chunks

Tócsi:
Potato pancakes with
caraway

Prézlis nudli
Potato noodles in breadcrumbs
(Photograph on opposite page)

2¼ lbs/1 kg floury potatoes
Generous 2 cups/250 g flour
1 egg
2 tbsp/30 g butter
Pinch of salt
Flour for work surface
2 cups/100 g breadcrumbs
⅓ cup/80 g lard or white vegetable fat

Boil the potatoes in their skins. Peel while warm, and mash. Cool slightly. Knead together with the flour, egg, butter, and salt. Roll out the dough to about ½ inch/1 cm thick on a floured work surface. Cut it into lengthwise strips 1¼ inches/3 cm wide, then across at intervals of about ½ inch/1 cm. Take a piece at a time and work it into an elongated roll, by rolling it with the heel of the hand on the work surface. Leave the finished rolls lying separately on the work surface to rest until you are ready to cook them. Cook in plenty of salted, boiling water over a high heat, moving the potato noodles around in the water frequently. Lift them out as soon as they rise to the surface, and drain well. Brown the breadcrumbs in the hot lard. Add the potato noodles. Cover with a lid, and shake to coat them in breadcrumbs. Serve with salt gherkins. Another popular way of serving these is as a sweet dish with confectioners' sugar or jam.

Szilvás gombóc
Plum dumplings
(Photograph below)

For the dumpling mixture:

2¼ lbs/1 kg floury potatoes
3 cups/350 g flour
1 egg
2 tbsp/30 g butter
Pinch of salt

Remaining ingredients:

1 lb/500 g plums
1 sugar cube per plum
½ tsp cinnamon
2 cups/100 g breadcrumbs
3½ tbsp/50 g butter
Ground cinnamon and confectioners' sugar

Prepare the dough for the dumplings as for potato noodles (previous recipe). Roll to ¼ inch/5 mm thick. Sprinkle with flour, and cut into 3 inch/8 cm squares. Wash and pit plums. Place one on each square, insert a sugar cube in space from which pit was removed, and sprinkle with cinnamon. Fold dough around the plum and press edges together to seal. Shape into dumplings. Place dumplings in boiling salted water. Wait for them to rise to the surface, then simmer for 4–5 minutes. Brown the breadcrumbs in butter. Drain cooked dumplings thoroughly, and transfer them to the pan with the breadcrumbs. Cover pan, and leave for 3–4 minutes before shaking to coat the dumplings. Sprinkle with cinnamon and confectioners' sugar to taste.

The ingredients for the dumplings: potatoes, salt, butter, flour, and eggs.

Mix thoroughly together.

Place a sugar cube in the center of the plum to replace the pit.

The dumplings need to simmer for a few minutes after they have risen to the surface.

PULSES

Rich in protein, carbohydrate, and minerals, pulses formed an indispensable part of the winter diet for centuries. The dried seeds are capable of being stored for years, which means they are available all year round. Hungarians mainly like to combine them with smoked meats and sausage.

A great variety of dried beans can be found for sale in Hungarian markets. They are used to make vegetable dishes, soups, and salads, and are especially popular in winter.

Sárgaborsó leves
Yellow pea soup

1 large onion
1½ cups/250 g yellow dried peas
Salt
2½ tbsp/40 g lard or white vegetable fat
3 tbsp flour
1 clove of garlic, crushed
½ tsp paprika
Generous pinch of pepper
1 bread roll (or white bread)

Peel the onion. Boil the peas and onion in a generous 4 pints/2 liters of water for 1 hour until tender. Season with salt. Melt the lard, and blend with the flour to make a roux. Remove from the heat, and stir in the garlic and paprika. Thicken the soup by blending with the roux. Season with pepper. Cut the bread into cubes, and brown them in a dry pan. Serve with the soup.

Bableves
(bean soup)

Bableves
Bean soup
(Photograph below)

1½ cups/250 g dried beans
1 medium carrot
1 medium parsley root
1 small onion
Salt
2½ tbsp/50 g lard or white vegetable fat
3 tbsp flour
1 clove of garlic, crushed
1 tsp paprika
1–2 tbsp vinegar (6%)
7 oz/200 g smoked sausage (of the type for boiling)
Scant ½ cup/100 ml sour cream

Soak the beans overnight. On the following day, clean the carrot and parsley root, and cut into strips. Peel the onion. Pour off the liquid from the beans. Place the beans and the prepared vegetables in a saucepan of cold water, then bring to the boil and cook for 1½ hours. Do not add salt until the beans are almost tender. Melt the lard, then blend in the flour and cook until the color darkens. Remove from the heat. Stir in the garlic and paprika. Thicken the soup by blending with the roux. Adjust flavor by adding a little vinegar. Remove the onion. Slice the sausage and add to the soup. Add the sour cream. Return briefly to the boil.
A variation is to use 1–2 bay leaves or a little tarragon instead of the root vegetables. The soup is often served in Hungary with *csipetke* (see page 39) that have been prepared beforehand.

Babos káposzta
Cabbage with beans

Scant 1 cup/150 g pinto beans
Generous 1 lb/500 g smoked rib of pork
10 oz/300 g sauerkraut
2 bay leaves
Salt to taste
1 large onion
1 clove of garlic
2 tbsp/30 g lard or fat
1 heaped tsp paprika
3 tbsp flour
¾ cup/200 ml sour cream

Soak the beans overnight. Also soak the smoked pork as necessary. Then place the sauerkraut in a saucepan. Drain and add the beans. Cut up the pork and add to the pan. Season with bay leaves, adding salt if necessary. The salt is better omitted if the smoked pork is strongly flavored.
Half fill the saucepan with water, and cook the ingredients over a low heat until tender, shaking the pan from time to time.
Chop the onion finely. Crush the garlic. Melt the lard, and sweat the onion and garlic until translucent. Remove from the heat and sprinkle with paprika. Blend the flour into the sour cream. Add to the onion. Blend with the sauerkraut and beans, and reheat until thoroughly boiling.

Babfőzelék
Vegetable dish of beans

3 cups/500 g dried beans (white or pinto beans)
1 small onion
1–2 bay leaves to taste
Salt
¼ cup/60 g lard or white vegetable fat
6 tbsp flour
1 tsp paprika
1 clove of garlic
1–2 tbsp vinegar
Sour cream to taste

Soak the beans overnight. Then place in a saucepan with the onion (and bay leaf or leaves as wished). Add just enough water to cover, then bring to the boil and cook for about 1½ hours. Top up with hot water as necessary during the cooking. Do not add salt until the beans are nearly tender. Melt the fat, then blend in the flour and cook until it darkens in color. Remove from the heat. Stir in the paprika and crushed garlic. Blend with the vegetables to thicken. Remove the onion before serving. Adjust seasoning with vinegar and stir in sour cream to taste.

Sárgaborsó főzelék
Vegetable dish of yellow peas

1 small onion
3 cups/500 g yellow dried peas
Salt
3½ tbsp/50 g lard or white vegetable fat
5 tbsp flour
2 cloves of garlic
Pepper
Onion rings
Oil for frying

Peel the onion and leave whole. Place the peas and onion in a saucepan of cold, salted water. Bring to a boil, and cook for about 1 hour, stirring frequently. The peas will cook down into a purée if they are cooked slowly. Further puréeing should then be unnecessary. Remove the onion at the end of the cooking time. Melt the lard, and blend the flour into it to form a roux. Add the crushed garlic. Blend the pea purée and the roux, then reboil thoroughly. Season with pepper. Brown some onion rings in oil, and scatter on top of the peas to serve.

Magyaros babsaláta
Hungarian bean salad

1½ cups/250 g large pinto beans
1 large onion
Salt
Vinegar
Sugar
Pepper
1–2 tsp oil to taste
Celery leaves or chives
1 hard-boiled egg (optional)

Soak the beans overnight. Pour off the liquid from the beans, then place them in a large saucepan. Cover well with fresh water, bring to the boil, and cook for about 1½ hours. Leave the beans in the cooking liquid to cool.
Then peel the onion and cut into fine rings. Mix with the beans. Season the liquid with salt, vinegar, sugar, and pepper, aiming for a pleasantly sharp flavor. Leave in the refrigerator to infuse for at least 1 day. The salad can be drizzled with oil before serving, if you wish. Garnish with finely chopped celery leaves or chives to serve. Sprinkle with a chopped hard-boiled egg, (optional). This makes a delicious winter family dish.

Szabolcsi töltött káposzta
Stuffed cabbage, Szabolcs style

Stuffed cabbage is a regional specialty of Szabolcs-Szatmár. It is made using white cabbage, and has a flavor that can hardly be bettered; nor even sauerkraut can rival the results.

1 white cabbage (about 2½ lb/ 1.2 kg)
1 medium onion
¼ cup/60 g lard or white vegetable fat
¼ cup/50 g rice
2¼ cups/250 g ground pork
1 egg
Salt
½ tsp pepper
4½ tbsp tomato paste
1–3 tsp sugar

Remove the stalk and outer leaves from the cabbage. Place the cabbage in boiling hot water for 5 minutes. Drain thoroughly and then separate the leaves. Cut out any thick veins and stems. Peel and grate the onion, and sweat in about half the lard. Then add the rice and fry briefly, stirring (1–2 minutes). Stir the onion and rice mixture into the meat, together with the egg. Season with salt and pepper, and mix well. Select some fairly small, tender cabbage leaves. Then spread them out flat and put 1–2 teaspoons of meat filling onto each. Roll the leaf around the filling, to make a cone-shaped package. The pointed end should be where the stalk was, and the other end tucked in.
Cut up the rest of the cabbage. Melt the remaining lard in a saucepan, and place the stuffed cabbage leaves in the pan with the chopped cabbage (one way is to layer them.) Dilute the tomato paste to four times its volume with water, then season with sugar and salt. Pour over the cabbage. Bring to the boil, and cook on a medium heat.

Cherries (main photograph) and many other types of fruit are on sale in Hungarian markets (above).

FRUIT SOUPS AND SAUCES

Soups and sauces made of fruit are very popular in Hungary. The soups have a creamy texture, and are best served cold. They make a refreshing meal on hot summer days.

The fruit sauces, which are thick, are served hot as an accompaniment to meat dishes, potatoes, and pasta pellets; sometimes even instead of a vegetable.

Those generally used are fruits with a rich, sharp flavor: apples, quinces, morello cherries, gooseberries, and rhubarb. If other fruits are used, lemon juice is usually added. Sugar or other sweeteners need to be added at the outset, and cooked with the fruit; the results are less good if the dish is sweetened at the end of preparation.

Almaleves
Apple soup
(Photograph above right)

1¼ lbs/600 g sharp-flavored apples
Small piece of lemon peel
Small piece of cinnamon stick
2 cloves
Pinch of salt
3 tbsp sugar
3 tbsp flour
¾ cup/200 ml sour cream

Almaleves (Apple soup)

Peel and core the apples, cutting away any brown marks and bruises. Slice thinly.
Place the lemon peel, cinnamon, and cloves in a cheesecloth bag or tea ball. Put the apples, salt, sugar, and the package of spices into a saucepan with about 3 pints/1.5 liters of cold water. Bring to the boil, and cook until the fruit is tender, but not too soft. Remove the spices.
Blend the flour with a little water until smooth, and stir in the sour cream. Use this mixture to thicken the soup.
Cool, and serve ice cold in chilled soup bowls.

Birsalmamártás
Quince sauce (Photograph below)

Generous 1 lb/500 g quinces
Pinch of salt
3 tbsp sugar
2 tbsp flour
Scant ½ cup/100 ml sour cream

Peel and core the quinces, and slice thinly. Place in a saucepan with enough cold water to just cover the fruit. Add the salt and sugar, and cook until the quinces are soft.
Blend the flour with a little water until smooth. Stir in the sour cream, and use the mixture to thicken the sauce.
Serve hot to accompany a meat dish, such as chicken.

Vörösboros meggyleves
Tipsy morello cherry soup

1¾ lbs/800 g morello cherries
4–5 cloves
Small piece of cinnamon stick
¾ cup/200 ml dry red wine
Juice of 1 lemon
⅔ cup/120 g superfine sugar
Pinch of salt
2 egg yolks
¾ cup/200 ml light cream

Wash and pit the cherries. Place the cloves and cinnamon in a cheesecloth bag. Cook the cherries in their own juice and 3⅓ cups/800 ml water, together with the red wine, strained lemon juice, sugar, salt, and spices. Take out half the cherries, using a slotted spoon. Purée these, and return to the soup. Bring to a boil. Meanwhile, mix the egg yolks into the cream. Add the cupful of the hot soup to this mixture, stirring constantly. Then pour the egg and cream mixture into the soup. Stir in, and reheat. Do not let it boil, or the egg will curdle. Finally, remove the spices.
Cool, and serve ice cold in chilled soup bowls.

Meggyleves
(Morello cherry soup)

Főtt tyúkhús birsalmamártással (Chicken with quince sauce)

WATERMELONS AND SWEET MELONS

Well chilled, juicy watermelons are one of the most refreshing delights to be found in the fruit market. Before the advent of the refrigerator, Hungarians used to chill melons either in their cellars, in a bucket let down into the well, or under running water. It was a frequent sight to see the father of a family returning home with a trophy from the market weighing 22–33 pounds (10–15 kilograms). Today, the preferred size is 9–11 pounds (4–5 kilograms), which means the melons can fit easily in the refrigerator.

Melons originally came to Hungary from the steppes of central Asia. They need plenty of light and warmth, and Hungary offered excellent growing conditions. The production areas around the villages of Heves and Csány, about 60 miles (100 kilometers) east of Budapest, are known the length and breadth of the country for the high quality of their produce. The growers have a fund of knowledge handed down from generation to generation, a sure guarantee of the

A knife with a rounded, convex blade is plunged into the melon to extract a plug of fruit for the customer to taste.

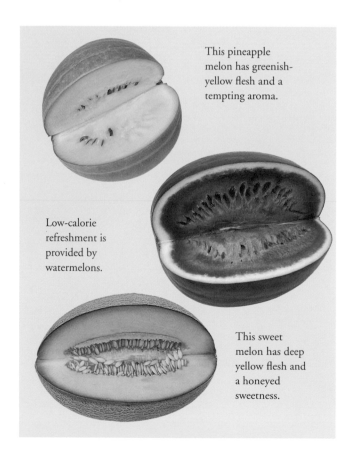

This pineapple melon has greenish-yellow flesh and a tempting aroma.

Low-calorie refreshment is provided by watermelons.

This sweet melon has deep yellow flesh and a honeyed sweetness.

finest standards. At harvest time, in July and August, tall piles of melons line the roadsides. A special place is cleared for them in the fruit and vegetable markets – an honor otherwise reserved only for the Christmas tree.

Something of a ritual attends the purchase of a melon in Hungary: customers pick out the melon themselves and examine it carefully by tapping it. If it emits a suitably hollow echo that meets with their approval, they hand it to the salesperson. It is then weighed and the obligatory question asked, "Shall I bore a hole in it?" This is usually met with an eager nod. After wiping the skin with a damp cloth, the salesperson plunges a convex-bladed knife into the melon, drawing out a cone-shaped plug of fruit. The customer can now taste the sample. If the taste is right, the deal is done.

Sweet melons are served as a dessert in Hungary, usually on their own, though sometimes in a fruit salad. To start a meal with melon is considered a snobbish indulgence. Family stories are told of melons being eaten in macho style in times past: tales of great-grandfathers who sprinkled their portion of sweet melon with snuff before devouring it. Those with a more sensitive digestion used paprika instead.

Melon seeds are today considered useless and simply thrown away, but a recipe dating back to 1601 had a way of using them: the crushed seeds were boiled in water and slightly sweetened with sugar to make a nourishing soup for invalids.

Early sweet melons are seen as a delicacy, fit for princes. Twigs and rushes were traditionally used to protect the ripening melons from hoar frost or overnight frosts. In the 17th century, the scientific researcher János Lippay recounted the case of a noblewoman who used real marten fur to cover her melons. "But thieves came in the darkness and took away the fur. So she lost not only the stolen fur, but the melons, too. They froze."

Dinnyekoktél
Melon cocktail

2¼ lbs/1 kg sweet melon
4½ lbs/2 kg watermelon
5 tbsp confectioners' sugar
Juice of 1 lemon
1¼ cups/300 ml muscatel wine
Scant ½ cup/100 ml apricot brandy
A few plums, morello cherries, or cherries preserved in rum, to taste

Cut away the tough center and seeds from the melons, then cut the flesh into fairly large cubes. Carefully mix the red and yellow melon cubes in a large glass bowl. Sprinkle with confectioners' sugar. Drizzle with the lemon juice, wine, and apricot brandy. Mix again carefully. Cover well, and leave to infuse for 4–6 hours in a refrigerator. Decorate with halved plums, morello cherries, or cherries preserved in rum before serving.

Bull's blood
EGER WINE

Above: István Dobó gave his men the Eger wine "Bull's Blood", to sustain them in battle against the Turks. The wine owes its name to the remarkable effect that this had on the enemy (see right).
Below: The picturesque baroque town of Eger is considered the most beautiful of its kind in Hungary.

At the foot of the Bükk mountains lies the town of Eger, one of the most beautiful and most frequently visited in Hungary. Its attractions include not only its history and artistic sights, but its world-famous wines, Egri Bikavér and Egri Leánkya. The former, widely known as Bull's Blood, is a potent, dry red wine that owes its deep ruby color to the grape skins which are fermented together with the grapes. It is a blend of several grape varieties. The main variety is Kékfrankos (Lemberger), which has replaced Kadarka, the grape formerly used. Its fine bouquet is nurtured by maturing with expert care and skill. Cabernet and Kékoporto, and occasionally Merlot, also contribute their share to the unique bouquet of Bull's Blood. The wine must bear the state-registered band around the neck, and cannot be sold without it. This was introduced to guard against imitations; it is the guarantee that this bottle of Bull's Blood genuinely comes from Eger.

The region has other excellent wines to offer, apart from Bull's blood. These include *Egri Medoc Noir* and *Egri Tramini. Egri Leányka* in particular, an outstanding white wine, deserves attention. The Hungarian grape variety Leányka (meaning "maiden"), which is found only in this area, ripens early. Its berries have a high sugar content, and the wine made from it has a slight sweetness and the scent of honey.

Eger's cellars are almost as famous as the wines themselves. Beneath the castle and great stretches of the town, there extends a network of passageways, formerly used for storage (especially of wine) or as a place of refuge in times of war. There are wine cellars throughout the area. The most famous place to find these is the "Valley of the Beautiful Women" (*Szépasszonyvölgy*), which has dozens of wine cellars side by side, serving the wines of the region. Originally, the cellars were simply carved into the rock. The wineries were then built in front of these.

It is said of the winemakers of Eger that they would be quite happy to spend their entire free time in the wine cellar. There used to be a special reason for this, up until about 30 years ago: it was considered improper for their wives to cross the threshold, so they were forbidden to do so. This provided a little peace for the men, whose wives could only stand at the door and try to persuade them to come home.

Many visitors to wine cellars take the opportunity of enjoying an extensive wine-tasting session. The winemaker pipettes the wine from the cask into glasses, then waits to see if more of that wine is wanted, or if it is time to proceed to the next cask. Calabashes, the hollowed-out fruits of the bottle gourd, were once used for this purpose. The plants were grown between the vines. Today, the decorated calabashes simply serve to adorn the winery walls; (bottle) gourds have long since been replaced by the glass variety for reasons of hygiene.

The winegrowers were legally granted the right to serve wine at the end of the 18th century. That was when the custom of selling wine literally by the draft originated. One draft cost 50 kreutzer, about five cents. Having paid, the customer was allowed to drink as much as he could swallow in one draft.

This custom has died out. However, in this region where wine has been grown for more than a thousand years, another tradition does survive: the proprietor always pours wine into his own glass first, but instead of drinking it, he pours it onto the ground. People unfamiliar with the custom might think he is rinsing the glass. But if asked, he will explain that the dead, too, should have their share.

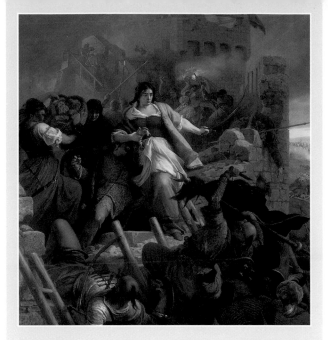

Bull's Blood

In 1552, Eger castle was besieged by the Turks. The defenders were vastly inferior in numbers, and by the fifth week of the siege, their strength was exhausted. The Turks began to storm the castle. The commander of the castle forces, István Dobó, then ordered the cellars to be opened, and the women gave red wine to the men engaged in the fighting. The besieging soldiers observed how the Hungarians, having imbibed the red liquid, were filled afresh with the spirit of battle. They thought that the Hungarians must have drunk the blood of bulls, giving them supernatural strength; without further ado, they retreated. It was 40 years before they dared risk another attack.

To judge from their behavior, the women must also have partaken of the wine. The historic chronicles relate that they, too, participated in the battle with courage and daring. They poured boiling water and pitch down onto the attackers, and threw rocks, playing a decisive role in what became a famous victory.

(Above: "The women of Eger" by Bertalan Székely)

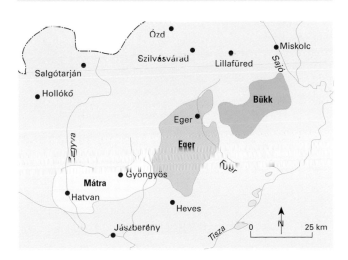

Monarchs of the forests
RED AND FALLOW DEER

Red and fallow deer are native to the whole of Hungary. Accordingly, the low mountain regions of Mátra and Bükk are ruled by the stag, that monarch of the Hungarian forests. The antlers of a royal stag are a universally sought-after trophy among huntsmen. Many of the world's finest antlers come from the forests of Hungary.

In past centuries, the stags of the Bükk mountains had a rival, a fellow monarch: the brown bear. The last of these was slain at the beginning of the 20th century, so bear's paw brawn will not feature on any menu in today's Hungary.

Szalonnás szarvascomb
Larded leg of venison

1¼ lbs/600 g leg of venison
3½ oz/100 g smoked bacon fat
Salt
1 large carrot
1 large parsley root
1 small onion
⅓ cup/80 g lard
1 clove of garlic
6–8 peppercorns
1 tsp capers
2 bay leaves
3 tbsp all-purpose flour
¾ cup/200 ml dry white wine
1 tbsp sugar
Juice of 1 lemon

Extract the tendons from the meat. Cut the bacon fat into strips. Stud the leg of venison all over with the bacon fat, and rub thoroughly with salt. Clean and slice the carrot and parsley root. Peel and chop the onion. Heat the lard in a large pot (suitable for braising meat), and brown the venison quickly on all sides to seal. Add the carrot, parsley root, onion, crushed garlic, peppercorns, capers, and bay leaves. Fry the vegetables, then add a little water. Cover, and cook the venison over a low heat. Remove the meat and keep hot.

Then make the sauce. Reduce the cooking juices in the pot (do not remove the vegetables). Sprinkle with flour, blend in and cook. Pour on the white wine, together with the same quantity of water, and deglaze. Finally, pass the sauce through a sieve, and adjust the seasoning with sugar and lemon juice.

Slice the meat and arrange on a serving dish. Pour over the sauce. Serve with potato croquettes.

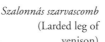

Szalonnás szarvascomb
(Larded leg of venison)

Savanyúleves szarvasborjúból
Piquant cream of young venison soup

1¾ lbs/800 g shoulder of young venison
1 large onion
¼ cup/60 g lard or white vegetable fat
2 cloves of garlic
1 tsp paprika
Salt
1 large parsley root
1 large carrot
2 bay leaves
1 large sweet bell pepper (capsicum)
1 medium tomato

2 egg yolks

¾ cup/200 ml sour cream

Juice of 1 lemon

Bone and dice the meat.
Peel the onion and chop finely.
Sweat in the hot lard until
translucent. Remove from the
heat, and stir in the crushed garlic
and the paprika. Add the meat
immediately, and season with salt.
Cover and cook on a low heat for
8–10 minutes.
Clean the parsley root and carrot,
then dice them and add to the
meat. Briefly continue to cook,
covered. Then add 3 pints/1.5
liters of water and the bay leaves.

Simmer for about 1½ hours.
Wash the sweet bell pepper,
remove the stalk, seeds, and ribs,
then cut into strips. Wash the
tomato, and cut into eight. When
the meat is almost cooked, add
the sweet bell pepper and tomato.
As soon as the meat is fully
cooked, beat together the egg
yolks and sour cream. Add to the
soup, stirring continuously. Do
not allow to boil, or the egg will
curdle.
Finally, season the soup with
lemon juice.

Szarvasgulyás
Venison goulash

Generous 1 lb/500 g venison (leg
or shoulder)

1 large onion

2 cloves of garlic

⅓ cup/80 g lard or white
vegetable fat

1 level tsp paprika

½ tsp caraway seeds

½ tsp pepper

A generous pinch of marjoram

Salt

7 oz/200 g potatoes

1 medium carrot

1 medium parsley root

Cut the meat into small cubes,
and place in cold water for about
1 hour. Peel the onion and chop
finely. Crush the garlic. Melt the
lard in a large saucepan and sweat
the onion and garlic. Then add
the meat and seasonings. Cover
and braise for about 1½ hours.
Meanwhile, peel and dice the
potatoes. Clean and slice the
carrot and parsley root. Shortly
before the end of the cooking
time, add the vegetables to the
saucepan, together with a
generous 2 pints/1 liter of water.
Cook until tender.

Buying and cooking game

The quality of game is not
immediately obvious from its
appearance, so it is important
to buy the meat from a reliable
supplier or huntsman.
Expert hanging – that is, the
initial storage of the meat – is
essential for it to develop its full
flavor and become tender. The
tough meat of older animals is
tenderized with the use of a
pickling liquid that also lessens

the strong gamey flavor.
Game is low in fat. It therefore
dries out easily, and is often
larded with bacon fat. Game
birds are often wrapped in
bacon for cooking.
Cooking methods are roasting
or braising. The meat should
always be cooked thoroughly to
ensure that any harmful
organisms are destroyed.

Old bottles of Tokay, covered with cobwebs and a thick coat of mold or bloom.

cause of the shriveling and rotting was the mold we call "noble rot," *Botrytis cinerea*, whose spores penetrate the grapeskins. The mold encourages the evaporation of moisture, reducing the acidity of the fruit, and increasing the sugar content, possibly to as much as 70%.

The grape harvest starts at the end of October, continuing through the whole of November. Only the shriveled grapes are selected from the bunches harvested. These desiccated grapes are mashed, either by being trodden to a pulp in a vat in the traditional manner, or by being crushed in a special mill.

Great labyrinths of cellars extend beneath the villages of the region. The layer of earth above them ranges from 16 to 165 feet (5 to 50 meters), according to the variations in ground level at the surface. In places, several cellars lie one above the other, connected by vertical shafts. Most were dug between the 15th and 19th centuries. In the early days, they served as places of refuge in war.

The cellars have an ideal level of humidity and a constant temperature of 50–54 °F (10–12 °C). The walls are covered in a thick layer of mold called *Cladosporium cellare*. It feeds on the alcohol evaporating from the casks. This creates the microclimate essential for the production of the unique aroma and flavor of Tokay wines. The wines begin their maturation in fairly small oak casks (either *Gönci*, with a capacity of 36 gallons or 136.6 liters, or *Szerednye*, 58 gallons or 200 liters). The wood is penetrated by the air carrying the beneficial mold.

Tokaji aszú

All the wines of Tokaj-Hegyalja are of excellent quality, but *Tokaji aszú* is the undisputed king among these aristocrats. According to tradition, the world has Zsuzsanna Lórántffy, wife of Prince György I Rákóczi, to thank for this wine. We are told that once, in the middle of the 17th century, the advance of the Turkish army caused her to postpone the grape harvest on the prince's estates near Tokaj. By the time the grapes were eventually pressed, they were shriveled and moldy. To everyone's astonishment, they yielded a quite exceptional wine. Its fame soon spread far beyond the country's borders. The

Opposite: The layer of mold on the cellar walls is important for preserving the humidity.

Tokay at a glance

Only white wines are made in Tokaj-Hegyalja. Over 90% of the grapes grown are Furmint and Hársevelű. Muscat lunell and a local variety called Oremus are used to boost the flavor and aroma. The wines (apart from a few exceptions mentioned below) are produced from several grape varieties.

Tokaji aszú: One of the finest liqueur wines in the world, with a high alcoholic strength; often served as an apéritif, or as a dessert wine. The best temperature for drinking is 57–61 °F/14–16 °C.

Tokaji aszú eszencia: The "king of kings," the rarest type of Tokay. This is a *Tokaji aszú* enriched with the juice squeezed from grapes with noble rot simply by the pressure of the berries in the wooden tub. One tub of desiccated grapes yields from 1–4¼ pints/0.5–2 liters of "essence," depending on the vintage. One liter of essence contains at least 250 grams of fruit sugar and 50 grams of non-sugar extract (4 oz fruit sugar and ⅚ oz non-sugar extract per pint). It achieves a maximum alcoholic strength of 6–10%/vol. The wine matures for a minimum of 15 years in wooden casks, to develop flavor, bouquet, and aromas. It never ferments completely on account of the high sugar content.

Tokaji szamorodni

The name Szamorodni comes from the Polish *samo rodni*, meaning "as it grows." It indicates that both plump and shriveled grapes are processed, instead of selecting the berries affected by "noble rot" from the bunches harvested. There are two categories:

Tokaji szamorodni, száraz (dry): An amber-colored, fiery wine with body and high alcoholic strength. Long years of maturation are the key to its fine qualities. The best temperature for drinking is 50–54 °F/10–12 °C.

Tokaji szamorodni, édes (sweet): The natural sweetness of this wine is lent an understated elegance by certain acids. Its bouquet is best appreciated at 54–57 °F/12–14 °C.

The following wines are produced from a single grape variety:

Tokaji furmint, száraz (dry): Rich in acidity, clean, crisp, and balanced, with a classy aroma. It is usually matured in wooden casks for two years, where it develops a slight storage bouquet.

Tokaji furmint, félédes (semi sweet): Matured for a minimum of two years.

Tokaji hárslevelű: A fiery, dry wine with a soft flavor and aroma. It spends two years maturing in oak casks before being bottled.

Tokaji muscat lunell: An elegant, semisweet wine with a delicate muscat nose. Matured for two years in oak.

Tokaj-Hegyalja has yet more excellent wines to offer. Usually bottled within a year, they are fresh and fruity and are becoming increasingly popular in Hungary.

One wooden tub (*puttony*) holds about 44 pounds (20 kilograms) of desiccated grapes.

Tokaji aszú eszencia

A very rare wine of the highest quality and practically without rival. It is enriched with juice, or essence, of high sugar content, and matured in oak for at least 15 years.

Tokaji aszú
A much sought-after rarity, a Tokay wine made using six *puttonyos* of selected grapes with "noble rot". 1957 is considered an outstanding vintage. Other good vintages in recent years are 1988, 1990, and 1993.

Tokaji furmint
A quality wine made from a single grape variety, Furmint. It is matured in two styles: dry and semisweet.

The sweet perfection of the morello cherry
CHERRIES IN BRANDY

Chocolates of this type, consisting of fruit preserved in strong alcohol and coated in chocolate, first appeared in the 19th century. This was when chocolatiers discovered how to create a chocolate coating that would not leak if used with a liquid filling. The hour had arrived for the cherry in brandy.

What distinguishes Hungarian *konyakmeggy* is the quality of the cherries. The chocolates are made exclusively from local varieties with a flavor that balances acidity and sweetness.

The chocolates are not all machine-produced; there are also handmade "cherries in brandy" such as the ones produced by the Szerencs chocolate factory, the most famous in Hungary. Manual production of these chocolates is performed using the same skills and techniques as those introduced at the beginning of the 20th century by the renowned Budapest firm of chocolatiers, Gerbeaud. Firm, ripe, unblemished morello cherries with a diameter of ¾–⅞ inch (18–22 millimeters) are selected. The cherries are steeped in alcohol for two to three months. On reaching an alcoholic content of 28%/vol, they are pitted and left to drain. They are then individually dipped in sugar fondant and placed on parchment or aluminum foil for the sugar coating to dry. The cherry is then placed on a blob of melted semisweet chocolate. This will harden into the firm base necessary to prevent the chocolate from leaking. The coated cherry on its base is then dipped in semisweet chocolate and placed on a tray. While the chocolate is still liquid, it is swirled into a decorative spiral.

As the coating of chocolate dries, it exerts pressure on the sugar coating underneath, and so on the cherry. The alcohol-soaked juice is pressed out, dissolving the sugar. It takes one or two weeks for the ultimate, full flavor to develop. The chocolates are finally wrapped in gold foil and packed into confectionery boxes.

After soaking in alcohol, the cherries are individually dipped in a concentrated sugar solution.

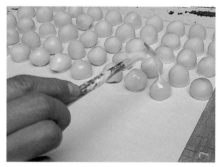

They are placed on parchment for the fondant to dry.

Once the sugar coating has set, a chocolate base is made for the cherries.

The sugar-coated cherries on their chocolate bases are dipped in semisweet chocolate.

Each individual chocolate is wrapped in gold foil as a final touch of elegance.

The alcohol-drenched juice takes one or two weeks to dissolve the sugar coating round the cherry.

Hungarian cherries in brandy were awarded a gold medal at the World Exhibition in Brussels in 1958.

Expert hands swirl the chocolate coating into a decorative spiral while it is still liquid.

Saint Nicholas brings his gifts

That good-natured old gentleman with the white beard, who arrives at Christmas down the chimney in Britain and America to fill children's stockings with gifts, is a busy man. Elsewhere, he places his Christmas packages under the tree. A short pause for breath, and he sets off for Russia to give the children their New Year trees. He starts his work at the beginning of December, in Hungary, where he is known as Mikulás (this comes from the Slav name Miklós = Nicholas). On the eve of the religious feast of Saint Nicholas, December 6, all Hungarian children (and any adults who feel they have earned a present) place their shoes and boots, nicely cleaned, on the windowsill. Overnight, these are filled to the brim with gifts wrapped in red paper. Many of the gifts are sweets, especially chocolate Santa Clauses and red Christmas boots. Noone being quite perfect, the gifts are usually accompanied by a birch, a bunch of twigs sprayed gold and tied with a red ribbon. It serves as a reminder of past "misdeeds" and a warning

not to repeat them. The obligatory red ribbon compensates for the stern mood of punishment that all this creates – at what is, after all, a time of joyful celebration. Not only that, if the birch is large enough, it is hung with candy wrapped in red foil (*szaloncukor*, see page 285). These are the traditional Hungarian Christmas tree decorations. They can be given before December 24, but only by Mikulás. As everyone knows, he is a kindly man, so he does not hand out the birch rods himself; this is done by his companions, little black devils called "Krampuses."

A time to dance and eat heartily
THE COUNTRY WEDDING

Foreign tourists in Hungary are often taken to see a traditional country wedding and its huge wedding breakfast. These events are by no means just a tourist attraction; they represent a living heritage. A great number of couples in both town and country still celebrate the happiest day of their lives surrounded by a mass gathering of relatives and friends, sharing a lavish feast and observing all the old customs.

Many and various are the wedding rituals that have been handed down through the ages: the earnest exhortations and the humorous rhymes of the best man, the weeping over the bride, the bridegroom's farewell, and, of course, the wedding dance. During this, the bridegroom has to discover his bride from among several girls of the same height, all swathed from head to foot.

There are regional differences in the food, and the order in which the dishes are served, but they all have one thing in

Astonishing quantities of food have to be prepared for a large wedding.

The traditional chicken soup for a wedding is prepared
Tyúkhúsleves, see page 35)

The pasta dough is cut into small squares, then shaped using a stick and a ribbed board to make curls or "snails." These are traditional. The soup served at the wedding feast usually contains such pasta curls.

A generous amount of meat is used for the chicken soup.

Enormous cooking vessels are needed for such large quantities.

234

Experienced cooks know how to make the wedding feast a success.

Many hands are needed in the kitchen.

Practice makes good teamwork.

Friends and relations lend plates and cutlery.

common: the table is so richly laden that there is plenty even for unexpected guests.

Preparations for the feast begin days in advance. Crockery and cutlery are borrowed from relatives or ordered from caterers. Piles of pots and pans mount in the space to be used as a kitchen, along with mountains of food; there, an innkeeper, restaurateur, or cook with long experience of wedding feasts holds sway, directing with military precision the preparation of the wedding menu so carefully decided long before.

Wedding celebrations are usually held in the open air in summer. A large marquee is set up to house the feast; the dancing takes place outside.

The meal begins with a rich meat soup containing noodle curls or "snails." By tradition, these are made by the friends of the bride. Following the meal, the cooks are all invited to dance, or to take part in the "snail-stamping," as it is popularly called.

The dancing continues through the night, traditionally accompanied by a band of gipsy musicians, though in these modern times, the music may come from a synthesizer.

The bride wears a white wedding dress for the ceremony (above), and a red one for the dancing (below). Guests can invite her to dance, in return for a gift of money for the new household.

Guests sit in the marquee (above and main photograph, below). The dancing takes place in the open (top).

A DUNÁNTÚL

TRANSDANUBIA

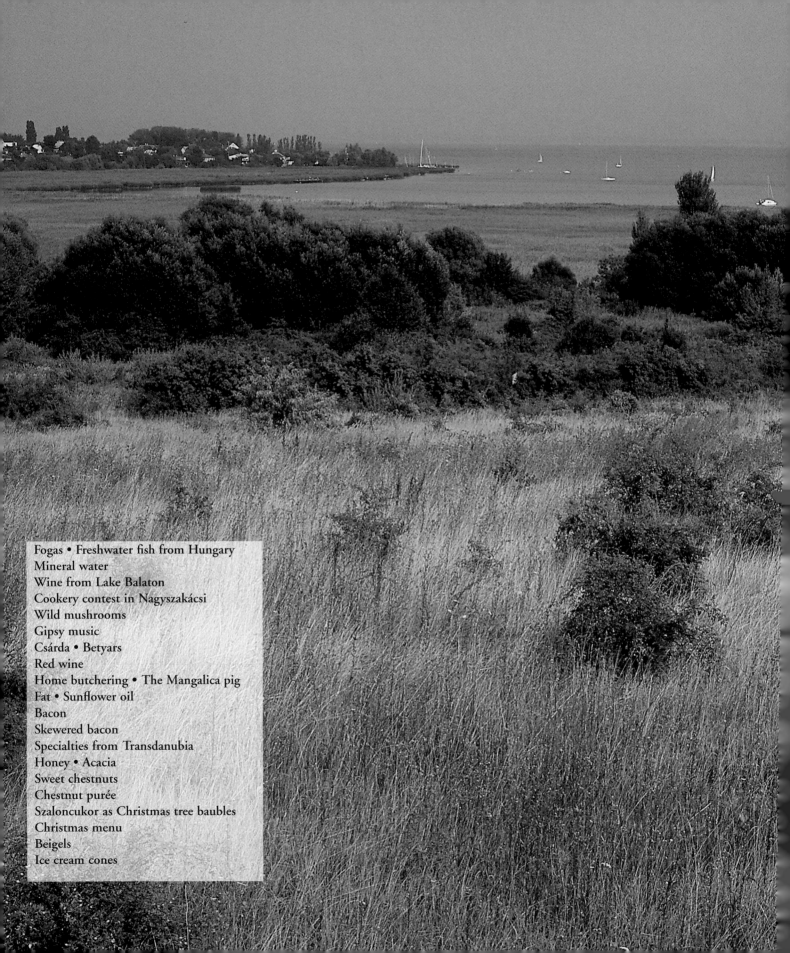

On reaching Hungary, the Danube flows from west to east for a while before turning sharply southward. To the west of its long north-south section lies the region of Transdanubia, once part of the Roman Empire. Due to its geographical location, its regional cuisine has stronger Austrian overtones than the rest of the country and provides the basis for Hungary's home cooking.

In the gentle foothills of the Alps to the northwest and the Mecsek Mountains, forests of chestnut trees thrive, their fruits roasted in winter or made into the much-loved chestnut purée. At the foot of the Alps extends a flat plane fragmented by watercourses. But most of Transdanubia is made up of gently undulating terrain, the center of which is dominated by the largest continental lake in Central Europe, Lake Balaton, which the Hungarians also refer to as their sea. It provides a habitat for many species of fish, one of which – the zander – has achieved a reputation outside the country. The woods of the neighboring Bakony Mountains are a paradise for wild-mushroom pickers and hunters. Above all, though, the mild maritime climate encourages an excellent viticulture, which has been attracting hoards of visitors for centuries.

The king of Lake Balaton
FOGAS

The noblest of all species of fish in Hungary is undoubtedly the *fogas* (zander) or, to be more precise, the Lake Balaton *fogas*. This is a species found only in Lake Balaton. Fish weighing up to 3¼ pounds (1.5 kilograms) are called *süllő* and it is only the larger fish, which can weigh up to 22 pounds (10 kilograms) and measure 37 inches (90 centimeters) long, that are referred to as *fogas*.

Foreign traders were fascinated by this tasty fish as early as the Middle Ages. A royal decree was issued in the 15th century, allowing the fish to be imported into Austria duty-free. So even in those early days fish from Lake Balaton were finding their way to Vienna.

The silver-gray zander is an extremely agile predator with a voracious appetite. Because it moves quickly and is highly active, its muscular, elongated body does not carry a single ounce of excess fat. It lives mainly off white fish, which it hunts in the deepest parts of the otherwise quite shallow, cloudy, sandy lake. It lives at depths of around 10–13 feet (3–4 meters), which are barely penetrated by the sun's rays,

Roughly 50 species of fish live in Lake Balaton; 16 to 18 species are caught by commercial fishermen. The largest catches of zander are made in the fall, early winter, and spring.

The silver-gray zander has a very delicate, fine-textured, white flesh. Being a predator, it is highly active and fast-moving, which means it also has very little body fat.

explaining why the flesh of this delicate, fine-textured fish is snow-white. Adult fish are particularly popular, as their bones are easy to remove. Time and again, Hungarian chefs have tried out new, innovative recipes with zander. But the favorite way of preparing it is still to coat the whole fish with a mixture of flour and paprika and pan-fry it.

The zander spawns between April and May. The female will lay up to 40,000 eggs a year, but only a third of these will develop, the remainder being eaten by the parents. The fishing seasons are controlled and spawning grounds maintained to protect stocks.

Freshwater fish from the length and breadth of Hungary

Ponty
(Scaly carp, common carp)
Evenly clad in scales; the original form of the carp lives in ponds; flavorsome fish.

Tükörponty
(Mirror carp)
A particularly high-backed, farmed carp with few scales; fatty, tasty flesh.

Csuka (Pike)
A predatory fish found lying in wait for its prey amid underwater plants. A

sweet, firm fish which is excellent for culinary purposes.

Bodorka (Roach)
A flat, high-backed body; large, red eyes; numerous fine bones; flesh of average quality.

Vörösszárnyú keszeg (Golden shiner)
Lives in stagnant or slow-moving waters; numerous bones, delicate flesh.

Harcsa (Catfish, sheathfish)
A scaleless, predatory fish with typical barb feathers; can grow to up to nearly 10 feet (3 meters) long and weigh 330

pounds (150 kilograms); firm, flavorsome, fatty flesh with virtually no bones.

Angolna (Eel)
Lives in rivers and lakes; very fatty meat, not easily digested.

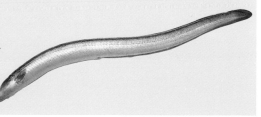

Egyben sült fogassüllő
Pan-fried zander
(Photographs below and right)

2 young zander (1–½ lbs/700 g each)	
Salt	
2 small pieces of potato	
1 cup/120 g flour	
1–2 tbsp mild paprika	
1–⅔ cups/400 ml oil for frying	
2 lemons for garnishing	
Salad leaves for garnishing	

Scale and gut the fish. Remove the fins, gills, and eyes, then wash the fish and pat them dry. Make slashes on both sides at intervals of about 1 inch/2 cm. Salt the cavity and outside of the fish, then leave until the salt is absorbed. Place a small piece of potato in each fish's mouth. Mix the flour and paprika (the mixture should not be too red) and use it to coat both sides of the fish. Heat the oil in a large, high-sided skillet. Fry the fish one at a time, bent into a crescent shape around the edge of the skillet, first on one side, then on the other, without altering the shape.

Arrange the fried fish in the arched position on a serving plate. Replace the pieces of potato with a slice of lemon. Garnish the plate with slices or quarters of lemon and salad leaves. Serve with potatoes in butter and parsley and tartare sauce (see page 301).

Because the fish is prepared whole, prices given on Hungarian menus are per 10 g (about ⅓ oz).

1 Scale, gut, and clean the fish. Next, make slash cuts on both sides.
2 Coat the whole, salted fish in a mixture of flour and paprika.

3 Fry the fish in a large, high-sided skillet in a crescent shape.
4 It is important to ensure that the fish retains its arched shape during frying.

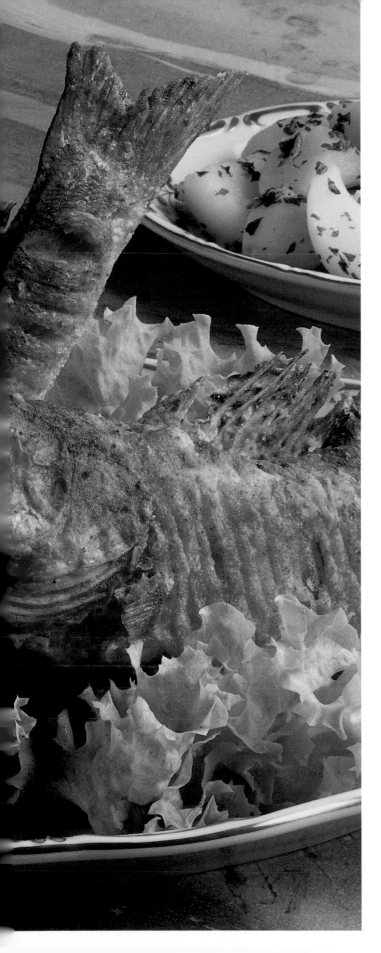

Töltött süllőtekercs tejszínes-paprikás mártással
(Zander rolls with cream sauce)

2 young zander (1–½ lbs/700 g each)
Salt
1 large onion
7 oz/200 g mushrooms
1 small bunch of parsley
3½ tbsp/50 g butter
Pinch of pepper
2 egg yolks
½ tsp mild paprika
Scant ½ cup/100 ml sour cream
4 tbsp flour
Scant ½ cup/100 ml light cream

Clean, gut, and scale the fish. Boil the bones in 4 cups/1 liter of salted water for 30–45 minutes. Gently pat the fillets, then salt them. Peel the onion and wipe the mushrooms, then either chop them both up finely or grate them. Chop the parsley. Gently fry a teaspoon of onion in a little butter until translucent. Add the mushrooms with a little salt and fry, then add the pepper and parsley. Mix in the egg yolks, and remove from the heat. Leave to cool. Spread the mushroom mixture on the fillets, then roll them up and secure with wooden picks. Quickly fry the remaining onion in the remaining fat, then remove from the heat. Sprinkle with paprika and pour over the strained fish stock. Add the fish rolls, then cover and cook. When ready, carefully lift out the fish and remove the needles. Arrange on a serving plate. Mix the sour cream and flour (see page 298) and use it to bind the cooking liquid. Add the light cream to the sauce and pass it through a sieve before pouring it over the fish. Serve with potatoes in butter and parsley.

Fogas jóasszony módra
Zander fillets
(Photograph below)

1 zander (about 3–¼ lbs/1.5 kg)
Salt
7 oz/200 g mushrooms
1 small onion
1 small bunch of parsley
3½ tbsp/50 g butter
⅔ cup/150 ml dry white wine
½ tsp pepper
¾ cup/200 ml light cream

Gut and scale the fish and remove the head. Skin both fillets, then wash and divide them into eight pieces. Boil the head and bones in 1¼ cups/300 ml salt water for 30 minutes, then strain the stock. Wipe the mushrooms and slice them thinly. Finely chop the onion and parsley. Salt the fillets and lay them side by side in a baking pan with a little butter. Add the white wine, ⅔ cup/150 ml stock, mushrooms, onion, parsley, and pepper. Cover with baking parchment and bake in a preheated (medium) oven. Transfer to a warmed serving plate and keep warm. To make the sauce, mix the remaining stock with the cream. Bring to a boil, then remove from the heat and whisk in the remaining butter until amalgamated. Pour the sauce over the fish.

Fresh from the spring
MINERAL WATER

In Hungary, a liter (about 2 pints) of mineral water must, by law, contain at least 1000 milligrams of soluble mineral substances or other essential components, such as trace elements. The regulations governing therapeutic waters are even more stringent. These waters provide the body with various substances that are essential to its biological system, such as calcium, magnesium, fluoride, and iodine.

The purity of the mineral water (*ásványvíz*) is guaranteed not only by protecting the source and its environment, but by another absolute requirement that the bottles are filled only on site and no other substances added (except for carbon dioxide).

The mixing of waters from different sources is prohibited. Mineral water must not flow through public water systems, either.

There is also a sort of "public" appraisal of the water quality. At many sources or springs, visitors can sample the waters themselves or take along containers to fill. The sight of locals regularly appearing with their wicker flasks or water cans for the next few days' supply is a sure guarantee that the water bubbling from the earth will both be wholesome and taste good. Many Hungarians regard this as a far better recommendation than official certification.

Mineral water is often sold right next to the source. Anyone traveling through Hungary should simply ask whether there is a good local source of mineral water.

Just under two miles from the north shore of Lake Balaton, in the Káli basin, lying surrounded by mountains, bubbles the Kékkút spring, whose waters were enjoyed by Roman settlers in the area as early as the 3rd and 4th centuries AD. Today, it is named for the Byzantine Empress Theodora, who is said to have drunk this water in the 11th century in preference to anything else.

Opposite (from left to right): *Óbudai Gyémánt, Balfi Ásványvíz, Parádi, Kékkúti ásványvíz, Margitszigeti kristályvíz*

At many Hungarian springs visitors are allowed to fill containers with mineral water themselves.

The various mineral waters are sold in glass or plastic bottles.

Wine for the wedding night
WINE FROM LAKE BALATON

Many years ago the locals living around Lake Balaton realized what ideal vine-growing conditions were offered by the vast expanse of water and outstanding soil conditions. In the 3rd century AD, the Roman emperor – and son of a gardener – Marcus Aurelius Probus, instructed his legions in the province of Pannonia, the present-day Transdanubia, to plant whole areas of vines, as they usually had little else to do during peacetime. This tradition was continued by all subsequent inhabitants of the region, including the Magyars. Each vine-growing district on Lake Balaton has one or two wines of character which merit particular praise.

Somló
This wine from the cone-shaped Mount Somló, which has a fieriness attributed to the ash of the extinct volcano, was once held in higher regard than Tokay. For centuries the men of the Hapsburg dynasty were served this wine on their wedding night, in the belief that it would promote the procreation of male offspring. Statistics have indeed revealed that more boys are born in this area than the national average.

Different wines originate from the individual mountain slopes, each of them pressed from eight to ten grape varieties, with a glowing greenish-white or golden yellow color and a fine acidity. Their true character develops during many years of maturation, which means they are intended for laying down. They are not, on the other hand, suitable for blending.

Right: Every sunny, autumnal day improves the quality of the wine.
Below: Grape harvest.

1 The color of the Riesling grape comes through later in the wine.
2 Each individual bunch is carefully cut off.
3 The buckets of grapes are transferred into large vats to be taken away for pressing.
4 The ripened grapes are a feast for the eye; the wine pressed from them, a pleasure to the palate.

5 After harvesting, the grapes first have their stalks removed.

6 Then they are crushed in a press.

7 Wooden wine presses are still used today.

8 Even the fresh must tastes wonderful.

Badacsony

This wine-growing area with its delightful countryside, which includes produce from Ábrahámhegy, Szent György-hegy, and Szigliget, was named for the box-shaped Mount Badacsony, which is still recognizable as such.

The region's main grape variety is the Olaszrizling (Italian Riesling). Wine made from this grape is usually bottled after only a year, so that it retains its bitter, almond bouquet. Its alcohol content is quite high at between 12.5 and 13.5%.

The popular Szürkebarát grape is a descendant of the French Pinot Gris grape, which in its native land produces a light wine that does not exactly merit the label "fine wine." In Badacsony, its grapes are juicier and its must sweeter. It produces a fiery, aromatic, golden yellow wine with an alcohol content of between 12.5 and 13.5%, which almost always contains unfermented sugar, so-called residual sugar. Another typical grape and vine variety from Badacsony is the ancient Kéknyelű, celebrated in folk songs and named after its bluish leaf stalks. It is an elegant, yellowish-green wine with an alcohol content of 13.5 to 14%; however, it seldom reaches

The wine harvest culminates in a huge celebration where guests dance with lively abandon.

The winegrowers' parade in Szigliget (above). The traditional "wine bell" (below) is an essential part of this.

Only 50 years ago the town crier announced the very latest news with his drum.

Above: The previous year's wine is served at the wine festival.
Bottom right: Lake Balaton wine regions.

the shops. The vines produce only a very low yield and winegrowers prefer to keep it for their own consumption or to sell it themselves, as a mark of tradition and prestige.
Other good wines from the region include Zöldszilváni (Green Silvaner), which originally came from Siebenbürgen, and Muskotály (Muscatel).

Csopak and Balatonfüred

After walking through the vineyards at Csopak and Balatonfüred visitors will find their shoes covered in red dust – an indication of the iron oxide in the loamy, volcanic soil, which gives the wine its particular bouquet. The Olaszrizling (Italian Riesling) thrives in this area. Its fruit produce a spicy, greenish-white wine with a bouquet similar to that of Reseda and a flavor of plums after several years' maturation. Although both wines have an alcohol content of 12.5–13.5%, the Italian Riesling varieties differ in character between the two towns.
The Riesling from the neighboring Dörgicse has a slightly lower alcohol content, but is more drinkable, making it an

ideal open wine. Another wine of justifiable popularity is the Furmint from Balatonfüred and Csopak.

Mór

The vineyards at Mór, just to the north of Lake Balaton between the foothills of the Bakony and Vértes Mountains, were left deserted when the population fled the Turkish invaders. Fortunately, however, the farmers who settled here from southern Germany in the 18th century included expert winegrowers who planted the Ezerjó, which has for some time been native to northern Hungary. The fiery Mór Ezerjó (*Móri ezerjó*), with its high alcohol content and acidity, has a pale yellow glow. It has a fine aroma and the unfermented sugar means it is frequently sweetish and, in good years, even sweet.

Dél-Balaton

The wine region's most important grape varieties from the southern shores of Lake Balaton are Olaszrisling (Italian Riesling), Chardonnay, Sauvignon, and Leányka.

The wine harvest

The vineyard must be tended and maintained by the winegrower the whole year round. Friends and relatives lend a hand in autumn, because grape-picking is a job for many busy hands and strong men are needed to carry the heavy vats. Each year the wine harvest is a welcome excuse to get the whole family together. Once the work is done, they settle themselves in the winepress building and begin drinking the wine, while the winegrower's traditional celebratory meal of mutton goulash bubbles away for several hours over an open fire. According to ancient tradition, the wine harvest ends with the winegrower's ball and parade.

Hearty dishes, such as stuffed cabbage (above), are served up at the winegrower's celebratory meal (below).

Szüreti birkapörkölt
Mutton goulash, winegrower's-style
(Serves 10)

5½ lbs/2.5 kg mutton with bones
4 large onions
Scant 1 cup/200 g mutton drippings
1 heaped tbsp hot paprika
Salt
1 mutton leg bone, optional
2–3 red bell peppers
3–4 cloves of garlic
1 tbsp caraway
Hot chili peppers, extra

Dice the meat and chop up the onions. Heat the drippings in a pot and fry the onion until translucent. Sprinkle on the paprika, then immediately add the meat and season with salt (if using a leg bone, break this up and add it to the pot before the meat). Seed the peppers and chop them up. Add to the meat along with the crushed garlic and caraway. Leave the *pörkölt* to braise in its own juices, then later gradually add water to the cooking liquid. Shake the pot regularly during cooking. Serve with hot chili peppers.

COOKERY CONTEST IN NAGYSZAKÁCSI

In 1414 the Hungarian King Sigismund (1387–1437) conferred upon his court chef, Ferenc Eresztvényi, and his close relatives the noble title *"specialis et fidelis coci nostre maiestatis."* The family arms depict a skewered pike arched above red flames, with a laurel bush at either end of the skewer, while the top of the crest bears a pike's head.

For over 300 years from the 13th century Eresztvényi's village, which by no coincidence is called Nagyszakácsi (master chef village), sent generations of master chefs to the royal court, while the kings also bestowed dominions there upon their highly esteemed chefs. Even the famous Renaissance chef György Veres received the epithet "von Nagyszakácsi." With the help of ten chefs and numerous kitchen hands, he ran the kitchens of King Matthias (1458–90), which were celebrated throughout Europe.

The Eresztvényi family arms.

Even today, villagers still boast such colorful surnames as Kövér (fat), Szita (sieve), and Bárány (lamb). Each year on the first Saturday in August chefs from throughout Hungary flock to Nagyszakácsi to compete for the title "Royal Chef" with dishes prepared from old recipes.

Above: The preparation of extravagant delicacies was commonplace in the lordly kitchens of early modern times.

Opposite: In the Nagyszakácsi cookery contest, food not only has to taste superb, it must also be beautifully and imaginatively presented.

Whether a dish is prepared to an original recipe or improvised is unimportant.

Even simple methods of preparation can produce first-class results.

Artistically decorated fruit and baking are a pleasure to behold.

A gift from the woods
WILD MUSHROOMS

The woods of the Bakony Mountains are home to vast quantities of wild mushrooms. Little wonder that dishes with the epithet "Bakonyer" frequently contain this ingredient – usually enriched with sour cream.

There are between 20 and 30 varieties of wild mushroom growing in Hungary and these are regularly used in the kitchen, either as a main dish in themselves or to enrich other food. However, it is cultivated mushrooms that are most commonly found on menus, button mushrooms for the most part.

Sonkával töltött gomba
Mushrooms filled with ham
(Photograph below)

Generous 1 lb/500 g mushrooms
⅓ cup/80 g butter
Salt, Pepper
14 oz/400 g cooked smoked ham
¾ cup/200 ml milk
4 tbsp flour
2 egg yolks
Paprika
Scant 1 cup/100 g grated cheese (e.g. Parmesan)

Wipe the mushrooms, which should be roughly the same size, and cut off the stalks. Grease a flameproof dish with 4 teaspoons of butter. Place the mushroom caps in the dish and season with salt and pepper.

Pass the ham through a grinder. Heat the milk. Melt 8 teaspoons/40 grams of butter in a pan, then stir in the flour (do not let it brown!). Gradually pour in the hot milk, stirring continuously, and simmer until the mixture thickens and leaves the sides of the pan. Stir in the ham first, followed by the egg yolks and finally enough paprika to give the mixture a pinkish color. Fill the mushroom caps with the mixture and sprinkle with grated cheese, then drizzle with melted butter.

Bake in a preheated oven at 460 °F/240 °C for about 15 minutes. Serve as an appetizer.

Lila tölcsérpereszke (Lilac blewit)
A good mushroom with a strong flavor, particularly good when picked young; should not be eaten raw.

Sárga rókagomba
(Chanterelle)
A tasty mushroom; particularly good braised in *pörkölt* and *paprikás* dishes.

Kékhátú galambgomba (Green agaric)
An excellent mushroom varying in color from bluish violet through brown to greenish.

Fenyőpereszke
(Earth blewir)
A good mushroom with a slightly mealy aroma, good in mixed mushroom dishes.

Májusi pereszke (May blewit)
A very good mushroom with a fine, mealy aroma; excellent for braising.

Nagy őzlábgomba (Parasol mushroom)
A very good mushroom, caps excellent for broiling, tender stalks; should not be eaten raw.

Sötét trombitagomba
(Autumn trumpet or trumpet of death)
A good mushroom; often used dried.

Késői laskagomba
(Oyster mushroom)
A very good mushroom; grows on tree trunks and stumps; mild flavor.

PLAY ON, CIGÁNY...

Even the Betyars posed as *cigányok* (gipsies) and today a simple evening meal still goes down far better if accompanied by the *prímás* playing nostalgic or lively melodies on his violin.

A *cigányzenekar* (gipsy band) needs no sheet music, it plays by ear. The *prímás*, or first violin, plays the melody, while the other musicians – second violin, bass violin, clarinet, and cymbals – add the harmony and rhythm. They are all masters of their instruments and splendid improvisers. With a practiced eye, the *prímás* will spot a tourist's nationality as soon as he walks into the bar and will insist on playing him a song from his native country during the course of the evening. It is not uncommon for a high-spirited guest to sing along at the top of his voice (although this does not usually happen in more fashionable restaurants).

Contrary to common conception, *cigányzene* (gipsy music) is not identical to Hungarian folk music, but rather a popular art music, which emerged at the start of the 19th century with the rise of national consciousness in Hungary.

The musicians' repertoire ranges from dreamy, melancholic tunes to lively melodies. Nowadays, tunes from operettas, movies, and musicals are also played.

Sült császárszalonna (roasted imperial bacon): Mildly smoked back bacon

Csécsi szalonna (Csécs bacon): Boiled neck bacon spiced with salt and mild paprika

Hédervári szalonna (Hedervar bacon): Cured, mildly smoked back bacon with mild paprika

Kenyérszalonna (bread bacon): Salted, smoked back bacon; long-lasting

Fött császárszalonna (boiled imperial bacon): Smoked, streaky back bacon

Fokhagymás abált szalonna (garlic bacon): Bacon spiced with garlic and paprika

Kolozsvári szalonna (Klausenburg bacon): Salted, cured meaty rib piece, cold-smoked for a short time

BACON

Anyone casting an eye over the refrigerated cabinet in a Hungarian supermarket or observing the display on offer at a butcher's will perhaps be surprised by the wide variety of different bacons.

You may find raw, salted and cured, smoked and cooked, or bacon that is produced by a combination of these processes. Bacon is available either with or without the lean meat and is sometimes also spiced. Not only does the method of preparation vary, but the breed and age of the pig are also

Below and opposite: Hungarian meat counters reflect the rich variety of the country's specialty bacons.

crucial factors, as is the way in which the meat has been processed – either singed or scalded – and then cut up. Bacon will taste different depending on whether it comes from the belly, neck, back, or sides. Smoked bacon is one of the basic provisions of every Hungarian household, being a crucial ingredient for both boiling and roasting.

When it comes to home butchering, variety takes second place to tradition and customary taste. However, the food industry offers a rich variety of bacon, thereby threatening the distinctive traditions of the individual regions. At the same time, it has to consider consumer wishes, which are subject to change. So it is that the formerly so popular and versatile *sózott* or *fehérszalonna* (salted or white bacon) is now hardly asked for at all.

A Budapest chestnut seller in the 1930s.

The prickly cups of the sweet or Spanish chestnut (*Castanea sativa*) contain two to four chestnuts.

Sweet (Spanish) chestnuts are high in carbohydrates. They have a pleasantly sweet taste when cooked.

SWEET CHESTNUTS

The chestnut (also known as the Spanish or sweet chestnut) is a subtropical plant that only grows in a few parts of Transdanubia with a special microclimate, sheltered by the mountains. These sites are to be found mainly in the foothills of the Alps, on the slopes of the Mecsek Mountains in the south of the country, and in a few sunny sections of the elbow of the Danube to the north of Budapest. Here, however, there grew real chestnut forests and the fruits of the trees became a much sought-after delicacy throughout the country.

Even up to a few years ago, the unmistakable harbingers of the cold months ahead were the chestnut sellers with their charcoal braziers, seen plying their trade around the towns, selling hot chestnuts in cone-shaped paper bags for the buyers to warm their hands on. Since this occupation seems to be dwindling, the chestnuts are more and more frequently roasted at home.

Chestnuts are also easy to roast at home.

Gesztenyés kifli
Chestnut horns

For the dough:

2⅔ cups/350 g flour	
1⅓ cups/300 g butter	
4 tbsp confectioners' sugar	
Pinch of salt	
2 egg yolks	
1–2 tbsp rum	
3½ tbsp sour cream	

For the filling:

¾ quantity chestnut mixture (see page 282)	
Rum, optional	
Cream, optional	

Other:

1 egg for glazing	
Vanilla sugar for sprinkling	
Confectioners' sugar for sprinkling	

Knead together the flour, butter, and confectioners' sugar; then add the salt, egg yolks, and enough rum and sour cream to produce a firm dough. Leave the dough in a cool place for 30 minutes, then roll it out on a floured board to a thickness of about ¼ inch/5 mm. Cut the dough into squares measuring roughly 3 inches/7.5 cm and spoon a small quantity of the chestnut mixture onto each square (adding a small amount of rum or cream to the mixture gives it a better flavor and makes it easier to work). Shape the dough squares into horns and transfer them to a baking sheet. Brush with beaten egg. Bake in a preheated (medium) oven until light brown. Sprinkle with vanilla and confectioners' sugar while hot.

Gesztenyével töltött pulyka
Turkey with chestnut stuffing
(Photograph below)

2¼ lbs/1 kg chestnuts	
Salt	
4¼ cups/1 liter milk	
1 bread roll	
Generous 1 pound/500 g leg of pork	
1 egg	
Scant ½ cup/100 ml light cream	
½ tsp pepper	
1 oven-ready turkey (5½–6¾ lbs/2.5–3 kg)	
7 oz/200 g smoked bacon	
3½ tbsp/50 g butter	

Peel the chestnuts and cook until soft in 3¾ cups/900 ml of salted milk. Soften the bread roll in the rest of the milk and squeeze it out. Grind the chestnuts, bread, and pork, then mix with the egg, cream, salt, and pepper. Rinse the turkey inside and out. Season with salt, then fill with the stuffing. Close the cavity with trussing needles or sew it up with cooking thread. Cut the bacon into small strips and use it to lard the turkey breast and legs. Melt the butter and pour it over the turkey; then roast in a preheated oven for around 2 to 3 hours at about 400 °F/200 °C, basting frequently. Leave for 15 minutes before carving. Serve with creamed potato and prune compote or stewed apples.

Sült gesztenye
Roasted chestnuts

Soak the chestnuts in water for a few hours, to prevent them from drying out during roasting. Drain them and then pierce the skins on one side using the point of a knife. Place on a baking sheet with the pierced side facing down and roast for about 20 minutes at 410 °F (210 °C), until the skin opens and the chestnut is crisp outside and soft inside. Transfer to a ceramic dish and cover with a dish towel, to prevent them from cooling completely.

Gesztenyével töltött pulyka
(Turkey with chestnut stuffing)

Chocolate	Strawberry	Lemon	Pistachio	Blackberry	Mint

Yogurt Raspberry Coffee

Children could lick an ice cream the whole year round.

On hot summer days
ICE CREAM CONES

Anyone visiting Hungary in the summer will see people all over the place, both young and old, with ice cream cones in their hands. Despite a massive advertising campaign by the ice cream industry to promote its packaged products, the good old ice cream cone, which each ice cream maker produces in their own special flavor, is still holding its own. The ice cream cone, regarded by many as the original fast-food product, is an American invention first displayed at the St Louis Fair in 1904. Its advantages meant it was destined to stay around, enabling ice cream lovers to make up their very own ice cream, perhaps also topped with whipped cream. The ice cream cornet can be taken anywhere and it can all be eaten, right down to the very last mouthful – so no litter from packaging.

Ice cream and parfaits
Experts distinguish between different ice cream preparations, depending on the milk or cream content and whether eggs are used. Fruit sorbets contain none of the above ingredients. They are simply made from water, sugar and fruit.

When it comes to frozen treats, parfaits must be the very best. They are usually based on heavily sweetened fruit juice, particularly strawberry, mixed with lots of cream. Parfaits can, however, be made in any flavor, such as vanilla and chocolate, and decorated with whipped cream. Nevertheless, most ice cream fans still prefer to lick a cone than savor a parfait.

Left: The ice cream seller is part of the summer street scene.

APPENDIX

The cuisine of the enchanted garden
TRANSYLVANIAN CUISINE

According to the renowned British gastronome, Egon Rónay, who came from Hungary, world cuisine has brought forth three key achievements: French cuisine, Chinese food, and the cuisine of Transylvania.

Transylvania, which was formerly part of Hungary and now belongs to Romania, not only has a uniquely beautiful, wild, romantic scenery that has earned it the name "enchanted garden," it also has a history and culture which is no less unique. For centuries Romanians, Hungarians, Saxons, Armenians, and Jews lived together peacefully in this land in the Carpathian Basin, halfway between Istanbul and Vienna, enriching each other's cultures, and yet simultaneously preserving their own identities. It is worth noting that the refinement and ennobling of Hungarian cuisine started here. After the division of Hungary into three, Transylvania was a flourishing, independent duchy. It maneuvered successfully between the Ottoman Empire and the ruling European houses as they pushed eastward, while in the other parts of Hungary the population suffered under the yoke of Turkish and Habsburg tax collectors. The oldest Hungarian cookbook was devised in this "blessed" land of Transylvania in the 16th century. In *Szakács Tudomány,* "The Art of Cooking," an unknown Transylvanian cook, who had visited many countries and acquired his expertise in many ducal courts, described some 900 refined recipes. His writings also suggest menus and provide serving hints which are testimony of a high class and refined food culture.

Flour *roux* and paprika are less characteristic of Transylvanian cuisine than Hungarian; instead it uses more green herbs such as dill, savory, tarragon, thyme, marjoram, rosemary, and basil. It also prefers baked farinaceous dishes to boiled. Dishes based on cornmeal, and especially the polenta which is made from it, are rarely used in Hungary, but are frequently served by Transylvanian Hungarians and Romanians. Another regional specialty is fruit soup flavored with smoked meat.

Right: At one time the tree cake was baked in Transylvania on festive occasions, especially weddings.

Kürtőskalács
Tree cake
(Photograph right)

This cake, which is unique in shape, flavor, and preparation is a specialty of Transylvanian cuisine. The traditional equipment for baking a tree cake consists of a wooden roller, measuring 4 inches (10 centimeters) in diameter and 16 inches (40 centimeters) in length. Strips of yeast dough that have been rolled out to a finger's thickness are wrapped around it. Before baking, the surface of the dough is coated with a glaze made from honey, egg yolk, and sugar or sugar with walnuts or almonds. The cake is baked by turning the spit with the roller slowly, by hand, over charcoal embers.

Sütőben sült kürtőskalácskák
Oven-baked tree cake

Little tree cakes can also be baked in the oven. Thin strips of dough are wrapped around a small metal pipe (in the past cobs of corn with the kernels removed were used) and baked on a baking sheet in the oven.

For the dough:

2 cakes/30 g compressed fresh yeast
3⅓ cups/800 ml milk
2¼ lbs/1 kg flour
1 egg
3 egg yolks
5 tbsp confectioners' sugar
6½ tbsp/100 g butter

Extra:

¾ cup/100 g walnuts for sprinkling
1 egg,
½ cup/100 g sugar for sprinkling

To make the dough: work all the ingredients together to form a firm yeast dough, and leave it to rise for 1 hour.
Coarsely chop the walnuts with a knife. Break off little pieces from the raised dough. Roll them out until they are ¼ inch (5 mm) thick, and wrap them loosely around a small metal pipe. Brush the surface with the beaten egg, then sprinkle over the confectioners' sugar and chopped nuts. Bake in a preheated (medium hot) oven for 15 minutes. Serve warm.

Juhtúrós puliszka
Polenta with ewe's milk cheese

2½ cups/300 g cornmeal
Salt
1 tbsp wheat flour
¼ cup/60 g butter (or drippings from 3½ oz/100 g diced bacon, sautéed)
9 oz/250 g ewe's milk cheese (e.g. feta)

Warm the cornmeal in the oven. Bring a generous 4 cups (1 liter) of water to a boil in a very large saucepan. Add salt and gradually sprinkle the cornmeal over the surface of the water, whisking all the time with a balloon whisk, to prevent lumps forming. Then stir constantly with a wooden spoon for 15–20 minutes, until the polenta is cooked. As soon as the polenta starts to thicken, add the wheat flour and continue stirring for a few minutes. Finally, leave the thick mixture to stand for a few minutes.
Scoop out spoonfuls of the polenta and cover the base of a buttered ovenproof dish with them. Drizzle melted butter or drippings over the polenta, and sprinkle crumbled ewe's cheese on top. Repeat this process until all the ingredients are used up, finishing with a layer of ewe's cheese. If you have used bacon drippings with the polenta, scatter the sautéed bacon on top. Bake in a preheated (medium) oven for 10 minutes or until the cheese melts and browns.

TIPS ON HUNGARIAN CUISINE

Oven temperatures

There are no precise cooking times and temperatures for these traditional recipes. Low, medium, or high heat is suggested instead. These rather generalized temperatures are:

    low   about 175 °F (80 °C)
    medium   350–425 °F (180–220 °C)
    high   425 °F plus (220 °C plus)

The oven temperature may be reduced for fan-assisted ovens. It is also unnecessary to preheat these ovens.

Thickening

In Hungary soups, sauces, vegetable dishes, and stews are frequently thickened with flour, sour cream, or egg yolk.

Flour *roux*: Most Hungarian dishes are still thickened with flour, as they have always been.

Sprinkle flour onto melted butter and cook, stirring all the time, until the flour foams and achieves the desired color. The fat to flour ratio is usually 1:1, but may be modified depending on the dish.

White *roux*, in which the flour is cooked for only 1 minute and is not allowed to color (as for Béchamel sauce, for example), is not typical of Hungarian cuisine.

For most vegetable dishes and vegetable soups, the flour is cooked for 2–3 minutes. If the flour is cooked for longer, it takes on a golden brown color. This "brown" *roux* should in no circumstances be allowed to turn dark brown.

Seasonings – such as crushed garlic, grated onion, finely chopped parsley, or dill – are added only when the roux is ready.

The addition of paprika requires particular care. When the *roux* has achieved the desired color, the pan is taken off the heat and the paprika quickly stirred in. Water is then added straightaway to prevent the paprika burning and the dish acquiring a bitter taste and brownish color.

The prepared, seasoned *roux* is diluted with liquid (usually water). Cold liquid is always added to hot *roux* and warm liquid to cold *roux!* The sauce is stirred to ensure there are no lumps, and then brought to the boil again with the main ingredients. Some dishes require a *roux* to be slightly sweetened. Stir the flour into melted butter and add sugar. Cook the mixture until it browns, stirring all the time, then proceed as above.

Flour: Reduce the cooking liquid until just the pan juices are left. Sprinkle over flour, and cook until browned, stirring all the time. Then add water or another liquid, and bring to the boil again.

Sour cream: Slake the flour with a little water in a bowl, and blend until there are no lumps. Then add sour cream (sometimes fresh cream or milk) and stir to remove any lumps. Pour it into the other ingredients in a thin stream, stirring all the time. The ingredients to which the sour cream is added should be hot or boiling.

Variation: Blend the cream and flour mixture with a little of the cooking liquid before use.

Egg yolk: Some dishes may also be bound with egg yolk. First beat the egg yolk until smooth with a little of the hot cooking liquid, then add to the soup or sauce, stirring all the time. The sauce or soup should not be brought to the boil again, or the egg will curdle.

Jelly roll sponge

Basic recipe: Separate 6 eggs. Whisk the egg yolks with 1 cup/120 g confectioners' sugar until the mixture turns pale yellow and thickens. Whisk the egg whites until very stiff. Carefully fold spoonfuls of the egg whites and 1 cup/120 g flour into the yolk mixture using a spatula or metal spoon. Butter the bottom (never the sides) of the cake pan or baking sheet and dust it with flour. Pour the batter into the pan and level off the top, then bake in a preheated oven at 350 °F/ 180 °C for 20–30 minutes. The oven door should not be opened during the first 5 minutes. Test the cake to make sure it is cooked, then turn off the oven, and leave the cake to cool in the oven with the door open for a few minutes. When the cake has cooled, slice it into three layers. Spread these with cream filling, according to the recipe, and sandwich them together.

Chocolate-flavored sponge: Prepare according to the basic recipe, but add 1 tablespoon of cocoa powder to the egg yolk mixture.

Nut-flavored sponge: Prepare according to the basic recipe, but use grated walnuts instead of flour.

Puff pastry

Make dough for puff pastry according to whichever recipe you prefer. The dough should be kept cool so that, when it is rolled out, the individual layers do not stick together. For this reason the dough should be rolled out on a cold surface (e.g. marble) and handled as little as possible. Puff pastry is usually rolled out, layered, and then rolled out again three times. The pastry may be folded either three or four times. Each option has its own associated technique.

• Three layers: Roll out the pastry evenly until it forms a long rectangle. Fold one of the short ends inward to the center of the pastry, then fold the other short end over it, so there are three layers of pastry.

• Four layers: Roll out the pastry evenly until it forms a long rectangle. Fold both of the short ends inward to the center, then fold the sheet of pastry together down the center (like closing a book).

If glazing the pastry with beaten egg, be careful that it does not run down over the edges of the pastry and prevent it from rising. Place the pastry on a floured baking sheet and bake in the preheated oven. The oven should maintain an even temperature. If the top of the pastry browns too quickly, lay a sheet of baking parchment on top.

Fat

Hungarian specialties are traditionally prepared with pork drippings, which give many dishes their typical flavor, or butter. More recently, the former is gradually disappearing from the kitchen and in its place sunflower oil, or margarine for baking, are more likely to be used.

If using margarine instead of butter, the quantity specified in the recipe should be increased by 10% if using reduced fat margarine.

Mixed salad

Recipe (serves 10): Cook 12 oz/350 g carrots and 7 oz/200 g parsnip in boiling, salted water, then drain and dice finely. Boil 12 oz/350 g potatoes, skin them and dice them. Peel and dice 7 oz/200 g apples. Dice 5 oz/150 g pickled cucumbers. The dice should all be the same size. Cook ⅔ cup (100 g) peas in boiling, salted water. Leave all the ingredients to cool, then combine them with 1¼ cups/300 ml seasoned mayonnaise. Refrigerate the salad for a few hours so the flavors can blend. If this salad is being prepared for cold platters, use a little less mayonnaise so the salad will be a little firmer.

Roasting a goose liver

Basic recipe: Rinse the goose liver and soak it in ice-cold milk for at least 1 hour. Drain it well and pat it dry carefully. Soak a generous 1 lb/550 g of goose fat thoroughly, and cut it into even-sized pieces. Put the goose fat in a saucepan and add a splash of water, then sauté it until the fat runs. Strain the fat into another pan and heat it up again, then carefully place the goose liver in the hot fat. Sauté briefly, until it takes on an attractive golden-brown color, then turn the liver carefully. Add sufficient water to not quite cover the liver. If desired, you can also add 1–2 cloves of garlic and half a small onion. Cover and braise over a low heat until the liquid has completely evaporated. Carefully remove the cooked liver and place it on a deep dish. Season it sparingly with salt. Strain the fat over the liver, and stir a little medium hot paprika into the fat. Put the goose liver in the refrigerator.

Variation: Rinse 1 goose liver and soak it in ice-cold milk for at least 1 hour. Then drain well and carefully pat it dry. Divide the goose fat in half and line a saucepan with half of the raw goose fat. Place the liver in the pan and add enough meat stock to cover the liver. Add garlic or onion to taste, and cover with the remaining fat. Cover the pan and braise for 30–40 minutes (to check if the liver is cooked, pierce it with a meat skewer; the liver is cooked if no meat adheres to the skewer when it is removed). Place the liver on a serving dish and sprinkle sparingly with salt. Bring the remaining cooking liquid to a boil and simmer on a high heat until reduced, then leave it to cool for a few minutes. Stir ground paprika into the reduced liquid, and pour it over the liver. Refrigerate the liver.

Testing cakes

To test whether a cake is properly cooked, insert a meat skewer or thin knitting needle into the center of the cake. It is cooked if the skewer comes out of the cake clean. If there is batter clinging to the skewer, then the cake needs to bake for a little longer.

Bacon coxcombs

Make incisions (½–¾ inch/1–2 cm deep) in the rind of a thick slice of rinded bacon at intervals of ½–⅝ inch/1–1.5 centimeters, and sauté the bacon until crisp and brown. Dip the tips of the "coxcombs" in paprika and keep them warm until ready to serve the dish. Coxcombs should always be prepared immediately before serving.

Yeast dough (Quantities according to recipe)

Activating yeast: Dissolve the sugar in a large cup of warm milk (blood hot). There should be no sugar left on the base of the cup! Crumble the fresh compressed yeast into the milk. Cover and leave it to work in a moderately warm place. After 8–10 minutes, the yeast should have frothed up to the rim of the cup.

Starter dough: In a bowl, mix together the activated yeast (see above) and flour, to make a runny porridge. Cover with a dish towel and leave to rise in a warm place until bubbles form (about 15 minutes). It can then be worked.

Yeast dough: All the ingredients should be at room temperature. Sift the flour into a deep bowl and make a well in the center, then add the starter as well as the salt, butter, and egg. Knead until a smooth, moderately firm dough forms and comes away from the sides of the bowl. If other ingredients (e.g. lemon rind, raisins) are specified in the recipe, these are worked in at this stage. Sprinkle flour over the dough, then cover and leave to raise in a warm, but not hot, place (maximum 95 °F/35 °C) that is protected from drafts, until it has doubled in size (about 30 minutes). Then turn out onto a floured surface, knead again, and shape according to the recipe.

Bakery products with a filling are left to rise again briefly. Brush with beaten egg and bake in a preheated oven at 400 °F (200 °C) for 30–40 minutes.

Stock

In Hungary stock, rather than water, is used for cooking vegetable dishes and vegetable soups. The bones (veal or pork) are simmered in lightly salted water for about 1½ hours. The stock is then strained and left to cool. The fat sets on top of the stock and may be skimmed off before the stock is used.

Preserving fruit

All the pans, jars, bottles, and lids used should not be damaged and, in addition, must be cleaned very thoroughly and sterilized so as not to impair the quality of the preserves.

Hot filling: Place the jars in a saucepan, or roasting pan, filled with warm water, and spoon the hot preserve into the jars.

Closing the jars: For screw-top jars, simply screw the lid tight. If using cellophane, place several rounds of the same size which have been soaked in water over the mouth of the jar, and secure with an elastic band. Preserving jars are fastened with special clamps.

Dry sterilization: Fill the jars with the hot preserve and seal them, then wrap them in several layers of paper. Line a large basket or box with pillows and blankets. Place the jars inside and cover tightly. Leave to stand for at least 24 hours, until the preserve has cooled completely.

Sterilization in hot water: If you haven't got a saucepan with a wire basket, line the bottom of a large saucepan with cloth or paper. Wrap the filled and sealed jars in cloth or paper so that they don't rattle together when boiling, and place them side by side in the pan. Pour enough water into the pan to come two-thirds of the way up the sides of the jars. If the contents of the jars are cold, use cold water; use hot water if the contents of the jars are hot. Sterilization starts when bubbles form in the liquid in the jars. Sterilization time is calculated from this point. The preserves should only simmer gently; they should not boil. The necessary temperature can be maintained by checking with a cook's thermometer. Take the jars out of the pan, place them on a damp, warm cloth, cover them with another cloth, and leave to cool at room temperature.

Mayonnaise

Basic recipe (the ingredients must be at room temperature): 1 egg yolk, salt, 1 tsp lemon juice, scant ½ cup (100 ml) oil. Whisk the egg yolk in a bowl until frothy, then beat in the salt and lemon juice. Add the oil a drop at a time, beating briskly. Later, when the mixture has achieved a very creamy consistency, you can add the oil in a thin stream and continue whisking until the mixture thickens.

Types of flour

Generally wheat flour is used. In Hungary a distinction is made between smooth and coarse flour. Finely milled, smooth flour (*finomliszt*) is used as a thickener and for most baking. The color is not always snow white, but rather yellowish due to a higher proportion of gluten. The more gluten the flour contains, the firmer the dough or batter will be. Wheat flour which is not so finely milled (*rétesliszt* = strudel flour) is used to make strudel and a few other cakes. A special wheaten bread flour is used for making bread. Less finely milled wheat, semolina, is also frequently used.

Plain pastry

There are many different versions of plain pastry. In every case the butter or margarine should be taken out of the refrigerator just before use. Chop the butter into cubes and rub it into the flour. Work very quickly so that the ingredients, which should all be very cold, are in contact with the hands as little as possible. Leave the mixture to rest in a cool place for at least 30 minutes. It is even better if it can be stored overnight in the refrigerator. Continue according to the recipe. The oven should be preheated well, and the pastry baked at 425° F/ 220 °C for the first 10 minutes. The temperature should then be reduced to 350 °F/180 °C. Do not open the door while baking is in progress!

Breadcrumb coating

Toss the portions of meat, fish, or vegetables in flour, then dip in egg beaten with a pinch of salt, and coat in breadcrumbs. The breadcrumb coating should be of even thickness. The breadcrumbed portions are then sautéed or deep-fried in plenty of hot oil.

Paprika

In general Hungarians use mild or slightly hot paprika. As an additional seasoning fresh green or dried hot red chiles are served. If you have accidentally bitten into a hot chile, don't try to cool your mouth with water or another liquid, it just makes it worse. It is better to eat a piece of bread.

Paprika is used not just as a seasoning in Hungary, but also to give the dish an attractive color. Because the natural dye dissolves only in fat, and not in water, heat a little butter (not hot, just moderately warm), then sprinkle a little paprika on top, and stir it in until there are no lumps. Add a splash of water and season to taste with salt. Bring to a boil, then take the pan off the heat and leave the mixture to settle. After a few minutes a red layer of paprika will form on the top, which can be added to various *paprikás* dishes before serving. Cold dishes, such as cucumber salad, or brawn, are simply sprinkled with paprika.

Smoked meat stock

To soften the flavor of smoked meat, or to remove excess salt, soak in water and boil before use in the main recipe. Soak the meat for a minimum of 30 minutes, and preferably several hours, in cold water, which should be changed several times. Then place the meat in a saucepan, cover with fresh water, bring to a boil and simmer until the meat has lost its strong, salty taste (at least 30 minutes). Finally, leave the meat to cool in the stock. In Hungary the smoked meat stock is used to cook other dishes, because it lends a piquant flavor.

Chocolate frosting

Melt 5 oz/150 g coverture in a bowl over a saucepan of hot water, then fold in ⅔ cup/70 g confectioners' sugar. Take the pan off the heat, beat in 2 egg whites with a balloon whisk and whisk until a thick frosting forms. Spread the frosting over the cake or other baked items, then place it in the still-warm oven, which has been turned off, for 1–2 minutes.

Seasoned mayonnaise

Season mayonnaise to taste with lemon juice, mustard, pepper, or other seasonings, such as finely chopped herbs, then blend in some sour cream.

In another variation, blend the mayonnaise to a smooth paste with white wine, a splash of freshly squeezed lemon juice, and the seasonings of your choice.

Sugar frosting

Sift 2¼ cups (250 g) confectioners' sugar into a small saucepan. Add 1–2 tablespoons of water and heat it, stirring all the time, on a low heat until the sugar dissolves completely and a thick, smooth syrup forms. Drizzle over the cake immediately.

Sugar syrup

Heat the volume of water specified in the recipe, and sprinkle on the sugar. Stir until the sugar has completely dissolved, then boil for a few minutes.

Sautéing onions

Numerous Hungarian specialties obtain their typical flavor from onions roasted in pork drippings (or another type of fat). The way and the extent to which the onions are roasted have a decisive influence on the flavor and quality of the dish, yet it is not possible to specify exactly the length of time for which the onions should roast, or the temperature of the fat, because this depends on the quantity and quality of the ingredients (you need a bit of practice to get it just right).

The onion is peeled and finely chopped or grated as necessary. For goulash soup, *pörkölt* and *paprikás* dishes, just sweat the finely diced onion. Add it to moderately warm melted butter, or oil, and cook over a medium heat, stirring occasionally, until the onion is translucent, or beginning to disintegrate a bit.

Depending on the recipe the finely diced onion can be sautéed golden yellow or golden brown in the butter. In both cases add the onions to very hot butter and then reduce the heat.

Sautéed onion rings are sometimes used as a garnish for certain dishes. Peel the onion and slice very thinly. Separate the rings a little and dredge in flour. Shake off the excess flour and fry the onion rings in lots of hot oil until crisp.